We're in an all-out war with an enemy who wants to destroy us. Whenever we're being attacked, it's important to remember that we don't wage war against flesh and blood—we're in a spiritual battle. That's why we're so glad our dear friends Mark and Grace Driscoll have written *Win Your War*, a book that looks at spiritual warfare through the eyes of a married couple. In it they help you see the practical and biblical nature of spiritual warfare in your relationship with God, self, others, and the church. If you want to better understand how to access the power of the Holy Spirit to defeat the enemy, we encourage you to read this book.

—ROBERT AND DEBBIE MORRIS
FOUNDING LEAD SENIOR PASTOR AND
EXECUTIVE WOMEN'S PASTOR, GATEWAY CHURCH
BEST-SELLING AUTHOR, *THE BLESSED LIFE*, *FREQUENCY*,
AND *BEYOND BLESSED*

There's a battle raging all around you, and this book is a fantastic field guide to the realities of spiritual warfare. With theological depth and personal warmth, Mark and Grace speak to some of the most profound truths of life. *Win Your War* is a book that is certain to end up dog-eared and underlined because you will come back to it again and again.

—JOHN LINDELL
LEAD PASTOR, JAMES RIVER CHURCH

Mark and Grace Driscoll have issued a wake-up call to the people of God in this life-changing book. Their gripping message is not only for married couples but for the church all over the world. You will find yourself thanking God that the enemy—Satan, the "angel of light"—has been exposed in so many ways. You will also rejoice that the gospel is put forward, making it a book for both Christians and those who have not yet come to Christ in faith.

—R. T. AND LOUISE KENDALL
R. T. KENDALL MINISTRIES
SENIOR PASTOR, WESTMINSTER CHAPEL (FOR TWENTY-FIVE YEARS)
AUTHOR OF MORE THAN SIXTY BOOKS,
INCLUDING *TOTAL FORGIVENESS*

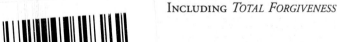

Never dull, always thought-provoking, Mark Driscoll is a cultural anthropologist with a unique gift of applying timeless truth to contemporary culture. In this book he plumbs the depths of spiritual warfare in a very practical, theological, and non-spooky way. I always learn something new from Mark that challenges the way I look at life. When you read the book, I think you'll see what I mean!

—GREG SURRATT
FOUNDING PASTOR, SEACOAST CHURCH
PRESIDENT, ASSOCIATION OF RELATED CHURCHES (ARC)

In *Win Your War* Mark and Grace Driscoll equip readers with the spiritual armor and biblical tools needed to achieve victory over the enemy. Filled with the truth of Scripture, this book shows us how to live in the power of the Holy Spirit, confident of God's presence in our lives, in four major areas: our relationship with God, our identity, our family and friends, and our church. Both timeless and timely, this book is a must-read.

—CHRIS HODGES
SENIOR PASTOR, CHURCH OF THE HIGHLANDS
AUTHOR, *THE DANIEL DILEMMA* AND *WHAT'S NEXT?*

Mark and Grace have walked through every page in this carefully crafted book. You will find hope, strong biblical encouragement, how to have a plan for victory in your relationship with God, and how to navigate healthy relationships with others where there may have been challenges. Not only will you find a fresh perspective with all your relationships, including church, but you will find hope for the future that God has for you.

—GREGORY L. JANTZ, PhD, CEDS
FOUNDER, THE CENTER | A PLACE OF HOPE

You can't win a war you don't know you're in. You need a thorough awareness of your enemies, your allies, and the weapons in your arsenal if you are to be victorious in the battle that is life. Mark and Grace Driscoll will give you the intel you need to come out on top in a culture where all around you people are racing to the bottom. *Win Your War* is an indispensable tool that you will wish you had read sooner.

—Levi Lusko
Pastor, Fresh Life Church; Best-Selling Author

To avoid the subject of spiritual warfare is to miss the central component of what it means to walk with God. So I am thrilled Mark and Grace Driscoll have written this vital book. The church needs it more than ever, as we are *all* called to this battle by the Lord for His wonderful purposes in our generation!

—Eric Metaxas
New York Times Number 1 Best-Selling
Author, *Bonhoeffer* and *Miracles*
Host, *The Eric Metaxas Show*

Timely. Powerful. Equipping. *Win Your War* will inspire holy confidence and instill supernatural strength as you seek to live full and free in the victory of Jesus. With compassion, wisdom, and truth, Mark and Grace Driscoll open our eyes to the weight inherent in every decision, action, and thought we face this side of heaven. I recommend this resource for any believer desiring to walk in the power and authority promised by the Spirit.

—Louie Giglio
Pastor, Passion City Church
Founder, Passion Conferences
Author, *Not Forsaken*

The Bible doesn't give us a lot of details (or answer many of our speculative questions) about spiritual warfare and the unseen realm. And sadly too many Jesus followers don't even know the things it does spell out clearly. Thankfully Mark and Grace Driscoll have written a book that explores the theology and practical implications of the battle for our souls in a straightforward and approachable manner. I found the chapters on inner vows and father wounds to be particularly perceptive. This is a book you need to read.

—Larry Osborne
Pastor, North Coast Church; Author

We have known Mark and Grace for over a decade as dear friends and trusted mentors. We've spent countless hours in their home, with their kids, observing their life and family. We have seen them walk in integrity when no one else was watching. We have seen them trust the Lord, serve others, and continue to give long after it had ceased being convenient. We have seen them live out the truths of this book in the real-time demands of frontline ministry. We've read dozens of books on spiritual warfare, each one leaving us theologically nervous or practically wanting. This book does neither. Mark and Grace have done in this book—saturated with Bible and practical application—what they have done personally with us over and over again through the years as friends: fanned faith, instilled hope, answered questions, and ultimately pointed us to Jesus. After we give a copy to our children, we will give one to everyone in our church family.

—JOSH AND SHARON MCPHERSON
SENIOR PASTOR, GRACE CITY CHURCH

Mark Driscoll is a gifted Bible teacher/practitioner who understands the nature of spiritual warfare regarding every primary relationship in our lives. His experience, his grasp of Scripture, and the solutions offered in this book are essential for every Christ follower!

—DR. JOSEPH MATTERA
FOUNDING PASTOR, RESURRECTION CHURCH
US COALITION OF APOSTOLIC LEADERS
CHRIST COVENANT COALITION

Mark and Grace Driscoll help us all by insightfully teaching the many dimensions of spiritual warfare. They correctly show that while our war with the devil includes releasing people from direct demonic oppression, the far more common and deadly war is against Satan's schemes to deceive, accuse, and tempt people, especially believers. The devil and his demons plot to steal, kill, and destroy our testimony, confidence, identity, and intimacy with God. The Driscolls' personal stories, combined with a strong biblical foundation and practical helps, make *Win Your War* an excellent study. Read with your Bible and your spirit open to Jesus, who came to destroy the devil's work.

—GERRY BRESHEARS, PhD
PROFESSOR OF THEOLOGY
WESTERN SEMINARY, PORTLAND

Win Your War is an insightful guide into the realm of spiritual warfare. Mark and Grace Driscoll illustrate their book with biblical teaching, personal experience, and practical wisdom. In a time when many people are confused about the reality of evil, it is refreshing to read a book that illuminates the unseen world. The Driscolls do not waste words or pretend to follow Christ. They have built their family and their church with the courage and love you will sense in this book. It will help you *win your war* and set you free.

—MARK BUCKLEY
LEAD PASTOR, LIVING STREAMS CHURCH

Win Your War is the most comprehensive book on spiritual warfare I have read in over twenty-five years! As Christians we live as warriors in a spiritual war zone. The battle is real, tangible, and experienced daily. In this book Mark and Grace break down theological truths, making them easily understood and personally applicable. Bringing solid theology with over seven hundred biblical references, *Win Your War* is both a textbook and a highly practical handbook every believer should read and apply to his or her daily Christian practice. The Driscolls' easy tone makes the often otherworldly subject of spiritual warfare normal, and their transparency encourages each of us to engage in our own battle for freedom.

—JIMMY WITCHER
SENIOR PASTOR, TRINITY FELLOWSHIP CHURCH

Perhaps you have sensed the increase in spiritual warfare. You may have even prayed for wisdom and power to face your adversary. Mark and Grace Driscoll have produced a powerful resource. This is more than a book on demonization. *Win Your War* excavates the underlying causes that empower dark forces to gain a foothold.

Not only do Mark and Grace unpack powerful biblical teaching on spiritual warfare; they do it with a pastor's heart and years of compassionate and practical victories in lives like yours.

—MARK MOORE
TEACHING PASTOR, CHRIST'S CHURCH OF THE VALLEY

We find ourselves, as sons and daughters of God, in a constant spiritual battle, which has been raging ever since Satan was cast out of heaven due to his rebellion. Ignorance in this battle is not bliss but certain defeat. Pastor Mark and Grace Driscoll, in *Win Your War*, bring a biblical perspective to the battles that we confront, and provide a Scripture-based road map to victory. The teaching in this book is down-to-earth, practical, and totally Christ-centered, providing the tools for us to apply in our lives the victory that Jesus Christ has won over Satan.

—CHRIS RICHARDS
SENIOR PASTOR, VINO NUEVO

The Bible describes the church and God's people not only as a family, or a temple, or a building, or a body, but also as an army where each member is a soldier. The reality is that we have wars within and without. In this book Mark and Grace Driscoll equip Christians with biblical tools to help them identify and overcome habitual sins that can cripple Christians' walk, thereby bringing freedom in Christ through the gospel.

—TOPE KOLEOSO
LEAD PASTOR, JUBILEE CHURCH LONDON

Mark and Grace Driscoll have walked with us through some tremendously difficult and demonic seasons of life and ministry, offering incredible insight into the unseen war that was really driving the issues that we were dealing with personally and professionally. When we heard they were coauthoring a book on spiritual warfare, we couldn't wait to get our hands on it. Our anticipation was met with an incredibly balanced field manual for pastors, couples, and any believer who wants a resource not only to endure the battle but to be standing firm after it subsides (Eph. 6:13). We are grateful for the Driscolls' ministry and know that this work will help so many people!

—PAUL AND FARRAH TAYLOR
LEAD PASTOR, RIVERS CROSSING COMMUNITY CHURCH

This newest work by Mark and Grace Driscoll is a must-read for the believer who deeply desires a new confidence to win in life. This book is biblically reliable and thoroughly practical. It's a powerful tool for the church as we unify to win the battles that matter the most.

—BRANDON THOMAS
SENIOR PASTOR, KEYSTONE CHURCH
PRESIDENT, PASSIONATE LIFE MINISTRIES

Mark and Grace Driscoll's *Win Your War* is a much-needed, thorough, masterful, and strategic walk-through of spiritual warfare—the best book on this topic that we have seen. This volume exudes clear, practical guidelines on how we can fight the spiritual, which creeps into the physical. We loved the real-world war illustrations, and the chapters on coveting versus contentment, division, and the Book of Revelation were excellent. The Driscolls' thoughts on dealing with the father wound are groundbreaking and life-changing. We are buying this book for our family and friends.

—J. D. PEARRING, DIRECTOR, EXCEL LEADERSHIP NETWORK;
LORI PEARRING, MARRIAGE AND FAMILY THERAPIST

WIN YOUR WAR

MARK AND GRACE DRISCOLL

CHARISMA
HOUSE

Visit the author's website at markdriscoll.org and Driscollbooks.com.

Library of Congress Cataloging-in-Publication Data

Names: Driscoll, Mark, 1970- author.
Title: Win your war / by Mark and Grace Driscoll.
Description: Lake Mary : Charisma House, 2019. | Includes bibliographical references.
Identifiers: LCCN 2019022514 (print) | LCCN 2019022515 (ebook) | ISBN 9781629996257 (hardback) | ISBN 9781629996264 (ebook)
Subjects: LCSH: Spiritual warfare.
Classification: LCC BV4509.5 .D754 2019 (print) | LCC BV4509.5 (ebook) | DDC 235/.4--dc23
LC record available at https://lccn.loc.gov/2019022514
LC ebook record available at https://lccn.loc.gov/2019022515

This publication is translated in Spanish under the title *Gane su guerra*, copyright © 2019 by Mark and Grace Driscoll, published by Casa Creación, a Charisma Media company. All rights reserved.

While the author has made every effort to provide accurate internet addresses at the time of publication, neither the publisher nor the author assumes any responsibility for errors or for changes that occur after publication. Further, the publisher does not have any control over and does not assume any responsibility for author or third-party websites or their content.

19 20 21 22 23 — 987654321
Printed in the United States of America

This book is dedicated to our five incredible and resilient kids, who have walked with us through our war and continue to walk with the Lord. We want to thank those who have been pastors to us along the journey—Robert, Jimmy, Larry, Roy, and Randal. We want to thank our extended family as well as friends such as Josh and Sharon, Ralph and Merry, Dan and Linda, John and Debbie, and Bill and Becky, among others, for being a means of God's grace to us. We are thankful for the team at Charisma, who have become friends. We wouldn't be moving forward without the love and support of our extended family, dear friends, partners at Mark Driscoll Ministries, and church family at The Trinity Church. We love and appreciate you all!

CONTENTS

FOREWORD

THE BOOK YOU are about to read is very unusual. In fact I know of no book quite like it. You will find it easy to read; it will grip you from the beginning. But you may not be prepared for it. And yet if you are a Christian, you will be edified and thankful for a book like this. If you are not a Christian but are open to what is reliable and trustworthy, this could be the instrument that will change your life—forever.

I met Mark and Grace Driscoll in Dallas for the first time a year ago. Various Christian leaders wanted us to meet. They said that Mark and I had a lot in common—being Word and Spirit men: Reformed in theology but open to the immediate and direct work of the Holy Spirit. I knew about Mark's ministry in Seattle, Washington, and that he moved to Phoenix, Arizona. Mark and Grace flew to Dallas to meet with me and others. I listened to Mark as he recounted what he and Grace had been through in recent years. Seldom have I run across a couple who have suffered as they have. I was stunned by Mark's candor and transparency. I will never forget the look of utter devotion on Grace's face as she sat next to her husband as he answered our questions. There is nothing more painful than the withholding of vindication. And yet God is at the bottom of such—which Mark and Grace know full well.

It is precisely their suffering that has prepared them for the making of the book you are about to read. This book was not written in an ivory tower—separate from the real world—as some are known to be. Mark and Grace have lived through what they write about. It is quite theological but immensely practical. You will be confronted with strong truth but blessed with simple and clear ways such truth can be applied in your life.

I have learned a lot from this book. I used to think I would write a book one day on angels and demons. But that is one aspiration I will permanently drop! Their book is better than I could have written.

Satan has one of two wishes for all people, namely, that either you would not believe in his existence at all or you would go overboard and give him undue attention. This book strikes a prudent balance between these extremes. You will come away with the conviction that the demonic world is very real—yes, but you will learn that the power of the blood of Jesus Christ is infinitely greater than Satan's lies. Greater is he that is in us than he that is in the world (1 John 4:4). But what impressed me even more is the *sense of sin* and a realistic view of human nature that emerge throughout the book. This book puts to rest any notion of the goodness of man—a worldview that has too long deceived humankind.

Win Your War is a team effort. Mark and Grace have given us a book that will enable you to overcome the world, the flesh, and the devil. But not in your own strength. It is because Christ overcame Satan at the cross!

—R. T. KENDALL
DPHIL, OXFORD UNIVERSITY
DD, TREVECCA NAZARENE UNIVERSITY
SENIOR PASTOR OF WESTMINSTER CHAPEL FOR TWENTY-FIVE YEARS
AUTHOR OF MORE THAN SIXTY BOOKS, INCLUDING *TOTAL FORGIVENESS*

FOREWORD

A S A YOUNG believer I knew nothing about spiritual warfare. And that is the exact state the devil wanted for me. His dream is for people to be completely ignorant of his evil intent for them and his specific schemes to defeat them and keep them in bondage. Since the Garden of Eden, when the devil took the form of a serpent, stealth has been his greatest advantage. It allows him to wreak havoc on innocent people without ever being suspected as the agent of harm.

And that is exactly what he did in my life and marriage. We were under assault and had no idea what was happening. But an event occurred that exposed the enemy's hand in our lives. My wife, Karen, and I had a good marriage and had actually experienced a miraculous healing in our relationship several years before this particular event.

But one day we started fighting. It just happened, and there really wasn't any specific reason for it. We were just irritated by each other's words and actions and our nerves were on edge when we were around each other. This went on for over a week, and it was escalating. Finally, one Wednesday evening around 6:00 p.m., Karen informed me that we needed to get ready to go to our Bible study, which we went to every week. It started at 7:00 p.m., and she didn't want to be late.

Out of spite I told her I wasn't going to go. I did it just to irritate her and get back at her, and it worked. She left the house angrily and went to the Bible study without me. Bob and Sarah Key were the leaders of the group, and they were wonderful people. Karen was at their home that night for several hours and then returned home.

I was sitting in the living room when Karen walked in. Her countenance and spirit were completely different than when she had left. She came into the room and sat across from me and said, "I need to tell you what happened at Bible study tonight." I replied, "OK, what happened?"

She said calmly, "Tonight Sarah Key told me that we had been on her heart all week when she was praying. And she told me that the Lord had showed her a vision of a lion's head in our living room, roaring, and it was here to destroy our marriage. She said it was a demonic spirit and we needed to hold hands and bind it and command it to leave in the name of Jesus."

Nothing like this had ever happened to us before. But as Karen spoke, I knew it was true. It was like the Lord was drawing back a drape and letting us see what was happening in the realm of the spirit we were ignorant of before. For the first time ever, I held my wife's hand and we prayed and bound the devil over our marriage and our home. It was a very simple prayer. I said, "Satan, in Jesus' name we bind you over our marriage and our home. We command you to leave us and never come back. Amen."

As soon as the words were out of my mouth, the atmosphere in our marriage and home was completely different. Tension was replaced by peace. Anger was replaced by affection. We had experienced an awakening, and our marriage would never be the same again.

In sharing this story, I'm not suggesting that every problem in marriage or life is the devil's fault. We have to learn many skills and spiritual lessons on many levels to be successful in life and love. But what I am saying is the devil is real, he is evil, and he is our personal enemy. We must learn to overcome him if we are going to live free, fulfilled, and victorious lives.

Mark and Grace Driscoll are two of my favorite people. I have so much love and respect for them. You can be assured as you read this powerful book that they live these truths out every day in their lives, marriage, family, and relationship with God. They are mature, victorious believers who have the authority to teach on this subject.

As I read through the pages of this book, I thought how I wished I could have read this as a young believer. It would have been such an incredible help then, but it is still a blessing to me today. There are so many rich truths and spiritual insights in this book. Mark and Grace have a unique ability to share deep biblical truths in a very practical manner.

Jesus died on the cross and rose from the grave to give us the ability to live an overcoming life of freedom and victory. And that is what this book will help equip you to do. This book is about helping all of us realize our destinies in the Lord and win every war against the enemy!

—Jimmy Evans
Senior Pastor of Gateway Church
Founder and CEO of MarriageToday
Senior Elder of Trinity Fellowship Church, Amarillo, Texas

FOREWORD

A S A BIBLICAL scholar I'm prone to only read scholarly works produced under peer review and highbrow academic publishers. The focus of my own work for both the academy and the person in the pew has largely been the supernatural worldview of the Bible. Consequently, when I was approached by Mark to read the manuscript of *Win Your War*, I was drawn out of my scholarly bubble by the twofold goal he and his wife, Grace, sought to accomplish in the book: to convince Christians that they need to embrace the reality of the supernatural world and to process every area of the Christian life (every personal "war") in accord with that belief.

The implication, of course, is that being conformed to the image of Christ involves more than the daily struggle to turn from self-destructive behavior, character flaws, and human evil. It also means *believing* that there are intelligent evil forces at work that not only impede the process of our growth in becoming more like Jesus but seek to manipulate our thinking and behavior to undermine our joy and usefulness to God. In short, God has enemies, and His enemies are our enemies—and they are not passive.

This may sound odd to some readers. How does it make sense to tell Christians that they need to embrace the supernatural? Don't Christians believe in God, that Jesus was God in the flesh, and that God the Holy Spirit resides within? Don't they believe what happened on the cross supernaturally resulted in the forgiveness of sin and everlasting life to all who believe that God sent Jesus for those purposes?

The answer put forth by Mark and Grace is straightforward. For many

Christians, belief in the supernatural ends with the points of doctrine noted above. Affirming the reality of intelligent evil the way it is portrayed in the Bible—where supernatural agents of darkness actively participate in misdirecting our thoughts and behavior to self-destruction, unbelief, and apathy—isn't on the table for many Christians in the modern Western world, driven by "enlightened" rationalism.

The unfortunate reality is that many Christians are *selectively* supernatural in their outlook, a stance that not only denies biblical authority on a range of ideas but anesthetizes believers as to what's really happening to them and their churches on social, cultural, and geopolitical levels. Most believers don't realize that demons occupy a low status in the pecking order of supernatural darkness. It's no accident that the Book of Daniel includes supernatural intelligences in the operations of empires (Daniel 10's "princes"). It's also no coincidence that Paul's vocabulary for intelligent evil (rulers, principalities, powers, thrones, etc.) follows suit—the terms are common ones for geographical dominion.

This is not to endorse a cartoonish view of *spiritual warfare*, a term that has become a buzzword in certain circles of Christianity. Mark and Grace are not finding demons under every rock (nor every church, corporate, or governmental board). While they refer to some truly strange supernatural incidents in their lives, they are quite clear from the outset that *Win Your War* is not about baptizing Hollywood's portrayals of the supernatural. Biblically speaking (and when we discuss supernatural darkness, we should indeed be speaking biblically), spiritual warfare should not be defined as soliciting angels, engaging in shouting matches with supernatural powers, or blaming our failures on demons. Rather, spiritual warfare is fundamentally about the conflict between two kingdoms, a conflict within and without for every true Christian, whether he or she discerns that or not. Followers of Jesus win their spiritual war when they spread the gospel, protect the gospel against false teaching, and live out the gospel by becoming more conformed to the loving, sacrificial character of Jesus.

Not surprisingly, these things are encapsulated in the last words of Jesus before He ascended to heaven (Matt. 28:18–20). It follows, then, that *these* are the things the supernatural powers of darkness fear, for they grow the kingdom of God and are the catalyst for the Lord's return. As the apostle Paul so eloquently noted, when the gospel spreads to the nations, the moment of the kingdom's consummation draws closer (Rom. 11:25–27; cf. Gal 3:7–9, 26–29). Believers weren't tasked by Jesus with "ghost-busting" in His name. We are instead supposed to be making disciples of all nations. But doing that requires each of us to be a useful and effective believer. The powers of supernatural darkness are on the clock, and they know it. We must win our spiritual war to do our part. This is why we face supernatural opposition.

Win Your War is a pastoral plea that needs to take hold in the hearts and minds of serious believers in every church that preaches the gospel. My hope is that *Win Your War* will prod readers toward realizing that the powers of darkness are real and that they work to influence our thinking and behavior to distract us from fulfilling—and enjoying—our lives in Christ and our kingdom tasks.

—Dr. Michael S. Heiser
PhD, Hebrew Bible and Semitic Studies
Executive Director, Awakening School of Theology and Ministry
Author, *The Unseen Realm, Angels,* and *Supernatural*

PREFACE

OUR WARS

*For we are not fighting against people made of flesh and blood, but
against persons without bodies—the evil rulers of the unseen world, those
mighty satanic beings and great evil princes of darkness who rule this
world; and against huge numbers of wicked spirits in the spirit world.*

—Ephesians 6:12, tlb

Our walk with God has been a march into war. Today we have five
kids (three boys and two girls) all walking with Jesus and serving in
The Trinity Church that we planted together as a family ministry in
Scottsdale, Arizona, in 2016. It sounds idyllic, but we've had our share of
struggles and pain along the way like everyone else. The release of this book
marks twenty-five years in ministry, nearly all of that as the senior leaders,
during which time a few dozen books of the Bible were taught, a few hundred churches were planted, and some ten thousand people—mainly young
men—were baptized. Through it all we've even had numerous personal
encounters with demonic activity that caused us to seek understanding
from God's Word. Our goal is to share those lessons with you in this book
so you can experience victory and freedom in your life and relationships.

For us it's been a lifelong discovery. Long before we met in 1988, got
married in 1992, graduated from college in 1993, and started planting our
first church in 1995, we grew up in very different families with different
levels of awareness of the spiritual realm.

I (Grace) grew up in a Christian home with two older sisters. My dad was an Evangelical pastor who graduated from Dallas Theological Seminary. My parents planted a church before I was born and served there for over forty years. My dad did his share of counseling with his gift of mercy, so he began a recovery ministry for addicts that brought him face to face with demonic activity.

Growing up, I remember stories of people who manifested demonic activity. Some were tormented until they experienced emotional deliverance. Others suffered physical torment until they were healed by the removal of unclean spirits. Dad told me stories of people who manifested superhuman strength, even throwing him across the room. At other times demons would inflict pain upon him when he touched a person. It all seemed kind of crazy to hear as a child, but I knew my dad was confident of God's power over the demonic, so I was too.

I (Mark) grew up in a Catholic home with a mom who was saved and healed at a prayer meeting with Charismatic and Pentecostal women. I did not know the Lord until age nineteen in college, reading the Bible that Grace bought for me. But I did have some encounters with the demonic.

My most vivid memory is from high school. I was coming down the stairs at a friend's house and felt a strong force pressing against my chest, prohibiting me from coming down the stairs. I pulled myself forward on the handrails and, letting go, found myself suspended in midair parallel with the stairs. When I told my friend about this experience, his mother explained that a priest had lived there. The house had an office as well as a confessional where people came to have meetings with the priest until the day he killed himself in the house. Then my friend's family moved in, and the father was very involved in the occult. As a result, unusual things were common in the home.

In spite of these encounters with the supernatural, neither of us came from a background where we learned how to engage in spiritual warfare. Grace had experienced an attack on her family through sickness and nightmares, but her dad was more involved with battling against it. I was a new Christian who slowly worked through a master's degree at a seminary with Conservative Baptist roots. In addition I interned at a church where the senior pastor believed that the supernatural gifts of the Bible had ceased and that Christians could not have much influence on demons.

So when demonic things started happening in our ministry, we did not know what to do. We began reading books on the issue and meeting with godly pastors who had some insight. More than anything we prayed and studied the Bible a lot, even looking up every single occurrence of Satan and demonic activity in the Bible. The Lord was gracious, and we learned about such things as discernment, offensive prayer, and how to see people liberated from spiritual oppression with the principles of Ephesians 6:10–20.

By God's power we saw people delivered from spiritual oppression. Many people stopped taking medications because their tormenting voices and panic attacks went away. Some people were also miraculously healed. We did not speak much about these things so as not to detract from our focus on Jesus or confuse our young people who were just learning the basics of Christianity.

Admittedly sometimes the works of the devil and his demons are overt and extraordinary. We have witnessed them firsthand. We empathize and relate to people who have endured these wars. However, we have come to believe that most of the demonic work is covert and ordinary. It is more subtle, less obvious, and therefore more like an undercover stealth agent than a public terrorist attack. For this reason we are not going to speak much about the overt and extraordinary demonic in this book. Instead our goal is to have a biblical, practical, and pastoral study of the typical ways that average Christians can win their war against the subtle and sly ways of Satan, the serpent.

The big idea behind the rest of this book is simple. There was a war in heaven that God and the spirit beings, including the angels, won. That war is now on earth, and everyone is born into that war. One day Jesus will return and win the war on earth as He won in heaven. The devil and his demons, along with all their works and effects, will be pushed down to hell for the eternal judgment they deserve.

The two sides of this war are as follows:

- In heaven, the kingdom of God, we find faith, the filling of the Spirit, freedom, supernatural living, humility, our identity in Christ, allegiance to God, cleansing, healing, forgiveness, godly people, truth, contentment, the Father's love, unity, shepherds and sheep, the true church, and true religion.

- Hell is the realm of Satan. It is filled with unbelief, demonic oppression, idolatry, natural living, pride, identity rooted in death, allegiance to the demonic, defilement, sickness, bitterness, godless people, lies, jealousy, no love, division, wolves, and false religion and spirituality.

Each day, in the practical decisions of life, you have a war to wage. You affect both kingdoms, and they affect you, whether you ever acknowledge it or not. Your daily thoughts, decisions, and actions will either invite heaven down into your life or pull hell up into your life.

We have learned that the enemy doesn't just attack you; he attacks your relationships. So to help you get the most from this book, we want you to think relationally. The Trinitarian God of the Bible is one God in three persons. That means God is relational, and He made you for relationship with Himself and others.

Before sin entered the world, God declared that everything He made was good. But there was one thing God said was *not* good: being alone. So God created Eve to be a wife for our first father, Adam. Immediately Satan showed up to attack their present and future relationships with God, themselves, each other, and those who would come after them.

As a result this book looks at spiritual war through the eyes of a married couple hoping to lovingly help you see the practical and biblical nature of spiritual warfare in your relationships with God, self, others, and the church. We've divided the book into four parts that deal with war on each of these relationship fronts. Each part contains several short chapters that help you recognize the "*un*holy spirit" at work behind your relationship struggles and access the power of the Holy Spirit to defeat him.

The good news is that no matter what your war, with God's grace and the Holy Spirit's help, you can apply Jesus' victory and win. The wars each of us face are all parts of a much bigger war that we will win in the end by God's grace. So let's get started. We'll focus first on your relationship with God. Waging your war begins by renewing your mind with a biblical worldview, which we will study next.

YOUR RELATIONSHIP WITH
GOD

CHAPTER 1

WIN YOUR WORLDVIEW WAR

The god of this world has blinded the minds of the unbe-
lievers, to keep them from seeing the light of the gospel
of the glory of Christ, who is the image of God.

—2 CORINTHIANS 4:4

OME YEARS AGO we hosted an *ABC Nightline* debate about the existence of Satan and demons. There were four of us on the panel. I
(Mark) enjoyed going head to head with Deepak Chopra. He is a
prolific author heralded by *Time* magazine as one of the top one hundred
heroes and icons of the century. For about an hour we disagreed on virtually everything pertaining to the spirit world. The following is how the
show started:

> DAN HARRIS: Good evening and welcome to a *Nightline* faceoff.
> Our question tonight is a very provocative one—does Satan exist?
> According to one recent poll, 70 percent of Americans believe yes,
> Satan does exist. But who, or what, is he? Is he a fallen angel, or
> is he some sort of formless, malevolent force in the universe? And
> if he doesn't exist, how do we explain why there is so much pain,
> suffering, and violence in the world today? This is a discussion
> that opens up a whole series of fascinating and fundamental ques-
> tions about good and evil, about human nature, and the nature
> of God. It is also a discussion that is likely to provoke some very

strong emotions. It is entirely possible that there are people here on this stage with me tonight who believe that others on the stage are doing, if only unwittingly, the work of Satan. It is also possible there are people on this stage who believe that believing in Satan is dangerous, wrong, and destructive. So let's get right to the discussion, and we're going to start with opening statements. We're going to go first to Pastor Mark Driscoll.

PASTOR MARK DRISCOLL: . . . Christians have always believed that there are great distinctions between the Creator and the creation. That God is eternal, He is good, He is loving, He is powerful. God made both that which is material and that which is spiritual. And God gave both angels and also human beings free will. Satan was an angel who rebelled against God, and in so doing led an insurrection. Other angels followed him. Our first parents joined that rebellion, and ultimately that is the cause of moral evil. It is rebellion against God. Everything God made He declared to be very good and all that is very bad is because of sin. That is our responsibility as well as Satan's. God is so good and so gracious that, though He is Creator and we are creation, He entered into creation as the man Jesus Christ. He came on a rescue mission to save us from sin, from death, from folly, and ultimately from Satan, who is our enemy. Jesus lived without sin, He contended with Satan. He was tempted and opposed by Satan, He never yielded to him, He never did sin. He went to the cross, and in great affection He substituted Himself for sinners like me and He died in our place for our sin. That is the essential belief of Christianity— that Satan is real, but so is Jesus, and He works out all things for good, and ultimately, He will redeem all that has been lost through Satan, sin, and death.

DEEPAK CHOPRA: I think our consciousness or, if you will, our soul, is a place of contrast because all creation goes through contrast. You have up and down, you have hot and cold, you have light and darkness. So, our essential state is one of ambiguity and ambivalence. And Freud, the great psychologist of the last century, said that neurosis and sometimes even psychosis is the inability to tolerate our ambiguity. The fact that we are sacred and profane at the same time, that we are divine and diabolical at the same time, that we can have forbidden lust on the one hand and unconditional love on the other. This is the human condition, that there is a part of us that is called the shadow. This is a relatively recent idea. The shadow is that part of us that is fearful, that is diabolical, that is scared, that has guilt and shame, that is in denial, and that believes in sin. It comes from separation from our divine source. If we want to understand the nature of evil in the world, we need to understand the nature of our own shadows. We need to embrace them, we need to forgive them, we need to share them with each other, and we need to confront them. It is my belief that people who obsess over sin, people who obsess over guilt and shame, and, unfortunately, there are religious institutions that have actually idealized guilt and shame and made it into a virtue, and when we obsess over these things and we collectively create this obsession, then we project it out there as this mythical figure that we call Satan. Healthy people do not have any need for Satan. Healthy people need to confront their own issues, understand themselves, and move towards the direction of compassion, creativity, understanding, context, insight, inspiration, revelation, and understanding that we are part of an ineffable mystery. That the moment we label that mystery as good and evil, right and wrong, then we create conflict in the world and that all the trouble in the world today is between religious ideologies. There are approximately thirty wars going on in the world and they're mostly in the name of God. So I would say, be done with Satan and confront your own issues.[1]

The world is filled with weeping, bleeding, and dying.

Why?

If we were good people getting better, and if history were evolving with us, you would rightly expect things to be trending brighter. Things are trending darker.

Why?

Something has gone terribly wrong. The world is a war zone, and various disciplines from philosophy to psychology and spirituality have attempted to tell us what has gone wrong and how it can be made right. However, only the Word of God gives us help to know the problem and hope to know the solution.

In preparing for this book, we have had numerous discussions. On one occasion our oldest daughter, Ashley, was at home on a holiday break from one of America's largest universities. She is bombarded continuously in classes, clubs, and conversations with beliefs that are at odds with biblical Christianity. Like most missionaries she enjoys praying with and for folks, having deep discussions about biblical Christianity, and helping people understand the good news of Jesus Christ.

Ashley was home for Thanksgiving, and when family and friends held hands in the kitchen to take turns naming what they were most thankful for in the past year, she said, "The prayer tent." She was referring to a tent set up by Christian students in the middle of campus where there has been at least one person continually present to pray for the campus day and night for weeks on end.

Ashley is one of the campus leaders, and she has had some amazing experiences in the prayer tent. People from every background and belief have come in for discussion and prayer—from atheists to alien-worshippers, from Muslims to Mormons, and seemingly everyone in between.

Ashley said that in her conversations she discovered four basic beliefs she finds lacking in most people's understanding. Like four legs on a chair, until she is able to establish these truths for someone to understand, the conversation eventually falls over.

THE FOUR LEGS OF A BIBLICAL WORLDVIEW

1. The unseen realm

You cannot believe God's Word or understand God's world unless you embrace the supernatural. From beginning to end the Bible is about an unseen realm as real as the visible world. Faith is required to believe in beings as real as we are who live in a world as real as ours and travel between these worlds, impacting and affecting human history and our daily lives. As a result everything is spiritual, and nothing is secular. What happens in the invisible world affects what happens in the visible world and vice versa. Furthermore, everyone is both a physical being with a body that is seen and a spiritual being with a soul that is unseen. Spiritual warfare is like gravity—it exists whether or not you believe in it, and it affects you every moment of every day.

Christianity has largely downplayed if not dismissed this truth for hundreds of years. Other than Pentecostal and Charismatic Christians, many denominations and their seminaries, seeking to win the approval of worldly scholarship, were too influenced by the rationalism, naturalism, and skepticism of modernity that corresponds in large part with the history of America.

Rationalism disbelieved most anything that could not be seen through a telescope or microscope and believed only that which could be proven through the scientific method of testing and retesting. This led to naturalism, a worldview that suggests all we have is the material and not the spiritual. The result was skepticism of anything spiritual, and eventually atheism and the denial of God altogether.

At the beginning of the Protestant Reformation, Martin Luther had a clear belief in the cosmic battle between God and angels and Satan and demons, including speaking against the demonic in a hymn he penned, "A Mighty Fortress is Our God." A noted historian on Luther wrote an entire book on Luther's experience with and teaching about the devil.[2] In *Table Talk* Luther wrote of the devil more times than the Bible, gospel, grace, and prayer.[3] Luther also speaks of multiple visits from the devil, including appearing in his room at Wartburg Castle in Germany as Luther sat down to translate the Bible. Startled, Luther grabbed his inkwell and threw it at the devil. For some years following, tourists would be shown the ink spot on the wall and told the story. But today the inkwell story is not told to visitors, and the ink spot cannot be seen. Some historians believe the inkstain evidence of the devil was painted over, forever hidden, as the story of the devil's visit to that very spot was also removed from the tour and dismissed as silly superstition.[4] Perhaps the painting over of demonic evidence explains the rest of church history since.[5]

As this worldly thinking overtook academia, belief in such things as angels, demons, healing, and prophecy was looked down on as primitive and naïve. Surely humanity had evolved beyond such archaic views. Christian colleges and seminaries seeking approval and accreditation eventually downplayed or dismissed the supernatural parts of the Scriptures.

As one example, the *Daily Study Bible* commentary series has been a favorite of pastors for generations. In that series one of the most popular

Bible commentators of the modern era, William Barclay, casts doubt on the miracles of Jesus Christ. Take, for example, the account of Jesus walking on water, which appears in three Gospels. Speaking of Matthew's account, Barclay says that we can either interpret the text to mean that Jesus walked on the water or that He walked on the shore of the water, giving the disciples the illusion of a miracle: "he came walking through the surf and the waves towards the boat, and came so suddenly upon them that they were terrified when they saw him. Both of these interpretations are equally valid. Some will prefer one, and some the other."[6] Commenting on Mark's account, Barclay says, "What happened we do not know, and will never know. The story is cloaked in mystery which defies explanation."[7] Lastly, Barclay says that in John's Gospel, Jesus walked on the seashore and not on the sea: "Jesus was walking on the seashore. That is what the phrase means in our passage....Jesus was walking...by the seashore."[8]

As Barclay interprets the miracles of Jesus in his Bible commentaries, you can almost sense the struggle he is facing as the Bible speaks of the supernatural but academia sees such things as superstitious and primitive. Much of Barclay's work is commendable and helpful, but sadly he is not alone in repeatedly giving two options on many miraculous texts—one that is true to the Bible, and one that is true to academia critical of the Bible. If you remember this story, Peter tried to walk on water and made it only a short while before the fisherman panicked and started to sink, and Jesus rescued him from drowning—things that would not make any sense on the shallow seashore. Jesus' miracles were signs pointing to Him as King of a supernatural kingdom. To be biblical, you must believe in the supernatural. Jesus did so many miracles that the Bible only records some of them: "Now Jesus did many other signs in the presence of the disciples, which are not written....Were every one of them to be written, I suppose that the world itself could not contain the books that would be written."[a]

On the flip side, much Christian teaching on the demonic in recent years that does believe in the supernatural is combined with wild speculation and sensationalism not anchored to sound biblical principles. As a result some Christians find talk of Satan and demons to be distracting from the glory of God and sound Bible teaching. The result is that, sure, we give a nod to the big supernatural issues like Jesus' virgin conception and bodily

a John 20:30; 21:25

resurrection, but beyond that many Christians live as skeptics rather than seekers of the supernatural.

Thankfully there is a growing increase in credible academic work on the supernatural. One example is the work of Dr. Michael Heiser, whom we will quote throughout this book.

2. Binary thinking

I (Mark) based another book I wrote[a] on an extensive research project commissioned with phone calls to nearly a million people and focus groups in three major cities. All of this research culminated in uncovering the single fundamental underlying difference between those who believe the Bible and those who do not. Christians think in terms of black and white (binary thinking). Non-Christians think in terms of shades of gray. Biblical thinking is binary thinking.

Biblical Christianity requires black-and-white thinking because it is dualistic. From beginning to end the Bible is thoroughly categorical: Satan and God, demons and angels, sin and holiness, lies and truth, wolves and shepherds, non-Christians and Christians, damnation and salvation, hell and heaven. An exhaustive list could fill a book—but you get the point. The Bible makes clear distinctions and judgments between opposed categories.

Mainstream culture is monistic. The culture does not allow black-and-white thinking. The culture refuses to allow any categories because that would mean making distinctions, which ultimately ends in making value judgments. Instead of Satan and God, we have a "higher power." Instead of demons and angels, we have spirits or ghosts. Instead of sin and holiness, we have lifestyle choice. Instead of lies and absolute truth, we have your truth and my truth. Instead of wolves and shepherds, we have spiritual guides. Instead of non-Christians and Christians, we have everyone defined as God's children. Instead of damnation and salvation, we have whatever works for you. Instead of hell and heaven, we have people who go to a better place when they die.

Monism is a religion. Although not always formal like Christianity, it is a religious view of the world that rejects dualistic thinking. Ultimately, if we believe Scripture, this is a battle between the God of the Bible, who is intolerant, and the gods of this world, who are at war against Him.

Throughout this book we are working from binary thinking and the

---

a The book and project *Christians Might Be Crazy* can be found at theresurgence.com.

premise that what God creates, Satan counterfeits. Satan creates nothing, but he does counterfeit, corrupt, and co-opt what God creates. Here are some examples:

GOD CREATES	SATAN COUNTERFEITS
angels	demons
obedience	rebellion
truth	lies
Spirit-filled	demon-possessed
cleansing	defilement
humility	pride
forgiveness	bitterness
worship	idolatry
contentment	coveting
peace	fear
unity	division
shepherds	wolves
God-esteem	self-esteem
covenant with God	inner vow with self
spirit	flesh
freedom	slavery
revival	riot
life	death
church	world
kingdom	hell

3. Group guilt

According to the Bible, God holds both spirits and people responsible for their behavior. The devil and his demons tempt others to participate in their evil plots and plans, and when someone surrenders to Satan and does something demonic, both the person and the demons are held responsible. Sadly, depending upon which Christian teachers you listen to, you will often find an imbalance. Some wrongly blame Satan for all of their wrongdoing and reduce human responsibility. Others wrongly blame people for all wrongdoing and overlook the role that the demonic realm plays in sinful human decision-making.

The Bible shows us how God perfectly deals with everyone who sins.

In Genesis 3 we see the record of the first human sin. There God holds everyone accountable. Following wrongdoing, God speaks first to the man, then to the woman, and lastly to the devil; this is the order of responsibility.

God judges the man first, holding him accountable for his sin and the failure to lovingly lead and defend his family. For spiritual defeats to stop and spiritual victories to begin, it is imperative that God's men accept their role and responsibility for godliness in their lives and families. Our first father, Adam, and most of his sons slyly try to shift the blame to the woman and the God who made her, but God has none of it. The man is responsible for his sin and cannot point to God, Satan, or the woman to make himself a victim instead of a villain.

God then judges the woman, holding her accountable for her sin and failure to follow God's command. She seeks to blame shift her sin to the devil, but God gives her consequences for her sin while not neglecting the role of the serpent. Lastly God judges the devil for his participation in the fall, rendering a verdict of eventual defeat and destruction once he is crushed under the feet of Jesus.

Who is responsible for the first sin? The man? The woman? The devil? The answer is yes. This is the principle of group guilt. Just as multiple people can be convicted and charged for involvement in the same crime, when sin occurs, numerous guilty persons are often involved.

4. Heaven down or hell up

As we will explore in the remainder of this book, there was a war in heaven that came to the earth. King Jesus has come down to the earth and will again come down, one last time, bringing the kingdom in His wake, to push the devil and his demons down to hell forever. Every day of our existence on earth we are living amidst a great battle that has been raging from long ago in heaven. Each day our decisions either invite heaven down or pull hell up into our lives.

Jesus' half-brother James used binary thinking, urging Christians not to pull hell up into our lives through popular and prevalent living, which is "false to the truth...earthly, unspiritual, demonic...and...vile," but instead to invite heaven down into our lives with the "wisdom from above."[a] Paul exhorted, "Set your minds on things that are above, not on things that are on

a Jas. 3:13–17

earth."[a] Jesus taught us to pray and then live heaven down, not hell up: "Your kingdom come, your will be done, on earth as it is in heaven."[b] When we see the Spirit fall on people in the Bible and to this day, this is living "kingdom down" rather than "culture up."

The same King who won in heaven came to earth to fight the same war on a new battlefront. We will study this war next.

---

a Col. 3:2
b Matt. 6:5–15

CHAPTER 2

GOD WON HIS WAR

War arose in heaven, Michael and his angels fighting against the dragon. And the dragon and his angels fought back, but he was defeated, and there was no longer any place for them in heaven. And the great dragon was thrown down, that ancient serpent, who is called the devil and Satan, the deceiver of the whole world—he was thrown down to the earth, and his angels were thrown down with him.

—Revelation 12:7–9

BEFORE HE PASSED away, Grandpa Gib (Grace's dad), as our kids called him, was on his way to Thailand to mediate a significant conflict threatening an entire missionary team working there. A bit older and disoriented after a long flight, Grandpa Gib got turned around during a layover in a foreign country and was far away from his connecting flight, potentially missing it. At that moment, Grandpa Gib was approached by a kind man who spoke perfect English and offered to take him directly to his departing flight. The stranger struck up a conversation about the Lord and was warm and loving. Grandpa Gib immediately and fully trusted him.

The stranger delivered Grandpa Gib and his bag to his flight in the nick of time, and when Grandpa turned to thank him, he was gone. They were not in a crowd, nor was there any other earthly explanation for his disappearance. The man had simply vanished. Grandpa Gib thanked God right then and there, convinced he had been visited by a ministering angel.

I (Mark) thought I knew a lot about angels growing up in a Catholic family in a home that had pictures of angels hanging on the walls. However, as I got older and started studying the Bible, I quickly realized that a lot of what we think about angels is myth, fable, and folklore. For example, the Sistine Chapel portrays angels as chubby babies with wings and harps sitting on clouds. This depiction has no basis in the Bible whatsoever and has contributed to an ongoing misperception of angels, including the myth that babies become angels when they die.

How about you? What are your thoughts about spirit beings, including angels?

The Bible has a great deal to say about spiritual beings, speaking of them as angels, watchers, holy ones, the host of heaven, sons of God, divine assembly, the gods, morning stars, glorious ones, and the armies of heaven.[a] One Bible dictionary, speaking specifically of angels, says "'angels' are mentioned almost three hundred times in Scripture, and are only noticeably absent from books such as Ruth, Nehemiah, Esther, the letters of John, and James."[1]

Another Bible dictionary says, "From the Garden of Eden to the renewed heaven and earth, angels are found repeatedly throughout the Bible. These beings are also spoken of as spirits, cherubim, seraphim, sons of God, [and] the heavenly host."[2]

No one really knows how many angels exist or if God ever makes more angels. The Bible, however, is clear: there are *a lot* of angels. It uses descriptions such as "innumerable angels" and "a thousand thousands served him, and ten thousand times ten thousand stood before him."[b]

Because they prefer the focus to be on God rather than themselves, it is not surprising that we only know the names of two angels in the entire Bible. One is Gabriel, who brings messages to Jesus' parents before His birth.[c] The other is Michael, who is referred to in military terms as an archangel and prince.[d] Since demons are fallen angels who counterfeit all that God creates, one of the best ways to understand the demonic realm is to understand the angelic realm first.

---

a Dan. 4:17; Ps. 89:5; Deut. 4:19–20; 1 Kings 22:19; 1 Sam. 1:11; Job 1:6; 38:7; Deut. 32:8–9; Ps. 82:1, 6; 89:6; Ezek. 28:2; Job 38:7; 2 Pet. 2:10; Jude 8; Rev. 19:14
b Heb. 12:22; Dan. 7:10
c Dan. 8:16; 9:21; Luke 1:19, 26
d Dan. 10:13; 12:1; Jude 9; Rev. 12:7

CHERUBIM AND SERAPHIM

Not only are there different ranks of angels, but there are also different types of angels and other spirit beings. When angels show up in the Bible, they look like human beings. However, that is not the case with all spirit beings from the unseen realm. Both cherubim and seraphim are sung about in the classic hymn "Holy, Holy, Holy." They appear throughout the Old Testament as winged heavenly beings, starting at the tree of life after Adam and Eve sinned, lovingly cutting them off to live forever separated from God.[a] Through the Bible cherubim angels often appear around the presence of God in the tabernacle and temple, guarding and worshipping.[b]

Seraphim appear in Isaiah 6:1–7:

> I saw the Lord sitting upon a throne, high and lifted up....Above him stood the seraphim. Each had six wings: with two he covered his face, and with two he covered his feet, and with two he flew. And one called to another and said: "Holy, holy, holy is the LORD of hosts; the whole earth is full of his glory!"...And I said: "Woe is me! For I am lost; for I am a man of unclean lips, and I dwell in the midst of a people of unclean lips; for my eyes have seen the King, the LORD of hosts!" Then one of the seraphim flew to me, having in his hand a burning coal that he had taken with tongs from the altar. And he touched my mouth and said: "Behold, this has touched your lips; your guilt is taken away, and your sin atoned for."

THREE WAYS ANGELS DIFFER FROM HUMAN BEINGS

Angels differ from human beings in at least three ways.

1. No human gender

Angels do not have a gender.[c] Since angels are spirit beings who do not reproduce like men and women, they are not male and female like we are. However, while on an assignment, an angel can appear as a male or female.

---

a Gen. 3:24
b Exod. 26:31–33; 36:35; 1 Kings 6:32, 35; 2 Chron. 3:14; Ezek. 1:4–24; 10:5–22; 41:18–19; Heb. 9:5; Rev. 4:6–8
c Matt. 22:30; Luke 20:35–36

2. No human body

Angels do not have bodies, because they are spiritual beings. Angels, however, may appear in physical bodies much like a soldier can go undercover for the sake of a mission. Genesis 19 explains an account between Abraham's extended family saved from death by "angels" who appeared as "men" and "seized him and his wife and his two daughters by the hand, the LORD being merciful to him, and they brought him out and set him outside the city" (v. 16). This is why "some have entertained angels unawares."[a] Yes, you may have had an angel show up in your life, but it was undercover, so you simply thought it was another person. Perhaps in heaven we will get to watch the proverbial film of these occasions and see our lives from God's perspective, which would be intriguing.

3. No human limitation

Because they do not share the limits of our humanity in a physical body, angels do not get sick, grow old, or die.[b]

SIX WAYS ANGELS AND OTHER SPIRIT BEINGS DIFFER FROM GOD

Angels and other spirit beings are amazing, but they are not equal to God. In fact we have found six ways that angels and other spirit beings are not on the same level as God.

1. God is eternal.

Angels are not eternal or the Creator like God. All spirit beings other than God had a beginning when their Creator created them.[c]

2. God is all-knowing.

God is all-knowing (*omniscient* is the theological term), but created spirit beings are not.[d] However, they (including fallen angels) have been observing human behavior throughout history, and as a result they have great insight and awareness, not unlike a highly skilled and experienced detective or therapist.[e]

---

a Heb. 13:2
b Luke 20:35–36; Matt. 22:30
c Neh. 9:6; Ps. 148:2, 5
d 1 Pet. 1:12
e 1 Sam. 28:3–25; Heb. 2:14; 1 Cor. 4:19

3. God is all-present.

God is all-present (*omnipresent* is the theological term) and not limited to a time or place. Spirit beings, however, are not present everywhere; they are limited to being in one place at a time and have to travel from place to place. For example, to bring the news to Mary that she would give birth to Jesus, "the angel Gabriel was sent from God to a city of Galilee named Nazareth."[a]

4. God is all-powerful.

Spirit beings are not all-powerful (*omnipotent* is the theological term) like God.[b]

5. God is sovereign.

Spirit beings are not in ultimate authority, or sovereign, like God. This is for the simple fact that they are created by God, who rules over them, as He does human beings, as the Creator of all persons in both the seen and unseen realms.

6. God is worshipped.

Spirit beings were made to be worshippers *of* God and not to be worshipped *like* God.[c]

Sometimes people get confused about angels and other spirit beings as if they were God. Sadly, people start praying to them or even worshipping them. Even John, who wrote five books of the Bible, was so overwhelmed in the presence of an angel that he apparently mistook it for God and worshipped it not once but twice.[d]

The confusion regarding angels and other spirit beings may explain, at least in part, the phenomenon of alien life. It is possible that what some people report as encounters with alien beings from another planet may in fact be encounters with alien spirits from another realm. Some reports of alien sightings indicate that the ways they move through the sky defy the laws of physical gravity. If true, these reports may be of such things as angels or demons. Some reports of alien revelation indicate that at least some of

---

a Luke 1:26
b 2 Pet. 2:11; Rev. 12:7; Dan. 10:10–14
c Heb. 1:5–13
d Rev. 19:10; 22:8–9

these aliens communicate things contrary to the Bible. If true, these encounters may be between a human being and a demon pretending to be an alien.

Not only do holy angels worship God, but they also want people to do the same. Admittedly the mystery surrounding angelic and other spiritual beings can be incredibly interesting. This can contribute to wild speculation about angelic and demonic activity, which the Bible forbids because it shifts the focus away from God.[a]

Angels and demons are real. However, our focus is to be on God alone. Jesus demonstrates this for us in Matthew 4:8–11. There Satan (a fallen divine being) tells Jesus to worship him. But Jesus says, "Be gone, Satan! For it is written, 'You shall worship the Lord your God and him only shall you serve'" (v. 10). After that the devil leaves Jesus, and angels minister to Him. Jesus focused on the Father, and the angels focused on Jesus because the focus of spirit and human beings should be God.

GOD'S DIVINE FAMILY

The Trinitarian God of the Bible (one God in three persons) is relational. The God of the Bible does not need spiritual or human beings but creates both to be His family in the seen and the unseen realms. The reason Satan and demons attack our relationships is because that strikes at the heart of God's nature since He is loving, unified, and relational.

Just as God reveals Himself as a Father and His human beings as a family throughout the Bible, God does the same with His spirit beings as a family. Just as in a human family some of the children are chosen to take on additional leadership and responsibility, so too there are levels of leadership in God's divine family: "In the ancient Semitic world, *sons of God*...is a phrase used to identify divine beings with higher-level responsibilities or jurisdictions. The term *angel*...describes an important but still lesser task: delivering messages."[3]

Speaking of God's divine family at creation, we read, "the morning stars sang together and all the sons of God shouted for joy."[b] *Stars* is ancient language for divine beings who are physically between people on earth and God in heaven just as angels are spiritually. As God was creating the world for humanity, both angels and the spirit beings called the sons of God sang

a Col. 2:18
b Job 38:7

in worship and cheered in much the same way that our kids got excited every time a new sibling was born into our family. The same thing happened at the birth of Jesus: "suddenly there was with the angel a multitude of the heavenly host praising God and saying, 'Glory to God in the highest, and on earth peace among those with whom he is pleased!' [Then] the angels went away...into heaven."[a] Additionally the investigation of Job's life occurred in the presence of God and the "sons of God."[b] God is a Father, the Trinity is a family, and God does ministry with His spiritual and physical children; ministry is a family business for God.

The Bible often speaks of God's divine family with the Hebrew word *Elohim*. On some occasions this word is used to refer to God. Other times it refers to the divine family as well as other fallen and demonic spirit beings. It is a general word for spiritual beings in the unseen realm, which can include God, the members of God's divine council, angelic and demonic beings at work in the world, and more.[4]

One example is found in Psalm 82:1, which says, "God [Elohim] has taken his place in the divine council; in the midst of the gods [Elohim] he holds judgment." Michael Heiser explains, "The Hebrew Bible uses the term *elohim* to speak of any inhabitant of the spiritual world. The word itself provides no differentiation among beings within that realm, though hierarchy is certainly present. Yahweh, for example, is an *elohim*, but no other *elohim* is Yahweh."[5]

GOD'S DIVINE COUNCIL

In the human realm we know that God works through human leaders in the Old Testament, New Testament, and to the current day. The same is true in the spirit realm, as God has a leadership team of spirit beings who are His divine council. The divine council is referred to throughout the Bible as "the assembly of the holy ones," "the council of the holy ones," "hosts," "the seat of the gods," "the mount of assembly," "the court...in judgment," and "the heavenly host."[c] The Bible gives us a clue that God has convened the divine council when He is revealed sitting on His throne. We get this same picture from Isaiah, Daniel, and John. Each one was taken from this realm into the unseen realm and placed amid the divine council gathered around God

---

a Luke 2:13–15
b Job 1:6
c Ps. 82:1; 89:4–8; Ezek. 28:2; Isa. 14:12–14; Dan. 7:9–10; Luke 2:13

enthroned.[a] Jacob also had a visit from God, angels, and the divine council. They came down a ladder to meet with him and he said to them, "How awesome is this place! This is none other than the house of God, and this is the gate of heaven."[b] Jacob then named that place Bethel, which means house of God, because it was at least temporarily the meeting place of God's divine council and the connecting place for the two realms and two families of God.

God's divine council does three primary things.

1. They observe God.

When God does something, His divine council is present to witness His work in much the same way that Moses watched God part the Red Sea or Mary watched Jesus die for the sin of the world. In these instances God speaks with His divine council, explaining what He is doing. When I was a little boy, my dad would take me to the job site as a construction worker. I would pack a little lunch and put on my boots, jeans, and hard hat to see what my dad did all day. Some of the time he did all the work while I watched, and he explained to me what he was doing. Examples of God doing this with the divine council are common, including the creation of man and woman in Genesis 1:20–28. Verse 26 says, "Then God said, 'Let us make man in our image, after our likeness.'" After our first parents sinned, we read in Genesis 3:22, "Then the LORD God said, 'Behold, the man has become like one of us in knowing good and evil.'"

2. They serve as messengers and ministers.

To pay our way through college, we spent our summers working at hotels. Hotel training teaches you to think of people as your guests; it is your job to make their lives better. As a result we would book reservations, drive to the airport, haul luggage, call cabs, make dinner reservations, deliver towels, and do anything else a guest wanted. The entire staff at the hotel had the same mission, and we worked long and hard hours to care for everyone. The hotel never closed, so the work never ceased.

In some ways divine beings (e.g., angels and the sons of God) are God's staff. Much like our resort kitchen staff, they bring food to hungry people.[c] Like the resort security staff, they also provide physical protection for God's

---

a Isa. 6:1–6; Dan. 7:9–10; Rev. 4
b Gen. 28:10–22
c 1 Kings 19:5–7; Ps. 78:23–25

people.[a] Since we usually worked in the lobby, we frequently gave people directions and guidance for the next leg of their journey, and divine beings do the same thing for God's people.[b]

God's divine staff members were created to do what most good resort staff members do—serve as messengers and ministers: "he [God] makes his messengers winds, his ministers a flaming fire."[c] As messengers, angels bring a word from God to people.[d] Angels helped bring the Law to Moses and helped Zechariah interpret his God-given vision.[e] An angel delivered the message of the coming birth of John the Baptizer, as well as the birth of Jesus Christ.[f] An angel also delivered the message of Jesus' time and place of birth to the shepherds.[g]

While on the earth as a man, Jesus Christ was ministered to by angels: "The Spirit immediately drove him out into the wilderness. And he was in the wilderness forty days, being tempted by Satan...and the angels were ministering to him."[h]

One Bible reference resource summarizes the ministering work of angels by saying, "Are not angels ministering spirits? (Heb. 1:14); he will give his angels charge of you (Ps. 91:11; Matt. 4:6; Luke 4:10); angels attended Jesus (Matt. 4:11; Mark 1:13); an angel strengthened him (Luke 22:43); angels are fellow-slaves with the brethren (Rev. 19:10; Rev. 22:9); an angel fed Elijah (1 Kings 19:5; 1 Kings 19:7); an angel of the Lord directed Philip (Acts 8:26); may the angel who redeemed me bless the lads (Gen. 48:16); if there is an angel as mediator (Job 33:23); he sent his angel and delivered his servants who trusted in him (Dan. 3:28); the poor man died and was carried by the angels to Abraham's bosom (Luke 16:22)."[6]

Some critics of the supernatural claim that God does not need angels to get His work done. That is true. In the unseen realm God chooses to work with and through angelic servants the same way He chooses to work with and through human servants in the seen realm. God has staff in both

---

a Gen. 19:15; 48:16; Ps. 34:7; 91:11–12; Dan. 3:28; 6:22; Matt. 18:10; Acts 27:23–24
b Gen. 24:7; Exod. 23:20–23; Acts 8:26
c Ps. 104:4
d Heb. 2:1–3
e Acts 7:52–53; Gal. 3:19; Zech. 4:1; 5:5; 6:5
f Luke 1:11–20; Matt. 1:20–25; Luke 1:26–35
g Luke 2:8–12
h Mark 1:12–13

realms and technically does not need either of them but includes spiritual and physical beings in His ministry.

3. God invites the divine council on some occasions to participate in ministry planning.

Just like God delegates certain decisions to human ministry leaders in the seen realm, He does the same with spiritual ministry leaders in the unseen realm. One example is found in 1 Kings 22:19–21: "I saw the LORD sitting on his throne, and all the host of heaven standing beside him on his right hand and on his left; and the LORD said, 'Who will entice Ahab, that he may go up and fall at Ramoth-gilead?' And one said one thing, and another said another. Then a spirit came forward and stood before the LORD, saying, 'I will…'"

God called a staff meeting with the divine council, told them His plan, and asked someone to step forward and volunteer for the mission, which one spirit being did. In this we see the relational nature of God's leadership, which is the same way He often operates with us. We see this same thing occur with the human being Isaiah, who was invited into the divine council meeting. God asked in the presence of the spirit beings, "Whom shall I send, and who will go for us?" to which Isaiah responded, "Here I am! Send me." God agreed, saying, "Go, and say to this people…"[a]

From the time our kids were little, we have included them in ministry. They have watched us do ministry, they have done ministry with us, and they have done ministry by themselves. We wanted our kids to learn ministry and enjoy loving God by serving people. As a result our kids had a large part in planting The Trinity Church in Scottsdale, Arizona, where we all serve the Lord together as a family, led by Grace and me. God's family—both human and spirit beings—do ministry together, following the example of Jesus our Big Brother, and every family should pattern itself after God's family.

THE GOVERNANCE WAR IN HEAVEN

Evil can be very hard to understand. Where does it come from? Why does it exist?

Since the early days of the church Christians have commonly referred to evil as a *privation*. In the simplest terms, evil is not so much a thing in itself but rather the corruption of the good, like cancer that preys on the host of

---

a Isa. 6:1–9

a human body. The body can live without cancer, but cancer cannot live without the body. Similarly, good can exist without evil, but evil cannot exist without good. Before the evil sin of rebellion by angels there was only good in God's kingdom. Today there is no evil in God's heavenly kingdom but rather only good. Moreover, when God completes His full project of redemption, all that will be in His kingdom will be good without any evil of any sort. Evil, therefore, can only counterfeit and corrupt God's good creation.

While only God truly knows why evil has come into this world, everyone knows that something has gone terribly wrong in this world. No matter how many wars we wage, elections we hold, tears we shed, dollars we spend, or medications we prescribe, evil and the suffering it causes continue unabated. God reveals to us in His Word both the way that evil entered this world and His plan to eradicate it forever. Perhaps because a loving relationship requires a choice, God gave divine beings (and later human beings) the capacity to choose between good and evil, which resulted in the rebellion of sin by some angels and all people. This was an act of war against God and His kingdom.

God is a King with a kingdom, and His divine family members serve much like His military soldiers. If you've ever known a military family who love one another but get focused and intense when sent on a mission, then you have a good idea of God's spiritual family.[7]

For example, an angelic army defends Elisha, angels start a war on earth in the days of Daniel, the commander of the Lord's army visits Joshua, and at the end of the age an angel will show up on the earth brandishing a sharp sickle with which to strike down the nations.[a]

When we read the Bible, we receive God's revelation and perspective on the war we were born into. Throughout the Bible spirit beings are deployed like soldiers to sustain and defend God's people.[b] We need to be careful not to assume God is only at work when we see it. There is much we do not see. Faith is trusting that God sees what we do not see and is at work through His angelic army warring for our well-being.

Much like a commanding military officer that seeks to incite a coup to overthrow a king and overtake a kingdom, one of the highest-ranking spirit beings, also called the "strong man" or "prince of demons,"[c] became filled

---

a 2 Kings 6:15–17; Dan. 10:12–21; Josh. 5:13–15; Rev. 14:19
b 1 Kings 19:5, 7; 2 Kings 6:17; Ps. 91:11
c Matt. 4:8–9; 9:34; 12:24, 29; Mark 3:22–27; Luke 4:6; 11:21–22; John 12:31; 14:30; 16:11; 1 John 5:19

with pride.[a] We now know him by various names such as Satan, the devil, the evil one, the prince of the power of the air, the spirit of the world, Belial, the enemy, the adversary, the serpent, the dragon, the tempter, the god of this world, and the counterfeit spirit.[b] Rather than glorifying God, he wanted to be glorified as god. Rather than obeying God, he wanted to be obeyed as god. Rather than living dependently upon God, he wanted to live independently as his own god. Rather than building the kingdom, he wanted to expand his own kingdom. The battlefield report from the unseen realm says, "Now war arose in heaven, Michael and his angels fighting against the dragon. And the dragon and his angels fought back, but he was defeated, and there was no longer any place for them in heaven. And the great dragon was thrown down, that ancient serpent, who is called the devil and Satan, the deceiver of the whole world—he was thrown down to the earth, and his angels were thrown down with him."[c]

God and the angels won that battle, but all humans, starting with our first parents, have our own little battles every day that feel like wars to us. After the great war in heaven, continuing with the story of Scripture, the scene shifts to a new battlefield—earth. Jesus says, "I saw Satan fall like lightning from heaven."[d] With Satan came the demons who are now called principalities, authorities, powers, thrones, counterfeit angels, rulers, hosts, elemental spirits, and demons throughout various scriptures. We will explore our battles in the next chapter.

---

a Isa. 14:11–23; Ezek. 28:12
b Rom. 16:20; 1 Cor. 5:5; 7:5; 2 Cor. 2:11; 11:14; 12:7; 1 Thess. 2:18; 2 Thess. 2:9; 1 Tim. 1:20; 5:15; Eph. 4:27; 6:11; 1 Tim. 3:6–7; 2 Tim. 2:26; Eph. 6:16; 2 Thess. 3:3; Eph. 2:2; 2 Cor. 6:15; Luke 10:19; 1 Tim. 5:14; 2 Cor. 11:3; Rev. 12:9; 1 Thess. 3:5; 2 Cor. 4:4; 11:4
c Rev. 12:7–9
d Luke 10:18

CHAPTER 3

ADAM AND EVE LOST OUR WAR

*The serpent was more crafty than any other beast of
the field that the LORD God had made.*

—GENESIS 3:1

I**N NORTH KOREA** a godlike leader controls the media and perpetuates the narrative that he is good and other nations are threats; people are brainwashed to believe they must live in complete obedience to their ruler or risk being destroyed by outsiders. This narrative is carried forth in the curriculum for schoolchildren, who learn about their dictator-god, sing songs to him, and pledge allegiance to him. They even learn the ten principles of the regime, which are their god's version of the Ten Commandments. This is another example of how God creates and Satan counterfeits—a crucial and constant theme of the Bible regarding spiritual warfare.

North Korean schoolchildren's curriculum includes propaganda paintings of soldiers from America and other nations murdering Korean children. During recess children are encouraged to take turns stabbing and beating dummies dressed to look like American soldiers. When referring to Americans, children are required to call them "American bastard" or "Yankee devil."[1]

Jang Jin Sung, a North Korean poet who worked in his former country's propaganda bureau before defecting to South Korea, calls this an "emotional dictatorship."[2] Author Yeonmi Park explains:

In North Korea, it's not enough for the government to control where you go, what you learn, where you work, and what you say. They need to control you through your emotions, making you a slave to the state by destroying your individuality, and your ability to react to situations based on your own experience of the world.

This dictatorship, both emotional and physical, is reinforced in every aspect of your life. In fact, the indoctrination starts as soon as you learn to talk and are taken on your mother's back to the *inminban* meetings everybody in North Korea has to attend at least once a week. You learn that your friends are your "comrades" and that is how you address one another. You are taught to think with one mind.[3]

When we consider that the children born into this reality are essentially captives in a war and brainwashed, it reminds us that the entire human race is a lot like North Korea. We've all been born on the wrong side of a war, under the leadership of a false god, and fed a steady diet of fear and propaganda through the media we consume, entertainment we enjoy, and schools we attend.

North Korea operates like a demonic cult. When the Bible says that Satan is the god of this world and people are captives, it is speaking of people born into a world that is like a cult.[a] Satan is the dictator of our planet, ruling as a god and controlling everyone in his kingdom by brainwashing them from birth.

While writing this chapter, we received word of mandatory "education" training in another state. Friends of ours who love Jesus have children there and received an email notifying them of a mandatory "Equity Summit" for all students, saying, "This will be a wonderful opportunity for students and staff to participate together in a day of gaining more knowledge and awareness about topics related to equality. The day will begin with a welcome from the...mayor."[4] You might think that seems harmless, but as you read further, ask yourself if it's any more indoctrinating or false-kingdom-building than North Korea. Here are some of the lecture options students were forced to choose from:

---

a 2 Cor. 4:4; Luke 4:18; Gal. 3:23; Eph. 4:8

Respectability of womxnhood

Who gets to define Womxnhood?...We will look at the historical legacies of colonization, patriarchy, and whiteness to dismantle the how and why we exclude certain womxn....What parts of our womxnhood do we suppress to please the male and white gaze? Let's learn how to dismantle these problematic and colonial constructs and step fully, and powerfully, into our self-defined womxnhood.

Let's talk about sex(uality and gender)

We are all gendered, sexed and sexual beings! And yet, a lot of us don't know the differences between sex, gender and sexuality....Participants will walk away with new information and strategies to make their community more inclusive on the path to equality! This workshop will especially benefit QTPOC, LGBTQ+ and POC students and allies.

Two to a few

Our society is filled with black and white, either-or...we'll explain our society's traditional lens of sexuality and gender and explain the benefits of shifting towards seeing ourselves on a spectrum, with many different possibilities and identities which are not represented through the binary model.[5]

Not surprisingly, much of the culture war is over matters of identity, gender, marriage, and sexuality. All of this started in Genesis 3 when Satan came to confuse human identity, invert gender roles, and wreck marriage, which results in sexual rebellion and dysfunction in the remaining chapters of Genesis and human history.

YOUR WAR COMES AFTER YOUR WEDDING

The story line of the Bible is wedding then war. Satan did not show up until a man and woman were married with a ministry call on their lives. The first thing the enemy did was attack marriage, separating a husband and wife so he could then wreck their family and legacy. Spiritual warfare starts by attacking the relationship of a married couple. If you are married now or will someday get married, you need to know that after your wedding comes a war for your family and legacy.

Genesis 3 is one of the most important chapters in all of the Bible. It explains the source of and solution for sin and death. The scene is the beautiful and perfect garden made by God for our first parents to live in together without sin and its many effects.

Why did Satan come to the Garden of Eden? Likely because it was the place of God's divine council meetings. Throughout the Bible, God has chosen a connecting point on earth between the seen and unseen realms. Examples include the tabernacle, temple, and of course the body of Jesus Christ. The first such location chosen by God for divine council meetings was Eden. "Eden was *God's* home on earth. It was his residence. And where the King lives, his council meets."[6]

The meeting between Satan, Adam, and Eve was likely common and not the first time the couple had met there with a spirit being. This might explain why they were not startled or scared. Until sin entered the world and separation occurred, God's human and divine family members likely interacted with one another, particularly in the divine council meeting place of Eden. This also explains why an angel guarded Eden after our first parents were removed from the divine council upon sinning—God's loyal family removed His fallen family from their shared home.

The entrance of the serpent known as Satan[a] marks the beginning of chaos in creation. He is called "cunning," which means that he is shrewd, deceitful, and incredibly dangerous. Satan began by tempting Eve to mistrust God's Word by changing its meaning, just as He did when likewise tempting Jesus. Rather than rebuking Satan, Eve entertained his lies and was subsequently deceived by his crafty arguments.[b] Satan boldly accused God of being a liar; he tempted their pride by declaring that if they disobeyed God, they could become His peers and gods themselves. Satan invited humanity, starting with a husband and wife, to join him and his demons in their coup attempt against God—he was now continuing on earth the same battle he had lost in heaven. Again, this attack was in the realm of the divine council meeting held in Eden where God and His two staff families—angelic and human—would

a Rev. 12:9; 20:2
b John 8:42–47; 2 Cor. 11:3; 1 Tim. 2:14

meet. God intended from the beginning that His two families would work together in both the physical and spiritual realms.

The Lord had made a "grace garden" with one "law tree." Adam and Eve were free to eat of any tree with one exception. Satan's tactic was and is to misrepresent God as having us live in a "law garden" with many rules and restrictions. The truth is, God is a gracious Father, and when He says no, it is only for the sake of keeping His children from harm. Otherwise we have great freedom. He is like a parent who stocks the fridge and pantry with good food and treats and tells the kids not to drink the bleach under the sink.

How does the enemy still use this strategy to destroy you? Do you struggle with what *feels* good, such as sex, food, drugs, and alcohol? Do you struggle with what *looks* good, such as pornography, the possessions of others, and your own appearance and reputation? Do you struggle with pride and the need to be first, be respected, be admired, be thanked, be appreciated, and be honored? If so, you are experiencing spiritual warfare.

GODLY GOVERNANCE HAS SINGULAR HEADSHIP AND PLURAL LEADERSHIP

The government of God has the Father as the singular head, and the Son and Spirit joining Him in plural leadership. The government of home has the husband as the singular head, and the husband and wife in plural leadership. Demonic attack is concentrated upon leaders because, since the war in heaven, Satan is seeking to make himself the singular head in every sphere. Understanding singular headship and plural leadership helps us understand the satanic war in Eden and explains why Satan attacked:

- the Father in heaven;
- Adam (as head of the human race on earth);
- Jesus (as the new head of the human race on earth); and
- Peter (as the human head of the early church).

Tragically Adam stood by silently while all of the coup attempts on earth occurred; he failed to lead his family in godliness. "She [Eve] also gave some to her husband [Adam] who was with her, and he ate."[a] Eve's sin was

---

a Gen. 3:6

commission—she did what was forbidden; Adam's sin was *omission*—he did nothing.

This demonic pattern continues. Satan attacks marriage and family while passive, silent, non-relational, inactive men say and do nothing. Practically, this looks like a home in which Mom reads the Bible, prays, and goes to church with the kids while Dad sits on the other side of their teeter-totter not doing those things or leading his family spiritually.

Adam joined his wife in sin, which brought shame, distrust, and relational separation between Adam and Eve, and between our first parents and God. God then came looking for the man, holding him responsible for the sinful condition of his family as its head. The pattern is crucial: though Eve sinned first, God held Adam firstly responsible because he was the singular head of his family. "The LORD God called to the man and said to him, 'Where are you?'"[a]

God asks the same question of all the sons of Adam. To the men reading this, "Where are you?" Are you doing your God-given job to lovingly lead at home, at work, at church, and in your community? The lesson from our first father is that if we do not head our homes, Satan will gladly take our place.

Rather than repenting of his sin and owning his epic failure, Adam argued with God by blaming Eve for his sin and blaming God for making Eve. Eve also failed to repent of her sin and blamed the serpent for deceiving her. We do the same blame shifting as our first parents.

Following the fall, God cursed the parties involved as a penalty for their sin. For joining the fallen angels in the coup attempt against God, our first mother was given increased pain in childbirth and struggle with maintaining harmony with her hubby.[7] Practically speaking, this is why many women struggle with being wives and mothers.

Our first father's work became toil as the curse of sin extended to all of creation, including the ground he worked. In practical terms, this means that as men seek to work their jobs and pay their bills, they will continually be as frustrated with what is supposed to be under *their* dominion as God is with the rebellious man who is likewise supposed to be under *His* dominion. For men this means struggles will mainly come in two forms: a career at work and a covenant with a wife.

a Gen. 3:9

God dealt graciously and kindly with the man and woman though they had sinned. God lovingly clothed Adam and Eve to protect them and cover their shame. God also banished the couple from the tree of life; otherwise they would have lived forever in sin with no hope of redemption. To ensure this, God placed one of His faithful angelic soldiers on guard. The first mention of any holy spirit being other than God in the Bible is in Genesis 3:24: "He [God] drove out the man, and at the east of the garden of Eden he placed the cherubim and a flaming sword that turned every way to guard the way to the tree of life." When Adam and Eve ate the forbidden fruit, the first evil they felt was their sin, the first evil they did was hide, and the first evil they said was blaming someone else. Therefore, the way to wage spiritual war and defeat the demonic is to own our sin, run to God, and confess the truth, owning fully what we have done.

BORN INTO BATTLE

As head, Adam was the representative and father of all mankind, and when he sinned and fell out of favor with God, so did every person who would ever live. One of the great demonic myths is that each of us is an isolated individual born into this world with a blank slate and able to determine our own destiny. The fact is, each of us is born on the wrong side of a war. When Adam sinned, he voted for every member of the human family.

> Sin came into the world through one man, and death through sin, and so death spread to all men because all sinned.[a]

> By a man came death…in Adam all die.[b]

You were born a rebel in the war against God. This rebellion is part of your nature, as according to the Bible we are sinners by nature from conception.[c]

After cursing Adam and Eve, God cursed the serpent for what he had done. He was told he would be defeated one day by the woman's "seed," who is Jesus.[d] Theologians have long called the promise of Jesus in Genesis

---

a Rom. 5:12
b 1 Cor. 15:21–22
c Ps. 51:5; 58:3; Isa. 64:6; Rom. 3:23; 5:10; Eph. 2:3
d Gal. 3:16, KJV

3:15 the *protoevangelion* (first gospel), as God preaches the hope of salvation for the first time. His angel will preach it to the earth the last time before eternity is ushered in.[a] In the middle of history we join God and the angels by proclaiming the good news of Jesus Christ.

Opposing the ministry of God to forward the kingdom are demonic forces, fallen spirit beings who are at war. Paul wrote some of the most focused biblical passages on the war with the demonic realm. His goal was to equip local churches because they are on the front lines of the war.

> These are the terms Paul uses when describing the "rulers of this age" (1 Cor. 2:6, 8), the rulers "in heavenly places" (Eph. 3:10), and "the ruler of the authority of the air" (Eph. 2:2). Paul often inter-changed these terms with others that are familiar to most Bible students:
>
> ⊙ principalities (*archē*)
>
> ⊙ powers/authorities (*exousia*)
>
> ⊙ powers (*dynamis*)
>
> ⊙ dominions/lords (*kyrios*)
>
> ⊙ thrones (*thronos*)[8]

It is important to note there is no possibility of salvation for sinful angels. There is only a possibility of salvation for sinful people. God could have treated us like the demons and simply cast every one of us into "the eternal fire prepared for the devil and his angels."[b] Clearly "God did not spare angels when they sinned, but cast them into hell and committed them to chains of gloomy darkness to be kept until the judgment."[c] Instead of this just fate in hell, people are given the possibility of heaven and forgiving grace through Jesus Christ. This is one of the great mysteries of our faith. Some wonder how God could send anyone to hell. The real question is, How could God take anyone to heaven? We will explore this in the next chapter.

---

a Rev. 14:6
b Matt. 25:41
c 2 Pet. 2:4

CHAPTER 4

JESUS WON YOUR WAR

The reason the Son of God appeared was to destroy the works of the devil.
—1 John 3:8

W E BOTH CONSIDER an old Baptist preacher named Charles Spurgeon to be one of our favorite Bible teachers. In one of his best sermons Spurgeon provides vivid imagery of the victory of Jesus Christ on the cross. The following excerpt from that sermon will help set the tone for the remainder of this chapter.

> Satan came against Christ; he had in his hand a sharp sword called the Law, dipped in the poison of sin, so that every wound which the law inflicted was deadly. Christ dashed this sword out of Satan's hand, and there stood the prince of darkness unarmed. His helmet was cleft in twain, and his head was crushed as with a rod of iron. Death rose against Christ. The Saviour snatched his quiver from him, emptied out all his darts, cut them in two, gave Death back the feather end, but kept the poisoned barbs from him, that he might never destroy the ransomed. Sin came against Christ; but sin was utterly cut in pieces...all your enemies, and mine, totally disarmed? Satan has nothing left him now wherewith he may attack us.... The crown is taken from Satan.... His reigning power is gone. He may tempt, but he cannot compel; he may threaten, but he cannot subdue.... If Christ on the cross hath spoiled Satan, let

us not be afraid to encounter this great enemy of our souls....Let us not fear. The result of the battle is certain, for as the Lord our Saviour hath overcome once even so shall we most surely conquer in him. Be ye none of you afraid with sudden fear when the evil one cometh upon you....Hold up the cross before you....Through this much tribulation shall you inherit the kingdom....Go ye up against them, put your feet upon their necks, fear not, neither be ye dismayed, for the battle is the Lord's and he will deliver them into your hands. Be ye very courageous, remembering that you have to fight with a stingless dragon. He may hiss, but his teeth are broken and his poison fang extracted. You have to do battle with an enemy already scarred by your Master's weapons....Be not afraid. The lion may howl, but rend you in pieces he never can. The enemy may rush in upon you with hideous noise and terrible alarms, but there is no real cause for fear. Stand fast in the Lord. Ye war against a king who hath lost his crown....Rejoice, rejoice ye in the day of battle, for it is for you but the beginning of an eternity of triumph.[1]

ANGELS AND JESUS

The Son of God was born as a baby to Joseph and Mary, taking the battle from heaven to earth. God sent an angel to tell them Jesus was coming. Can you imagine the enormity of this experience? No one ever went to the backwater town of Nazareth. Then an angel showed up to announce the choice of an unlikely young woman for the most important task ever assigned to any mere mortal.

This was just the beginning of angelic ministry in the life of Jesus. In fact angels served in Jesus' earthly life in thirteen ways:

1. An angel promised the birth and ministry of John the Baptizer.[a]

2. An angel named Jesus.[b]

3. An angel told Mary she was chosen to be Jesus' virgin mother.[c]

---

a Luke 1:11–17
b Matt. 1:21; Luke 1:13
c Matt. 1:20–21; Luke 1:26–37

4. An angel told Mary and Joseph to parent Jesus.[a]

5. Angels told the shepherds Jesus was born.[b]

6. Angels worshipped Jesus at His birth.[c]

7. Angels warned Jesus' parents of the coming genocide so they could flee to Egypt.[d]

8. Angels strengthened Jesus after His temptation battle with Satan.[e]

9. An angel strengthened Jesus in Gethsemane before the cross.[f]

10. An angel rolled the stone away from Jesus' tomb.[g]

11. An angel told two women at the empty tomb that Jesus had risen.[h]

12. Two angels comforted Mary Magdalene and reunited her with Jesus.[i]

13. Angels promised that Jesus would be coming again.[j]

And still yet to come, angels will declare Jesus' victory and ride into history with Him for war in the end.[k]

SATAN'S ATTACKS ON JESUS

Not only did angels serve Jesus, but Satan's attack on Jesus also commenced when Jesus was only a boy. King Herod decreed that all firstborn sons be put to death in an effort to murder Jesus as an infant. Through an angel God warned Jesus' parents of the plot, and they fled to Egypt as refugees to spare Jesus' life.

---

a Matt. 1:20–21
b Luke 2:8–15
c Luke 2:13–14
d Matt. 2:13, 20
e Matt. 4:11
f Luke 22:43
g Matt. 28:2
h Matt. 28:5–7; Luke 24:4–7; John 20:11–14
i John 20:11–14
j Acts 1:10–11
k Rev. 1:1; 19:9; 22:1, 6, 16

Jesus was later attacked by Satan the tempter, who offered Him a much easier life than the one planned for Him by God the Father. God sent Jesus to earth to live a sinless life and die on the cross for sinners. In contrast, Satan offered a kingdom without a cross and promised that Jesus could rule in glory and power without any opposition or crucifixion so long as He bowed down in honor to Satan. Both the Father and the devil offered Jesus the same thing: He would sit at the right hand of a king and rule over a kingdom. The only difference was that the Father offered a path of pain, and the devil offered a path of pleasure.

An old Puritan preacher named Thomas Brooks wrote an insightful book on spiritual warfare, *Precious Remedies Against Satan's Devices*. Brooks uses a fishing metaphor to explain that the enemy will bait your hook with anything you find desirable—sex, money, power, pleasure, fame, fortune, and relationships. Satan's goal is for you to take the bait without seeing the hook. Once the hook is in your mouth, he then reels you in to club you and gut you. Often he slyly baits you with good things offered for sinful uses.

The backdrop of the entire life of Jesus is spiritual warfare. Leading up to the cross, Satan nearly got Peter to join the demonic rebellion, but Jesus prayed for him: "Simon, Simon, behold, Satan demanded to have you, that he might sift you like wheat, but I have prayed for you."[a] Satan will try and recruit you into his rebellion as well, but the good news is that Jesus continually prays for you as He "always lives to make intercession."[b] The next time you are in a war with the enemy, pause and envision Jesus Christ sitting at the right hand of the Father, praying for you to win your war.

Christ Jesus...is at the right hand of God...interceding for us.[c]

Judas Iscariot welcomed Satan[d] and conspired with him to betray Jesus and hand Him over to be crucified. All of this was spiritual warfare. Through the cross Satan and his demons thought they had finally defeated Jesus. If we picture the Lord Jesus hanging on the cross, bloodied and dying, it looks like the devil has finally won. Isaiah 45:15 says, "Truly, you are a God who

---

a Luke 22:31–32
b Heb. 7:25
c Rom. 8:34
d John 13:27

hides himself, O God of Israel, the Savior." On the cross Jesus hid His victory in defeat, hid His glory in shame, and hid our life in His death.

On the cross Jesus bled and died for you, and by faith as you look to the cross, you see that He would go to any length to conquer your common enemy. Consequently Jesus' words, "It is finished," from the cross are His heralding of your deliverance. Crucifying Jesus was the biggest mistake the devil ever made. "None of the rulers of this age understood this, for if they had, they would not have crucified the Lord of glory."[a] Satan and the demons did not see their fatal mistake because they lacked the sight of faith and did not understand the humility of Jesus.

JESUS THE DRAGON SLAYER

One of the most emotionally powerful Scriptures about Jesus' victory over Satan, sin, and death says:

> And you, who were dead in your trespasses and the uncircumcision of your flesh, God made alive together with him, having forgiven us all our trespasses, by canceling the record of debt that stood against us with its legal demands. This he set aside, nailing it to the cross. He disarmed the rulers and authorities and put them to open shame, by triumphing over them in him.[b]

The imagery in this verse from Colossians comes from the great battle victories celebrated in antiquity. Jesus is our dragon slayer who came to defeat our enemy the dragon and set us free.

We long for the final defeat of the dragon with the return of Jesus. But the authority of the devil and his demons in our lives has already ended. Jesus has thoroughly freed us from all our obligations to and agreements with the dragon, enabling us to live according to the following scripture:

> Walk in a manner worthy of the Lord, fully pleasing to him: bearing fruit in every good work and increasing in the knowledge of God…strengthened with all power, according to his glorious might, for all endurance and patience with joy; giving thanks to the Father, who has qualified you to share in the inheritance of the

a 1 Cor. 2:8
b Col. 2:13–15

saints in light. He has delivered us from the domain of darkness and transferred us to the kingdom of his beloved Son, in whom we have redemption, the forgiveness of sins.[a]

Though defeated, Satan and his demons will not be destroyed until the final judgment at Jesus' white throne.[b] Subsequently their work continues on the earth, which means you must walk wisely. The devil and his demons have no legal authority over any believer. They may take advantage of our sin, folly, weakness, fear, unbelief, and the like. However, their ownership, dominion, and condemnation of us were canceled at the cross of Christ. For those who belong to and believe in Christ, all demonic ties formed through sin, cultic vows, generational sin, and participation in the demonic realm were rendered null and void forever by virtue of the complete and total victory of Jesus Christ. Your ministry is to believe and exercise that authority.

Despite the fact that he is a doomed, limping enemy, the old dragon remains crafty, as Scripture says. His goal is always the same: to hinder and harm your relationships, starting with your relationship with God. To fool you, Satan, the *un*holy spirit, will use various tactics that the Bible, our field guide for war, warns us about.[c] The rest of this book is a battle plan to learn the tactics of the unholy spirit and employ strategies to win your war through the power of the Holy Spirit. In the next chapter we will study in depth what is meant by John 8:36, "So if the Son sets you free, you will be free indeed."

a Col. 1:10–14
b Rev. 20:11–15
c 2 Cor. 2:11

CHAPTER 5

WIN YOUR WARS

The horse is prepared for the day of battle, but
deliverance and victory belong to the LORD.

—PROVERBS 21:31, AMP

ORLD WAR II was the biggest and bloodiest war in the history of the planet. More than thirty nations were involved in the battle for six years starting with the Nazi invasion of Poland in 1939 under the leadership of Adolf Hitler. Historians estimate that between 40 and 50 million people died because one man sought to rule as a demonically empowered false god over many nations.

At the war's conclusion, despite Hitler's suicide and his successor Karl Dönitz's signed surrender, individual skirmishes continued. As is often the case in war, some German soldiers kept fighting long after their nation was defeated and the triumphant nations had cleaned up their victory parades. Some refused to accept the reality that their kingdom had fallen. Others did not care that they were defeated and simply wanted to inflict as much pain and death as they possibly could.

The war between God and Satan is much like World War II. At the cross of Jesus Christ, Satan was defeated. But skirmishes rage on until our King returns to once and for all round up the rebellious people and spirits and sentence them to an eternal prison as His kingdom overtakes every nation of the earth. These skirmishes in your life are not the big battle—King

Jesus already won that! Your battles are fought in the context of a war that is over with a foe who is defeated and will ultimately be disarmed and destroyed.

WHEN WARS CEASE

We were snuggled up on the couch watching television late one night, flipping back and forth between channels. When watching the History Channel, even though they were showing footage of World War II with building suspense, we were not anxious or alarmed. On the other hand, as we watched real-time footage on the news channel, we were noticeably more agitated and anxious. Why? We know the ending for the old news but not for the current news, which caused us to respond differently to old versus current reports.

For God everything is the History Channel, and nothing is the nightly news. God sees everything in its finished state and invites us to trust Him for a happily ever after ending for all of His people. To walk with Jesus is to march in the angelic army with the God who overcomes the world. We are to believe this by "our faith" until we see it by sight as God does.

The enemy and his empire are crumbling and will be crushed. Knowing this and by faith believing that the Bible accurately records the end of history will give you the courage you need to win your wars. In our daily battles against sin Satan tries to tempt us to join his army. He wants us to hate others rather than love others, hurt others rather than help them, and punish them rather than share the good news that Jesus was already punished for them. This not only harms them but also harms us as we experience anxiety instead of peace, angst instead of joy, and acrimony instead of harmony.

Not only is Satan a deceiver, but he has also apparently deceived himself into thinking he can rewrite the story line of the Bible and defeat God once and for all. This might explain why Satan continues to wage war even though the Bible is clear that he loses in the end.

Nevertheless, the same Jesus who *defeated* the devil in His first coming will finally *destroy* the devil in His second coming.

FOUR KEYS TO EXERCISE YOUR GOD-GIVEN SPIRITUAL AUTHORITY

Our King Jesus said, "All authority in heaven and on earth has been given to me."[a] If you belong to Jesus Christ, you need to believe the following four things so you can exercise the authority He delegated to you as you wage your war.

1. You have moved from the kingdom of darkness to the kingdom of light.

When you were born, you were born into the world system, which is a counterfeit kingdom at war against the kingdom of God since "the whole world lies in the power of the evil one."[b] When you were born again of the Holy Spirit, your citizenship transferred from this world to the kingdom. Your residence may still be in this world, but your citizenship is in heaven, as "He has delivered us from the domain of darkness and transferred us to the kingdom of his beloved Son."[c] Furthermore, King Jesus protects you in this enemy territory: "We know that everyone who has been born of God does not keep on sinning, but he who was born of God protects him, and the evil one does not touch him."[d]

For Christians this life is as close to hell as we will ever be; it is as bad as it will ever get. Conversely, for non-Christians, this life is as close to heaven as they will ever be; it is as good as it will ever get.

2. Demonic attack is not uncommon.

In school we study the history of wars; in church we study the war behind the wars. Not only are soldiers marching into battle throughout history, but so are spirits. Like physical soldiers, demon warriors are skilled persons who communicate, possess great intelligence, have emotions that drive them, and have a will by which they make tactical decisions.[e]

When two nations are at war, every citizen is also involved in that war. When an enemy army marches into a town, the residents find themselves under siege for the simple reason that there is a war and everyone is on one side or the other.

---

a Matt. 28:18
b 1 John 5:19
c Col. 1:13
d 1 John 5:18
e Luke 4:31–37; 8:28–30; Mark 1:23–24, 27

In wars only the noteworthy warriors become legends. The Bible names some of these demonic warriors: Baal[a] and other demons working together as the Baals,[b] also called the host of heaven;[c] Ashtaroth/Asherah;[d] Chemosh;[e] Molech;[f] Artemis;[g] Legion;[h] Hermes;[i] Zeus;[j] Dike, also called Justice;[k] Castor and Pollux, the twin gods;[l] Kiyyun, the star-god;[m] the queen of heaven;[n] and Lilith, also called the night creature or screech owl.[o] We also see fallen divine leaders, the princes of Persia and Greece, at spiritual war with God's divine leader. God's chief prince, Michael, and the Lord's angels and other divine beings are all engaged in the battle.[p]

Like any army, we do not know the names of most of the enemy troops as there are many demonic "unknown god(s)."[q] New Testament scholar Clinton Arnold has noted that in addition to the named demons in Scripture, "one scholar has counted 123 different demons identified by name in the rabbinic literature."[1]

The Bible also speaks of demons in terms of dangerous beasts, starting with Satan as a serpent/dragon and a lion,[r] and other demons called such things as a python spirit,[s] goat demons,[t] and wild animals including ostriches, bulls, hyenas, birds, and scorpions.[u]

This is not surprising, as the Bible also refers to evil people, in addition to evil spirits, in animalistic terms such as vipers, serpents, goats, cows,

---

a Num. 25:1–5; 2 Kings 17:16; 21:3
b Judg. 2:11, 13
c 2 Kings 21:3; 23:4
d Judg. 2:13; 1 Kings 15:13; 2 Kings 17:16; 21:3
e Judg. 11:24; 1 Kings 11:7, 33
f Lev. 18:21; 20:2–5; 1 Kings 11:7; 2 Kings 23:10; Jer. 32:35
g Acts 19:24–35
h Mark 5:9, 15; Luke 8:30
i Acts 14:8–18
j Acts 14:8–18
k Acts 28:1–6
l Acts 28:11
m Amos 5:26
n Jer. 7:18; 44:17–19
o Isa. 34:14, NIV, KJV
p Dan. 10
q Acts 17:23
r Gen. 3:1; Rev. 12:9; 20:2; 1 Pet. 5:8
s Acts 16:16–18
t 2 Chron. 11:15; Isa. 13:21; 34:14
u Isa. 13:21; Ps. 22:12–13; Isa. 34:14; Luke 10:17–20

dogs, wolves, leeches, donkeys, and evil beasts.[a] This might also mean that the "wild beasts" Paul fought in Ephesus were actually people operating by demonic powers.[b]

Demonic attack is constant, often seducing the flesh within us because we are living in the midst of a war that has been raging since it erupted in heaven. Knowing about this war can cause panic, but God invites you to cast "all your anxieties on him, because he cares for you. Be sober-minded; be watchful. Your adversary the devil prowls around like a roaring lion, seeking someone to devour. Resist him, firm in your faith, knowing that the same kinds of suffering are being experienced by your brotherhood throughout the world."[c] You have peace with God but war on earth, as Jesus promised, "In me you may have peace. In the world you will have tribulation. But take heart; I have overcome the world."[d]

There is no place you can go to avoid this battle since the war is waged throughout the world. But the fact that you are sometimes under attack should oddly comfort you. A loyal subject of the king is the most likely target in a war. If you are loyal to King Jesus, then it is normal to walk through a demonic minefield now and then.

3. You come with your King's authority.

Sometimes as a guilty pleasure we will watch a few minutes of the television show *Cops*. Full disclosure: I (Mark) have had at least one cousin on the show, and he was *not* one of the cops. We have noticed that something curious happens in episode after episode. Someone who is raging and out of control suddenly changes his or her behavior once a police officer shows up on the scene. Often the person committing the crime simply surrenders.

Why?

Because the cop shows up with the full authority of an entire police force. When someone with more authority shows up, you must surrender. You can do this *willingly* by getting on the ground and throwing your hands up, or you can do this *unwillingly* by getting slammed on the ground

---

a Matt. 3:7; 12:34; 23:33; 25:32–33; Amos 4:1; Phil. 3:2; Rev. 22:15; Matt. 7:15; 10:16; Prov. 30:15; Gen. 16:12; Titus 1:12
b 1 Cor. 15:32, NIV
c 1 Pet. 5:7–9
d John 16:33

and having your hands wrenched behind your back for handcuffs. Either way, when someone with higher authority shows up, you will surrender.

When a demon comes into your life, it does not need to surrender to you. You have no authority apart from Jesus. Every demon must submit to Jesus because He has all authority.

No one and nothing has authority equal to Jesus Christ. Today Jesus is at the right hand of the Father "seated... in the heavenly places, far above all rule and authority and power and dominion, and above every name that is named, not only in this age but also in the one to come," with everyone and everything "under his feet."[a]

However, there is more. In Paul's letter to the Ephesians we read that God "raised us up with him and seated us with him in the heavenly places in Christ Jesus."[b] The children of God will be seated for all eternity in authority with King Jesus. In fact a day is coming when God's people will "judge angels."[c] How staggering is that concept? When all is said and done, God's people will exercise authority over fallen angels for all eternity. Therefore, when a demon shows up in your life, he is the criminal, you are the cop, and you come in the name and authority of the highest power in all eternity: Jesus.

4. Your defeated enemy has to surrender to your victorious King.

Do you remember the kids' game called uncle, or mercy? The gist of the game is that two kids squeeze one another's hands until one of them surrenders by shouting, "Uncle!" or "Mercy!"

Satan and demons seem to like playing their own spiritual version of this game. They will bring some sort of trouble, trial, or temptation and squeeze until you surrender to them, thereby allowing them to win. Demons want you to believe the lie that they will never stop squeezing until you surrender so you will give up and give in to get it over with as quickly as possible.

The truth is that you do not have to play their game. Rather than surrendering to unholy spirits, you can yield to the Holy Spirit. If you surrender to the Spirit and command the demonic to depart, it must leave you: "Submit yourselves therefore to God. Resist the devil, and he will flee from you."[d] Jesus modeled this. As we surrender to the Spirit, the devil must sur-

---

a Eph. 1:15–22
b Eph. 2:6
c 1 Cor. 6:3
d Jas. 4:7

render to Him as well. You do not have to give up or give in. The Spirit of God in you is greater than the demonic spirits against you, and if you do not surrender to the demonic but instead surrender to God, they will also surrender to Him and leave you as they did Jesus.

THE SUPERNATURAL POWER OF SPIRITS

The limitations we have are natural. As created beings with limited energy, we all reach the point where we have depleted ourselves and say things like, "I'm out," "I need a break," "I cannot do any more," "I just need to sit down," and "I've got nothing left to give."

Sound familiar?

Now, consider the different reality in which angels and other divine beings live. They do not share in the limits of our humanity. Instead they sing and serve "day and night."[a] What is the longest church service, worship event, Christian conference, or retreat you have sat through? Even the most devout believer would not be able to hold church and worship God "day and night," day after day and night after night.

What is true of angels is also true of demons. Satan's nonstop attack on believers is "day and night."[b] Demons do not need a nap, a day off, food, water, or sleep because they do not get tired or sick.

Do you see the problem for you? If you have human limits, and demonic spirits who attack you do not share those limits, how can you possibly win a war against that foe since "we do not wrestle against flesh and blood, but against the rulers, against the authorities, against the cosmic powers over this present darkness, against the spiritual forces of evil in the heavenly places"?[c]

To win your war, you cannot fight by your own natural power. A natural person cannot win a spiritual battle against a supernatural demon. No one ever defeated the demonic by his or her own strength. No matter how self-disciplined you are, how hard you try, or how tough you may be, eventually the supernatural always defeats the natural.

Sometimes evil people live by the power of demonic forces and have a superhuman energy level. They harass and hound you until you are over-whelmed, exhausted, and overtaken. Jesus delivered two "demon-possessed

---

a Rev. 4:8; 7:15
b Rev. 12:10
c Eph. 6:12

men" who were "so fierce that no one could pass that way."[a] People took the long way around the region where these men lived. Two men controlled an entire region—until Jesus cast their demons out.

In Mark 5:1–20 Jesus encounters "a man with an unclean spirit." Because of his demonic strength, "no one could bind him anymore, not even with a chain, for he had often been bound with shackles and chains, but he wrenched the chains apart, and he broke the shackles in pieces. No one had the strength to subdue him. Night and day among the tombs and on the mountains he was always crying out and cutting himself with stones" (vv. 3–5).

You know you are dealing with a demonized person when they do evil, never grow weary, and force everyone else to work around them, avoid them, and live in fear of them. The only way that you can win your war against demonic power is by the supernatural power of God the Holy Spirit: "Be strong in the Lord and in the strength of his might."[b] Our strength comes from the Lord's strength and not our own. The Christian life is super-naturally lived "in the Spirit" by God's power at work for you, in you, and through you. The counterfeit of being Spirit-filled is being demon-possessed. When someone is filled with an unholy spirit, your only defense is to be filled with the Holy Spirit.

SPIRIT-FILLED LIKE JESUS

The only way to win a war against an unholy spirit is by the power of the Holy Spirit, because "you are from God and have overcome them, for he who is in you is greater than he who is in the world."[c] Jesus Christ models this truth for us. When God entered history as Jesus Christ, He joined us in our humanity and experienced our limitations. After a long walk through the desert Jesus sat down at a well to rest because He was tired from the journey.[d] After fasting for forty days and nights, He was hungry.[e] On the cross Jesus said, "I thirst."[f] Jesus' body was pushed to its human limits.

During His earthly life Jesus could have made things much easier for

---

a Matt. 8:28–34
b Eph. 6:10
c 1 John 4:4
d John 4:6
e Matt. 4:2
f John 19:28

Himself. He could have chosen not to live humbly and endure the limits of humanity, but instead He chose to humble Himself to become like you so that you could become like Him. Jesus was pushed to the limits of humanity as you are.

Prior to His death on the cross Jesus' greatest spiritual battle was with the devil himself. Knowing Jesus was isolated, hungry, thirsty, and tired after forty days alone fasting in the wilderness, Satan sought to exploit Jesus' humanity. Satan offered the hungry Jesus bread to eat. Satan also offered self-indulgence to meet every physical longing that we humans have, such as food, drink, sex, sleep, and comfort. The Father offered self-denial to resist every sinful longing and temptation that we face. In all honesty, which path would you choose—the pleasure path of self-indulgence or the pain path of self-denial?

Jesus won His war. How did He do it? Jesus' march into war "was led by the Spirit."[a] After winning His war, "Jesus returned in the power of the Spirit."[b]

You can win your war by the same power that our Christ did. The supernatural power of the Holy Spirit is "the Spirit of Christ" that "dwells in you."[c] The same Spirit that empowered the life and resurrection of Jesus Christ while He was on the earth is available to you.

Often we think of the ministry of the Holy Spirit as being miraculous things, but the Holy Spirit also ministers in the mundane. He is there to help you in times of trouble, trial, and temptation so you can live by a supernatural power, the most incredible power source there could possibly be!

Perhaps an illustration will help. While writing a previous book, *Spirit-Filled Jesus*, I (Mark) was under a deadline and had hours of writing time on a flight. I opened my laptop to find that my battery was nearly dead. I was admittedly frustrated as I had a long flight and lots of work to do to help people learn to live by God's power, but my laptop had no power. My laptop died, and ironically, I spent the remaining hours wishing I *had* power so I could *write about* power.

To make matters worse, after the flight landed, I dropped a pen. As I bent over to pick it up, I saw that under my seat was a power outlet that I

---

a Luke 4:1
b Luke 4:14
c Rom. 8:9

had overlooked. Yes, I had an unlimited free power source available to me that I simply failed to access.

The power of God in the unseen realm is available to God's people in the seen realm through the Holy Spirit. He plugs us into the power of God so that we can defeat the same demonic forces that were already defeated at the wars in heaven and on the cross.

Many, if not most, Christians are living life by their own power until they wear down and wear out. The devil and his demons know this, so they beat us down until they bring us down. Meanwhile God the Holy Spirit is available as the power source we need to live a life of victory. Sadly, we fail to plug into His power. We often have a far better and more intentional plan of plugging our phone or laptop into a power source than we do to keep our soul plugged into the Spirit. How? Prayer, worship, Scripture, fellowship, and inviting God's presence and peace before, during, and after our wars. The key to all spiritual war is to overcome our demonic influence, as we will learn in the next chapter.

CHAPTER 6

WIN YOUR WAR AGAINST DEMONIC INFLUENCE

Nothing can ever separate us from God's love... neither angels nor demons... not even the powers of hell can separate us from God's love. No power in the sky above or in the earth below— indeed, nothing in all creation will ever be able to separate us from the love of God that is revealed in Christ Jesus our Lord.

—ROMANS 8:38–39, NLT

I (MARK) WAS A nonpracticing Catholic who did not know Jesus when I met Grace. We started dating in high school, at which time Grace bought me a beautiful leather-bound Bible with my name engraved on the front. I became a Christian reading that Bible in college, and before long Grace transferred so we could attend the same college and church. At my first men's retreat God spoke to me and told me to marry Grace, preach the Bible, train men, and plant churches. We were married in college, and after graduating, we started officially doing ministry by leading college students roughly our age.

To be nearer to the university students, we moved into a former college rental house. We were young, inexperienced, and naïve. We read about loving people and practicing hospitality in the Bible, and in our lack of wisdom we turned our home into the base of our ministry. We lived upstairs with our young children, and on the main floor was the ministry office along with our kitchen, living room, and dining room. In the basement lived interns and broke college kids who needed a place to crash.

Nearly every night of the week we hosted Bible studies in our home. We welcomed a few thousand people into our home each year, and that's no exaggeration.

We moved out of that house after one final late-night event pushed us over the top. We awoke to the sound of someone vigorously shaking the handle to the front door and trying to get in through various closed windows on the main floor. I grabbed my gun, instructed Grace to call the police and stay upstairs no matter what, and started praying that I would not have to preach the funeral for someone I shot.

Peering outside through the narrow glass window next to our front door, I recognized the man. He was sweating, yelling, and agitated. I thought he was possibly on drugs, as we lived in an area that had a lot of black tar heroin overdoses during the grunge era—including one man who died on the back steps of the punk rock venue where we held church.

Within minutes the police arrived. As they approached, the man started growling very loudly and boldly like a lion. The police were trying to calm him down. I stepped outside, and the man immediately escalated. He tried to run toward me and was thrown to the ground by the police, and they had trouble subduing him as he fought back. In the struggle the man somehow got to the patrol car, where he threw his arms and legs around a tire and held on tight while they tried to arrest him. The entire time he growled like a lion at the top of his lungs. Eventually they cuffed him, wrestled him into the patrol car, and arrested him.

Obviously suffering from some combination of demonic and mental problems, the man was later tested, and no drugs were found in his system. However, he escaped a psychiatric ward and walked for miles in his underwear—until he was arrested walking down the middle of the busy street in front of our home. We are happy to report that, with spiritual and medical help, this person was delivered and seems to be doing well today. No one is beyond God's power for transformation.

This story is reminiscent of the line, "The devil made me do it." It was made popular in the 1970s by Flip Wilson, a comedian who hosted a television show. In one of his sketches Flip did an impersonation of a woman who used this as her excuse for any sort of wrongdoing.

The first person to blame shift their sinning to Satan was our mother Eve: "The serpent deceived me."ᵃ Satan is at work in the world, but can we really blame the devil for our misdeeds?

Whenever the topic of Satan and demons comes up, the first question often asked is, "Can a Christian be possessed by a demon?" We want to address this question now so that we can set a framework for the rest of our study together.

For the non-Christian, it is possible to give oneself over to sin, rebellion, and evil to the extent that an unclean spirit takes up residence in and ownership over someone. The New Testament Gospels are filled with reports about Jesus' ministry of deliverance. Curiously Jesus is the first person in the Bible to cast a demon out of someone; the Old Testament has no record of this ever happening prior to Jesus' ministry. However, all demonic deliverance accounts in the New Testament follow Jesus' pattern. Here are a few examples from just one New Testament book.

- Matthew 4:24 (CEV) says, "People with every kind of sickness or disease were brought to him. Some of them had a lot of demons in them, others were thought to be crazy, and still others could not walk. But Jesus healed them all."

- Matthew 8:16 (CEV) says, "Many people with demons in them were brought to Jesus. And with only a word he forced out the evil spirits and healed everyone who was sick."

- Matthew 9:32–33 (CEV) says, "Some people brought to him a man who could not talk because a demon was in him. After Jesus had forced the demon out, the man started talking."

- Matthew 12:22 (CEV) says, "People brought to Jesus a man who was blind and could not talk because he had a demon in him. Jesus healed the man, and then he was able to talk and see."

- Matthew 15:22, 28 (CEV) says, "A Canaanite woman from there came out shouting, 'Lord and Son of David, have pity on me! My daughter is full of demons.' . . . At that moment her daughter was healed."

---

a Gen. 3:13

- Matthew 17:18 (CEV) says, "Jesus spoke sternly to the demon. It went out of the boy, and right then he was healed."

The Bible is very clear. Demonic spirits can overcome some non-Christians to the point that they suffer mental and physical anguish. Not all mental and physical anguish is the result of demonic control, but some of it is. In such circumstances a doctor to serve the body, a counselor to serve the mind, and the power of God to deliver the soul can all be helpful to minister to the whole person.

CAN A CHRISTIAN BE DEMON-POSSESSED?

How about a Christian? Can a Christian be demon-possessed? On this issue, as they say, the devil is in the details. *Oxford English Dictionary* gives the following as the first three definitions of the word *possess*:

1. Have as belonging to one; own.

2. Have possession of as distinct from ownership.

3. Have as an ability, quality, or characteristic.[1]

Definition #1

In the first sense, a Christian cannot belong to Satan; he cannot own us. The transfer of ownership for people is always and only one way—people who belonged to Satan and darkness become God's people in the light. "He has delivered us from the domain of darkness and transferred us to the kingdom of his beloved Son."[a] Salvation is a miracle of God where we "turn from darkness to light and from the power of Satan to God."[b]

Some people ask if a Christian can lose his or her salvation, which is the wrong question. Salvation does not belong to us, but rather "salvation belongs to the Lord!"[c] Therefore, the question is, Can God lose a Christian? The answer to that is no. With total confidence the Holy Spirit says through Paul, "I am sure that neither...angels nor rulers...nor powers, nor height nor depth, nor anything else in all creation, will be able to separate us from the love of

---

a Col. 1:13
b Acts 26:18
c Jon. 2:9

God in Christ Jesus our Lord."[a] This is because a Christian is forever "sealed" with the Holy Spirit as the "guarantee" of eternal life.[b]

We have five children. We both love babies. When the kids were little and entirely dependent upon us, we would often snuggle up as a couple with them. The safest place for our children was in our arms. Jesus uses this kind of word picture, saying, "I give them eternal life, and they will never perish, and no one will snatch them out of my hand. My Father, who has given them to me, is greater than all, and no one is able to snatch them out of the Father's hand."[c]

Definition #2

In the second sense of the word *possess*, a Christian can be internally influenced by the demonic without ownership of their soul transferring to the devil. Think of your life like your home, since you live in both. You are the legal resident of your home, and no one else has the right to move in unless you give them permission. Now, let's say that some bad people come to your house, you open the door to welcome them in, and they decide to stay and make your life miserable. They possess no legal right to be there, but they are willing to squat until you exercise your legal authority and demand that they vacate your home. On rare occasions, through habitual sin, deep unbelief, dark addiction, or occult activity, a Christian can open the door to internal demonic influence that does not have any legal authority and can be evicted in Jesus' name.

In Acts 5:1–11 we meet "Ananias, with his wife Sapphira." After watching Barnabas sell land and give the proceeds to the church, they decided to do the same. They sold a piece of property, but rather than tithing the entire amount they had promised to the Lord, with the wife's consent the husband "kept back for himself some of the proceeds and brought only a part of it and laid it at the apostles' feet" (v. 2). These church members were guilty of lying to the Lord and their leaders while stealing. Pastor Peter asked, "Ananias, why has Satan filled your heart to lie to the Holy Spirit?" (v. 3) Then he told the couple, "You have not lied to man but to God" (v. 4). Internally influenced by Satan, both the husband and wife died right there on the spot, causing awe and fear among the other Christians.

Because Satan internally influenced them, some speculate that these two

---

a Rom. 8:38–39
b Eph. 1:13–14
c John 10:28–29

were not, in fact, Christians. Here is what one New Testament commentary says:

> Were Ananias and Sapphira really believers? Scholars answer in at least two ways: 1) they were members of the church (so-called nominal Christians) who never entered in faith into a personal saving relationship with Jesus; 2) they were Christians whose sin (possibly the sin unto death of 1 John 5:16–17; cf. 1 Cor. 11:27–30) God punished as an example to the church but who gained eternal salvation. The entire narrative seems to indicate that these people were born-again Christians and very much a part of the Jerusalem congregation. It is not unusual in the Scripture to find death coming to believers at the hand of God.[2]

Christians can open themselves up to the internal influence of demonic powers through participating in evil, even though they still belong to God as His possession. Some argue that God and Satan cannot occupy the same space, but that is possible if the Lord permits it. As one example, in Job 1, Satan clearly comes into God's presence, and they have a conversation regarding Job.

Definition #3

In the third sense of the word *possess*, it is possible for a Christian to manifest demonic character or say things with demonic origins. As Jesus was teaching about His death, "Peter took him aside and began to rebuke him, saying, 'Far be it from you, Lord! This shall never happen to you.'" In response Jesus "turned and said to Peter, 'Get behind me, Satan!'"[a] Peter was a believer, but in that instance he echoed what Satan was saying and rebuked the Lord as if Jesus were sinning. Jesus identified Satan as the ultimate origin of what Peter was doing and saying.

In summary, a Christian can be lied to, tempted by, and attacked by Satan just as Jesus Christ was. However, it is impossible for a demon to own a believer as its possession.

While God cannot lose a Christian, a person can fake having faith. This was precisely the case with Judas Iscariot. He was incredibly covert, hiding the fact that for years as Jesus' bookkeeper "he was a thief, and having charge

---

a Matt. 16:21–23

of the moneybag he used to help himself to what was put into it."ᵃ Even though Judas outwardly looked like a believer, he was not. Knowing that many would wrongly assume Judas was a believer whom "Satan entered,"ᵇ Jesus made it clear that Judas was never a real Christian. Jesus said of His disciples minus Judas, "I protected them and kept them safe…None has been lost except the one doomed to destruction."ᶜ

For the real Christian there is no excuse for permitting internal influence to demonic forces. The problem is not out there in demons but ultimately in us. We cannot control what demons do, but we can control what we do since "each person is tempted when he is lured and enticed by his own desire."ᵈ Demons cannot control believers or make us do anything because we have the weapons to win our spiritual wars. There is always a way to escape a demonic attack.ᵉ

Becoming a Christian is both receiving Jesus and rejecting Satan. On the Old Testament Day of Atonement, two animals were sacrificed for this very reason. The first animal was spotless (symbolizing sinlessness) and died as a substitute for the sinner, showing the receiving of Jesus. The second animal was a scapegoat to which sin was reckoned as it was driven away, showing the renouncing of Satan. Heiser adds this interesting detail in his book *The Unseen Realm*:

> The wilderness was where Israelites believed "desert demons," including Azazel, lived. The Azazel material is especially telling, since…[the] Jewish practice of the Day of Atonement ritual in Jesus' day included driving the goat "for Azazel" into the desert outside Jerusalem and pushing it over a cliff so it could not return. The wilderness was a place associated with the demonic, so it's no surprise that this is where Jesus meets the devil.³

Similarly the baptismal formula of the early church included both receiving Jesus and renouncing Satan: "The renunciation of the devil at baptism is a custom which goes back certainly to the 2nd century."⁴

We further learn, "The first witness for renunciations…is Tertullian.…When

---

a John 12:6
b Luke 22:3
c John 17:12, NIV
d Jas. 1:14
e 1 Cor. 10:13

entering the water, we make profession of the Christian faith in the words of its rule, we bear public testimony that we have renounced the devil, his pomp, and his angels."[5]

The key to living free from demonic influence as a Christian is twofold. One, you must receive Jesus Christ and His defeat of the demonic. Two, you must renounce any ground you give to the demonic through such things as sin, rebellion, unbelief, pride, and the other matters we discuss throughout this book. This is precisely what James 4:7 means when it says, "Submit yourselves therefore to God [receive]. Resist the devil [renounce], and he will flee from you" (amplification added).

NIGHT TERRORS

One key way to resist demonic attack is to "Stay alert!"[a] This may indicate that when we are asleep, we are more vulnerable to the demonic realm, which never sleeps. For some people the physical darkness that descends at bedtime comes with corresponding spiritual darkness. Many people suffer from nightmares and night terrors as fear grips them during sleep.

Trauma survivors such as soldiers, first responders, and sexual assault victims are more prone to nightmares. People with recurring nightmares and night terrors are prone to self-harm and even suicide. One news story reports:

> Trauma survivors—specifically those suffering from Post Traumatic Stress Disorder (PTSD)—are more likely to experience nightmares. In fact, while only 2.5 to 10 percent of adults experience nightmares…up to 90 percent of those with PTSD have reported "disturbing dreams with some degree of resemblance to the actual traumatic event"…more than 50 percent of Vietnam War veterans with PTSD said they experienced nightmares "fairly often," while only 3 percent of civilians reported the same.[6]

During the writing of this book, several different times when Mark was away preaching out of state or the country, I (Grace) was suddenly awakened by dark, fuzzy shapes moving in our bedroom. One even flew at me, seemingly to attack. I immediately spoke Jesus' name to command them away. I continued to pray against fear and the enemy and pray for protection of

---

a 1 Pet. 5:8, NLT

our home and family until I was able to fall asleep again. Sadly this is not uncommon, particularly in seasons of intense ministry.

Like most people we have both experienced nightmares and the terror they bring. Your heart races, reacting to the dream as if it were a real event, until you eventually wake up, disoriented and unsure about what is really happening. Our children have had the same experience, and this is not uncommon. The Sleep Health Foundation says that roughly 10 to 50 percent of children experience nightmares.[7]

We know of a godly young pastor's child who started acting unusually moody and out of sorts. The parents began disciplining the child, but over the course of a few days he grew more despondent. Worried, the parents sat the child down, lovingly prayed over him, and asked him to share anything else that might be happening. The child refused to disclose anything, but the parents could tell something was being concealed. Eventually the child said a "mean man" was appearing in his room at night "saying bad things" about Jesus and the family and threatening that if the child told the parents he would "hurt their family." The poor child was sleep deprived and traumatized, and a demonic wedge was forming between the child and his parents.

We also know of other children who have had night terrors brought on by demons that they referred to as "invisible friends." Some children put place settings at their tea parties or talk about conversations they have with their "invisible friend." Sometimes this is an active imagination or fictitious and fun role-playing, like a child dressing up as a princess or firefighter, but at other times this is literally a demon that deceptively pretends to be a friend. These kinds of demonic encounters can and do contribute to some night terrors for children and can continue into adulthood.

Job describes a night terror, saying, "Amid thoughts from visions of the night, when deep sleep falls on men, dread came upon me, and trembling, which made all my bones shake. A spirit glided past my face; the hair of my flesh stood up. It stood still, but I could not discern its appearance. A form was before my eyes; there was silence, then I heard a voice."[a] Sometimes a night terror is demonic as Job describes; sometimes it is simply our minds playing tricks on us. Science still seeks to understand everything about the ways our body works while we sleep.

When it comes to night terrors, there is hope for God's children: "If you

---

a Job 4:13–16

lie down, you will not be afraid; when you lie down, your sleep will be sweet. Do not be afraid of sudden terror."[a] The authority that we enjoy in Christ includes our times of sleep. "You will not fear the terror of the night."[b]

A nighttime routine that invites the presence of God into your home is essential. This can include such things as praying over the home, Bible reading, personal prayer, worship, repenting of any sin, and what we call "offensive prayer." By this we mean prayer that takes an offensive stance against the enemy. Too often Christians are on the defensive, waiting for an enemy strike and then responding. In any war it is better to be on the offensive, striking your enemies before they strike you.

Throughout the Book of Psalms you can find prayerful worship songs to pray and worship offensively against foes both spiritual and physical (e.g., Ps. 18; 27; 31; 35; 83). In the worst season of spiritual war, a season in which we felt under attack day and night, we wrote out Psalm 31 and posted it in our bedroom to remind us of God's promises and to pray offensively. We can confirm that as we wage war against the demonic realm by praying and worshipping God, the presence and peace of God occupy the center of our lives and drive out whatever is dark and demonic. Not only are such things as demonic influence and night terrors driven out by prayer and worship, but so are potential idols in our lives that seek to take God's place, which we will learn about next.

a Prov. 3:24–25
b Ps. 91:5

CHAPTER 7

WIN YOUR WAR AGAINST IDOLATRY

So, my beloved, flee from idolatry.

—1 Corinthians 10:14, mev

THE SAMARITANS WERE sexually confused, started a cult, and even sacrificed their children to demons who masqueraded as gods. While others walked around Samaria, God came to earth and went for a long walk to that very place.

In the heat of the desert Jesus sat down at a well to have a conversation with a Samaritan woman, as John 4 reports. She was an outcast, married five times, and living with some guy who had taken advantage of her abused and confused state.

Jesus was Jewish. The woman was Samaritan. Between these two groups was a war over worship. In the days of Ezra and Nehemiah the Jewish exiles who had returned to Jerusalem began repairing and rebuilding the temple so they could worship God there. The Samaritans offered to help but were told that as godless idolaters who did not possess salvation, their assistance was unwelcome.[a]

In response the renegade Jew Manasseh married a Samaritan woman and constructed another temple on Mount Gerizim, which was in the heart of

---

a Ezra 4:1–5

Samaria, to serve as their competing site of worship and priesthood.[a] God created a temple in Jerusalem, and Satan counterfeited it in Samaria. Today we would simply call this a cult. The counterfeit Samaritan temple remained in use for roughly three hundred years, until the Jews burned it to the ground.

Sitting with Jesus, the Samaritan woman asked Jesus *the* theological issue dividing their religions, races, and worship: Where should she go to worship God?

Jesus' answer changed the course of human history.

Jesus declared an end to both Samaritan and Jewish worship, and instead favored worshipping in spirit and truth. The Father was actively seeking worshippers. Because of the Spirit, people would no longer need to go to a place or temple; they could worship anyplace because God would make their bodies temples.

Jesus speaks all this to a sole sinful Samaritan woman. He knows her, and now she knows Him, so their eternal relationship begins. Stunned, she runs into town telling the good news of Jesus as one of the first and greatest evangelists in the entire New Testament, sparking a revival in Samaria.

This woman's story is what it means to be "turned to God from idols."[b] She had many problems—relational, marital, spiritual, sexual, and social— yet under all her problems was idolatry.

This woman was passionate and kept worshipping even though she was worshipping the wrong thing. Anyone who marries five times and is taking another run at it is really passionate about having a relationship. That person is a desperate worshipper, devoting all his or her passion to the wrong thing. God created us to worship Him, but idolatry is the counterfeit of worship. Like the Samaritan woman at the well, we worship our way into trouble by worshipping counterfeits, and we can worship our way out of trouble by worshipping our Creator.

WORSHIP

Worship versus idolatry is one of the main themes of the Bible. God provided the Ten Commandments in order of importance. The first commandment teaches us *who* to worship and who or what *not* to worship.

---

a Neh. 13:23–31
b 1 Thess. 1:9

The second commandment teaches us *how* to worship and how *not* to worship.

It's impossible to worship the one true God while disobeying the remaining commandments. Dishonor, murder, adultery, greed, lying, and envy happen because we choose to commit idolatry, worshipping someone or something counterfeit in place of God the Creator. Our false gods lead us into slavery *to* sin rather than freedom *from* sin.

Worship starts with God. God is a worshipper. For all eternity the Father, Son, and Spirit are pouring themselves out in love and service to one another in perfect relationship. God made us in His image and likeness as worshippers. Worship is not merely a part of what we do and something that starts and stops; worship is what everyone does all the time. The issue is not *if* we worship but who, what, and how we worship.

IDOLATRY

When rabid sports fans pay big bucks for tickets, show up early to tailgate, wear team gear, paint their faces, and stand up screaming for a few hours, it is, for many, a day of worship at their "church" shaped like a stadium. When the fan club shows up for the concert of their favorite band at great expense and with great expectation as they sweat and sing along to every word, you can be sure that it is their version of a revival meeting. When someone spends all his or her time and money on golf, boating, fishing, sex, gambling, watching television, surfing the internet, or ranting about politics, he or she is making a sacrifice, which is an act of worship. The alcoholic worships the bottle, the drug addict worships the high, the codependent person worships his or her relationship partner, the greedy person worships the demon god Mammon as a lover of money, the control freak worships being in charge, and the helicopter parent worships his or her kid.

Worship is what happens when we worship the Creator God in the right way, in "spirit and truth" (John 4:24). Idolatry is what happens when we worship a counterfeit god or worship the right God in a counterfeit way. What constitutes a counterfeit god or object of worship? "Martin Luther's answer, reflecting on the first commandment in his larger catechism, was 'whatever your heart clings to and relies upon, that is your God; trust and faith of the heart alone make both God and idol.'"[1]

While idolatry manifests externally, it originates internally. As Christians we commonly ask people if they have accepted Jesus in their hearts; the counterfeit is people who "have taken their idols into their hearts."[a] Christian counselor David Powlison says, "Idolatry is by far the most frequently discussed problem in the Scriptures."[2]

Underlying idolatry is the lie that someone or something other than God can do a fine job being the object of our worship. When we believe the lie, we commit idolatry and exchange the real God, who created everyone and everything, for someone or something God made as our counterfeit god.[b]

God made us to worship Him by enjoying everyone and everything that He graciously provides for us. Satan wants us to love the gifts more than their Giver. Satan does not care what you worship so long as you worship someone or something other than God. Idolatry occurs when we take a good thing and put it in God's place. Idolatry occurs when someone or something becomes too important to us, displacing God as the center of our lives, and we start sacrificing our time, money, energy, health, and even relationship with God to serve the idol. This can be a dating relationship, grade point average, job, spouse, child, possession, hobby, sport, or even a feeling such as comfort, relaxation, or safety.

Because He sees behind the natural into the spiritual forces at work propping up entertainment, politics, sports, education, and various spiritualities and religions, God repeatedly connects idolatry with the demonic. Demonic powers will make the worship of idols profitable, pleasurable, and preferable to worshipping the real God. Pagan practices have never really been updated because they remain constant best sellers—sex, money, power, fame, beauty, comfort, and the like never really go out of demand.

How does God feel about idolatry that demonic powers cause to be pervasive, powerful, and popular? Jealous. The jealousy of God is mentioned frequently in the Bible in the context of idolatry.[c] Jealousy happens when someone is in our place. God loves us, and when we love someone or something instead of Him, He feels much like married people would feel if they came home to have dinner with their spouse and found the person their spouse is committing adultery with sitting in their seat at the family table.

---

a Ezek. 14:1–8
b Rom. 1:25
c Exod. 20:5; 34:14; Deut. 5:8–10; Nah. 1:2; 1 John 5:21

SPIRITUAL SLAVERY

It's a short walk from *sin*, which is infrequent, to *habitual sin*, which has a more frequent cycle, to *addiction*, which is frequent. People often descend the slippery slope from one level to another without a conscious awareness, which is why honest friends and trained professionals can help us see our blind spots.

The Diagnostic and Statistical Manual of the American Psychiatric Association defines *drug addiction* as "characterized by compulsion, loss of control and continued use in spite of adverse consequences.... The compulsive behavior is reinforcing (rewarding or pleasurable) initially, but tolerance and dependency lead to its decreasing effectiveness to produce the pleasure. Eventually the individual loses the ability to limit intake and addiction process progresses. The ability of the drug to produce the associated pleasure is replaced by a need to fend off withdrawal."[3]

Different people have different struggles and addictions, so feel free to insert your own vice in place of the drugs (i.e., your "drug" of choice might be sex, porn, food, alcohol, high-risk behavior, people pleasing, anger and rage, gambling, shopping, or something else).

The world is the counterfeit of the kingdom of God. In the kingdom people worship God by practicing self-control. In the world people worship pleasure as god and lose self-control, so their sinful flesh controls them.

For Christians, struggling with addiction makes them miserable. Paul speaks of his struggle with sin. The Christian's "desire to do what is right" feels like fighting gravity where sin has gotten a grip on an area of life so that "the evil I do not want is what I keep on doing."[a]

Whereas the culture uses the word *addiction*, the Bible uses the word *slavery*. "For whatever overcomes a person, to that he is enslaved."[b] If you cannot stop a sinful pattern, you are a slave. Some people will deny this truth and claim they can stop their addictive behavior at any time, but until they actually take the first step toward freedom, admit they have a problem, and stop making excuses and instead make changes, they remain in bondage.

If you were free, you would be free to stop. If you cannot stop, though,

---

a Rom. 7:14–25
b 2 Pet. 2:19

you are indeed a slave who is not free at all. When Christians are addicted, they really only have four options.

1. **Minimization**: Try and manage sin to keep it from getting worse. These efforts are doomed to failure. Sin is like cancer; either you kill it or it kills you.

2. **Compartmentalization**: Try and hide it, live a secret double life, anxiously hoping you don't get caught, exposed, and found out.

3. **Celebration**: Accept it as your new identity and be proud of it even though you should be ashamed of it. This explains why the world has parades for things when it should have funerals.

4. **Liberation**: Walk in the freedom God intends by killing what is killing you. "Put to death therefore what is earthly in you: sexual immorality, impurity, passion, evil desire, and covetousness, which is idolatry."[a] We will examine how this is possible in the remainder of the chapter.

FREEDOM FROM SLAVERY

Slaves need freedom. To be set free from slavery, a redeemer is needed, which is a mega-theme of Scripture. The big idea is that all people are held captive by someone or something, unable to free themselves; unless a redeemer steps in, they are helpless and powerless.

The word *redemption* and its derivatives (e.g., *redeemer, redeem*) appear roughly 150 times in the English Bible. The prototype for redemption is the Exodus story, where God by divine power delivered people from slavery to worship Him freely.[b]

Satan is the ruler behind the temptations of this world. "You used to live in sin, just like the rest of the world, obeying the devil—the commander of the powers in the unseen world. He is the spirit at work in the hearts of those who refuse to obey God. All of us used to live that way, following the passionate desires and inclinations of our sinful nature."[c]

---

a Col. 3:5
b Exod. 15:1–18; Deut. 7:8; 15:15; 2 Sam. 7:23; 1 Chron. 17:21; Isa. 51:10; Mic. 6:4
c Eph. 2:2–3, NLT

Eternal life does not begin the day we die. Eternal life begins the day we meet Jesus. When Jesus redeems us, we get a new ruler who loves us and blesses us so that we experience the fullness of life. Captives of the demonic realm need to be set free by Jesus. Jesus began His public ministry promising, "He has sent me to proclaim liberty to the captives...to set at liberty those who are oppressed."[a]

THE PLEASURE PATH

Everyone starts life as a slave to sin. Slaves to sin need to trust in Jesus as their Redeemer, who died that they might live. Jesus comes to crush whatever is ruling over you, setting you free to worship God in all of life! Satan wants you to sin, and he wants that sin to kill your marriage, kill your family, kill your health, and ultimately bring you to eternal hell with him. Only through Jesus can you be redeemed from the slavery that keeps you tied to the devil and his demons.

When you are addicted or enslaved to a particular sin, it is because you are empowering your flesh to rule over you. When the Bible speaks of your flesh, it is talking about a rebellious seed of folly and death that lives in you and wants to drag you into sin and slavery. All of humanity has inherited that seed from Adam. Only through Jesus can you walk away from your slavery to sin. "Our old self was crucified with him in order that the body of sin might be brought to nothing, so that we would no longer be enslaved to sin. For one who has died has been set free from sin."[b]

The slavery of sinful addictions is both a physical and a spiritual problem. God made us one person in two parts with a physical body and spiritual soul. Therefore, in addition to understanding the spiritual nature of slavery, it is also helpful to understand the physical nature of slavery. In recent years the field of biopsychology has discovered how the slavery of addiction rewires the human brain. For example, a Christian named William Struthers has looked at the physical side of the addictive slavery to pornography. In his book *Wired for Intimacy* he uses a helpful analogy upon which we will expand.

Imagine that you went for a walk in the woods. There was no path, but at the end of your walk you greatly enjoyed what you discovered—something

a Luke 4:18
b Rom. 6:6–7

like a waterfall, beautiful view, fresh river, and so on. Imagine if on frequent hikes you traced your same steps until a path formed—let's call this your pleasure path. The more you walk that path, the wider and deeper it becomes until you can quickly make the same trip over and over with less and less conscious intent. The senses of your body—your eyes seeing the path, your feet remembering the steps—would make that trip faster and easier each time you headed down the pleasure path.

With most any pleasure, this same thing happens in our brains and bodies as a neural pathway is carved out through repeated behavior. Struthers says it this way: "The orbitofrontal cortex is our emotional modulatory system. This is our decision-making system. To be addicted to something is to release dopamine, which causes you to want it and to make the decision to pursue it. That's our addiction pathway."[4]

God created the pleasure path for His glory and our good. We were made to enjoy God and all that God provided for us to enjoy in this world. Had sin not entered the world and our bodies, we would only have pleasure without all the pain. Had sin not entered, we would only know the freedom of enjoying what God gives without falling into slavery.

The problem with idols is that they lie. Their demonic deception is that sin can satisfy. In reality the addict is never satisfied, which presses him or her into deeper levels of addiction, leaving behind a path of desperation, destruction, and death.

Only God—life with God, obedience to God, and freedom through God—can satisfy. Practically speaking, this is why God wants us to practice chastity before marriage and fidelity in marriage—so that we will have only one neural pathway toward enjoying intimacy with our spouse alone. This is also why God calls us to fill ourselves with the Spirit rather than getting drunk, because drunkenness invites unholy liquor "spirits." Likewise we shouldn't allow our "stomach" to become our "god," thereby eating ourselves to obesity, disease, sickness, and death.[a] No counterfeit can replace the Creator.

The good news is that we can build new pathways. When you are angry, rather than raging, you can start to carve out a new path into God's presence through worship and prayer. When you are scared and anxious, you can spend time in God's Word rather than drinking too much to calm your nerves.

---

a Phil. 3:19, NIV

When you are feeling intimate, you can lovingly build a complete and healthy relationship with your spouse rather than running into sexual sin. Over time you can build momentum so that your brain, body, and soul more naturally and quickly take the path toward God's presence rather than the demonic pleasure path, paved with lies that leads only to pain. To experience this freedom requires humility, which we will explore next.

YOUR RELATIONSHIP WITH
SELF

CHAPTER 8

WIN YOUR WAR AGAINST PRIDE

Pride... is not from the Father but is from the world.
—1 JOHN 2:16

YEARS AGO WHEN we were planting our first church, neither of us remembers ever previously having a prophetic dream or really knowing anything about them. I (Mark) actually was not sure that such miraculous things happened in this era and was skeptical of prophetic dreams altogether. Unexpectedly, while I was sleeping, God gave me a dream in which I was standing in the foyer of our rented church on the opening night of our church plant. As I turned around in my dream, an older man walked in alone. He was carrying a Bible in a brown leather case and wearing a blue shirt, green shorts, sandals, and a homemade cross around his neck. He revealed that he had been covertly plotting to take over the baby church. God then spoke Acts 20:28–31 and 1 Peter 5:1–4, exhorting us to protect the flock from wolves.

I awoke to tell Grace that God revealed that the older man was a wolf sent by Satan and that Jesus wanted us to protect and lead the small flock He had given us. We prayed together that night but were both a bit in shock. The next day I told my church planting coach and a few others about the odd occurrence. We fasted and prayed for the week leading up to our first public service. We were hoping for a big turnout of maybe a hundred or so people.

On the opening night of our church plant in October of 1996, the service was just getting started when Grace realized that she had forgotten her Bible in the foyer. I jumped up to get it, and as I turned around, I found myself standing alone in the foyer just as I had been in the dream. An older man then walked in the door wearing the same outfit as in my dream and spoke every word of the dream. Stunned, I was momentarily speechless. Regaining my thoughts, I told him to leave our church and never come back. After removing the older man, I walked down the church aisle and handed my wife her Bible on my way up to preach the first sermon and launch the church.

A few months later an older pastor contacted me and said that his denomination had disciplined the "wolf" on suspicion of undermining young pastors and taking money from new churches. God supernaturally saved our baby church with baby Christians from a proud older man who was intent on taking over and causing division.

OUR LOVING GOD ALSO HATES

What do you hate? If you were to put together a short list of things you hate—things that make your stomach churn, blood boil, and head ache—what would they be?

Did you know that our loving God has multiple lists of things He hates? Proverbs 6:16–19 says, "There are six things that the LORD hates, seven that are an abomination to him." At the top of the list are "haughty eyes." The Amplified Bible (AMP) translates this as "a proud look [the attitude that makes one overestimate oneself and discount others]." We all know this person, the one who literally considers himself above others and looks down at them with disdain, disgust, or disregard.

Not only does God hate pride, but He also declares war on it. Echoing Proverbs, both Jesus' half brother and His lead disciple say, "God opposes the proud."[a] If we insist on our way, our fame, our glory, and our best interest, the living God of the universe will work against us in direct opposition. Our pride puts us in this demonic position of picking a fight with God.

We are certainly not qualified to write about humility and against pride. The sad truth is, none of us is qualified. You're proud. They're proud. We're all proud in different ways. It's easy to point out pride in others while

a Jas. 4:6; 1 Pet. 5:5

remaining unaware of our own blind spots. Some of us think we deserve more money. Some of us think we deserve more respect. Some of us think we deserve more comfort. Some of us think we deserve more praise.

TAKING THE PRIDE TEST

Perhaps a bit of self-examination will help. Consider each of the following statements and score yourself this way:

Always–5 points
Frequently–4 points
Sometimes–3 points
Rarely–2 points
Never–0 points

- In conversations I prefer speaking about myself or having others talk about me rather than listening about other people.

- In most situations I am thinking about how things will benefit me, reflect on me, or work in my favor.

- If I'm honest, when making decisions I tend to do what I think is best for me rather than what would glorify God.

- When someone says I have hurt or offended them, I tend to think they are the one with the problem.

- When good things happen for other people, I tend to get jealous and have a hard time being happy for them.

- I desire a lot of attention and affirmation.

- I think I'm generally better than most people.

- I am not a generous person and am more prone to take than to give.

- I feel like the world would be a better place if people just agreed with the way I think they should behave.

- I have a hard time not winning and am an overly competitive person.

- It is more common for people to serve me than for me to serve them.

- It bothers me when I do something good and do not receive credit for it.

- I have a hard time giving compliments to others, speaking well of others, and honoring others.

- I feel like certain menial tasks are below me and should be done by someone else.

- I hide my Christian convictions when I am with people who might disagree with me, judge me, or reject me.

- I have a hard time taking orders, receiving correction, or being under authority.

- I think about myself more than I think about God and other people.

- I prefer to be the teacher informing others rather than the student who is learning.

- I care a lot about how I appear to others—my appearance, possessions, and people with whom I associate.

- I tend to brag about myself and criticize others.

On a scale of 0–100, how did you score? How much work do you have to do?

Before we arrogantly jump to judge others, we must carefully and humbly judge ourselves. Before we use the Bible as binoculars to look at other people, we need to use it as a mirror to look at ourselves.

One Bible dictionary says of the King James Version, "The ten Hebrew and two Greek words generally used for pride refer to being high or exalted in attitude, the opposite of the virtue of humility, which God rewards and praises so often. One other Greek word refers to a person being puffed up or inflated with pride or egotism. The idea is that one gives the impression of substance but is really filled only with air (see, e.g., 1 Cor. 5:2; 8:1; 13:4; Col. 2:18)."[1]

Anyone who thinks pride is something they *used* to struggle with is likely among the proudest. Pride is perhaps most incessant with religious folks who feel superior to and judgmental of those struggling to make moral or theological progress. Such arrogant people fail to realize that pride is possibly the worst sin of all.

Humility is a direction in which we travel, not a destination at which we arrive. The question is not, "Are you humble?" but rather, "Are you even trying?" The Bible urges us to humble ourselves because the way up in God's kingdom is to go low. God's people are told to humble themselves, and those who do so are recognized for it.[a] "Humble yourselves before the Lord, and he will exalt you."[b]

Some people live under the myth that circumstances can humble a person. The truth is, circumstances can *humiliate* you, but the only thing that can *humble* you is you. While circumstances are often meant to bring humility, we sadly respond in pride or control so that they don't happen again rather than learning from them.

THE COUNTERFEIT TRINITY: ME, MYSELF, AND I

Unfortunately none of us take our pride as seriously as we ought. None of us take our pride as seriously as God does. Have you ever wondered why God hates pride with such passion?

Pride is demonic.

Pride came to the earth with Satan and demons: "Your heart is proud, and you have said, 'I am a god.'"[c] Satan and demons, as well as people they have

---

a Exod. 10:3; 2 Kings 22:19; 2 Chron. 34:27; Dan. 10:12
b Jas. 4:10
c Ezek. 28:2

deceived, do not recognize authority beyond themselves. This is how proud people live, as if they were the gods of their own lives. The truth is, no one will die and give an account before a mirror; you will answer to a very real God, not to yourself. In any war, the enemy sets traps for their opposition. In his war against God, Satan sets the trap of pride for us. Paul warns young Christian leaders about the devil's pride trap.[a]

In the Book of Job, Satan declares war on Job because of his humility. Satan's scheme is for Job to become arrogant and turn against God because of his immense and undeserved suffering. Job suffers in the visible realm and has no idea that God and Satan are at war in the invisible realm.

Part of Satan's trap for Job—and for us—involves a demon spirit named Leviathan[2] who seeks to tempt our pride so that we lash out at God and blame Him for suffering caused by the demonic realm. Pride is the counterfeit of humility.

The way out of the devil's trap is to resist his temptation to be proud and instead to humble ourselves before God as Job did. God "gives more grace" to those who seek humility, which means that if you are battling pride with humility, God will help you win your war. If in humility you "submit yourselves" to God, you can by God's power "resist the devil." By either not stepping in his pride trap or stepping out of his pride trap in repentance, eventually "he will flee from you."[b]

Marketing efforts have been well-funded by the kingdom of darkness to package pride as self-esteem, self-love, and self-actualization—but it's still the pride trap. In the sin of pride the counterfeit trinity is me, myself, and I, with little room to consider God or others apart from how they benefit me. Pride replaces God as the center of the universe with me. Luther called this a theology of glory in which God and others exist to glorify me rather than all of us existing to glorify God.[3]

Augustine the church father likened pride to a mother who is pregnant with all other sins.[4] In pride Satan rebelled against God because he desired to be God. In pride Adam and Eve ate the forbidden fruit because they wanted to be like God. In pride we reject God's wisdom, will, and Word because we think we are a better god. All sin is birthed out of

---

a 1 Tim. 3:6–7
b Jas. 4:6–7

pride—and all virtue, all holiness, and all glory to God are birthed out
of humility.

PRIDE COMES FROM HELL; HUMILITY COMES FROM HEAVEN

After Satan brought pride to the earth, Jesus came to bring us humility. He
was born in poverty rather than wealth, to simple parents instead of royalty,
in a small town instead of a big city, and He was placed in a feeding trough
rather than a golden crib. Unlike Satan, unlike Adam and Eve, and unlike us,

> [Jesus] did not count equality with God a thing to be grasped, but
> emptied himself, by taking the form of a servant, being born in
> the likeness of men. And being found in human form, he humbled
> himself by becoming obedient to the point of death, even death
> on a cross. Therefore God has highly exalted him and bestowed
> on him the name that is above every name, so that at the name of
> Jesus every knee should bow, in heaven and on earth and under the
> earth, and every tongue confess that Jesus Christ is Lord, to the
> glory of God the Father.[a]

Jesus was humble, and God the Father glorifies Him as a result. Likewise,
if we repent of our pride and pursue humility by the Spirit's power, we will
one day be glorified with Him. We war against our pride by focusing not
on our humility—which is just another way of focusing on ourselves—
but rather on the humility of Jesus Christ. Someone has wisely said that
humility is not thinking less of yourself, but rather thinking of yourself less.

Just as Jesus came down in humility, so the Holy Spirit comes down
to empower proud people to become increasingly humble followers of our
humble Jesus. In any war the key to not getting shot is to keep your head
down and stay low to the ground. This is the spiritual equivalent of humility.

Satan is so cunning that he will even allow us to experience a spiritual
victory to set us up for pride and a spiritual defeat. The Bible describes
this exact scenario: "The seventy-two returned with joy, saying, 'Lord, even
the demons are subject to us in your name!' And he said to them, 'I saw
Satan fall like lightning from heaven. Behold, I have given you authority to
tread on serpents and scorpions, and over all the power of the enemy, and

---

a Phil. 2:6–11

nothing shall hurt you. Nevertheless, do not rejoice in this, that the spirits are subject to you, but rejoice that your names are written in heaven.'"[a]

Overjoyed at their newfound spiritual power, these believers were awed by their delegated authority over demonic forces. Intentionally Jesus shifted their focus from authority over demons to God's love for them. In pride we can focus on ourselves and our spiritual progress and prowess so much that we stop looking to God.

In closing, not only it is important that we learn about humility but also that we do not become proud of the lessons we are learning and humility we are demonstrating. When dealing with the demonic, it can be tempting to even think that we have the power and authority to command unclean spirits to submit to and obey us. Sadly this is common in circles with bad teaching, as ministry leaders stand up, often with haughty hearts, to yell at the devil, give orders to the devil, and make demands of the devil. In contrast, "the archangel Michael, contending with the devil…did not presume to pronounce a blasphemous judgment, but said, 'The Lord rebuke you.'"[b]

If one of the most powerful divine beings ranking as a general in the Lord's army deals with the demonic humbly and not by his own power or authority, then we must do the same. One key to maintaining humility is understanding your spiritual identity, which we examine next.

---

a Luke 10:17–20
b Jude 9

CHAPTER 9

WIN YOUR WAR AGAINST YOUR IDENTITY

The accuser of our brothers and sisters, who accuses them before our God day and night, has been hurled down.... Woe to the earth and the sea, because the devil has gone down to you! He is filled with fury, because he knows that his time is short."

—REVELATION 12:10, 12, NIV

WHEN I (GRACE) first started dating Mark as a teenager in high school, my Uncle John was the closest thing I had to a grandfather. Uncle John was an old man with no children of his own, and we loved each other dearly. Sadly, his wife Gladys developed Alzheimer's and lived in a full-time care facility because he could no longer care for her. She could not remember who she was or who her husband was.

Nevertheless, every single day, Uncle John would go out to breakfast and have fresh fruit boxed up to take to Gladys. At least once every day he would lovingly sit and visit with his wife, who had completely forgotten their identities.

I wonder if God often feels like Uncle John. He is present in the lives of the members of His beloved bride, the church, but day after day we forget who He is and who we are in relationship to Him. Many Christians loved by God have forgotten who they are.

If you had to pick one word to describe who you are, what would that word be? Your answer to that question is identity forming and therefore life shaping, emotion causing, and relationship defining.

How you see yourself is your identity. Our culture talks about identity as self-image or self-esteem. As Christians we know that we do not define ourselves by ourselves but rather find ourselves in relationship with God. The Bible tells us first who God is and then tells us who we are in relationship with God.

The question of identity is one with which humans have struggled since the first sin. Only by seeing ourselves rightly and biblically between God and the animals can we have both humility and dignity. We understand whom God intended us to be by knowing our position under God as created beings, and being humble toward and dependent upon God. By understanding our position of dominion over creation, we embrace our dignity as superior to animals and expect more from others and ourselves as God's image bearers.

This is a question that I (Grace) have to repeatedly return to when I'm struggling to not believe lies from the enemy. Even while I was writing this book, he tried to tell me I wasn't smart enough, godly enough, or confident enough to contribute. There were days I had to call friends for prayer, reread scriptures that reminded me of truth, and cry out to the Lord to tell me who I am in Him. The enemy prowls, but our Father provides for His kids.

You were created by God to glorify Him while here on earth, and when you die, if you are in Christ, you will be with God forever, glorifying Him perfectly. It is crucial to know your identity because it determines what you do. When you know who you are, you know what to do. Knowing your identity is the primary thing that changes everything.

Satan declares war on your identity because he knows it is perhaps the surest way to wreck the relationship between you and your God. Satan refused to accept his God-given identity and instead sought to form a new identity apart from God. He tempts us to do the same, which is demonic. God created you with an identity, and Satan wants you to instead live out of some counterfeit identity.

THE WAR FOR YOUR IDENTITY

The demonic war on identity started when our first parents, Adam and Eve, encountered the serpent who was "more crafty" than anything else made by God.[a] And the serpent started by attacking the very identity of God.

The Bible speaks of God as a Father. There are basically two kinds of dads. The red-light dad says no most of the time; has many rules; is controlling, domineering, and demanding; and as a result is not very relational or fun. The green-light dad says yes most of the time; has only a few rules; is very freeing, encouraging, and helpful; and as a result is very relational and a lot of fun.

The God of the Bible is a green-light Dad and not a red-light Dad. He told Adam and Eve that all of creation was a green light and that "You may surely eat of every tree of the garden."[b] Did you catch that? Everything was a green light (yes) with only one red light (no), "but of the tree of the knowledge of good and evil you shall not eat, for in the day that you eat of it you shall surely die."[c] Our Father said yes to everything but one thing, and told us He forbade that action because it would hurt us. Dad wants us to live in freedom and joy. It is vital that you understand the identity of God as a loving, relational, helpful, safe, wise, green-light Dad. Do you?

Satan attacked the identity of God. Satan actually sought to present God as a red-light Dad who was withholding good from His kids: "He said to the woman, 'Did God actually say, "You shall not eat of any tree in the garden"?'"[d]

As a Christian you must base your identity upon two things, perhaps the most important things you can learn studying the Bible: (1) who God really is, and (2) who God says you really are. It is no surprise that demonic attack starts on those two fronts, with Satan giving a counterfeit identity for God and you. If you have a wrong view of God and/or who you are in relation to God, then everything in your life spins out of control, as it did for Adam and Eve.

Did you notice the satanic strategy? Satan wanted them to achieve an identity by rebelling and living apart from God so that "you will be like God."[e] Do you remember what God said about their identity? Just prior, "God said, 'Let us make man in our image, after our likeness.'...So God created man in his own image, in the image of God he created him; male

---

a Gen. 3:1
b Gen. 2:16
c Gen. 2:17
d Gen. 3:1
e Gen. 3:5

and female he created them."[a] God made us in His "likeness," and all we need to do is receive this identity. When Satan tempted our first parents to become "like God," he was lying; they were already made in God's likeness, and all they needed to do was trust that fact by faith.

Satan tried this same trick on Jesus. In Luke 4:1–13 we read that Jesus spent forty days in the wilderness "being tempted by the devil." Then "the devil said to him, '*If* you are the Son of God...'" (emphasis added). Did you see the trick? Satan was attacking Jesus' identity as the Son of God. Once again Satan was tempting Jesus not to live from the identity He received from the Father. Just prior, at Jesus' baptism, God the Father said, "You are my beloved Son; with you I am well pleased."[b]

There is no authority in all of creation equal or superior to God the Father. When He says Jesus is the Son of God, that is a forever fact. With the Trinity present at Jesus' baptism, the Holy Spirit comes down to empower Jesus to live out His God-given identity and now does the same for Christians.

Do you also see how Jesus would work from the identity received from the Father and not work for an identity achieved by Himself? Before Jesus preached a sermon, performed a miracle, or cast out a demon, the Father was "well pleased" with Him. The same is true of you. You are a child of God, and that identity is secure. You can work from that identity with joy and gladness, knowing the Father's love is secure.

Not surprisingly Satan declares war against the identity of our Father and our family. Revelation speaks of the war in heaven between "the great dragon... that ancient serpent, who is called the devil and Satan, the deceiver of the whole world."[c] Since he landed on earth, "the accuser of our brothers... accuses them day and night."[d] Many of these accusations are in regard to your identity.

When Satan accuses you in order to attack your identity, you need to remember the following:

- Your identity is received from God, not achieved by you.

---

a Gen. 1:26–27
b Luke 3:22
c Rev. 12:9
d Rev. 12:10

- Your identity is something you work from, not something you work for.

- Your identity comes from a relationship with God, not from living independently from God.

- You aren't defined by what has been done to you or by you, but rather by what Jesus has done for you.

- What you do doesn't determine who you are; who you are in Christ should determine what you do.

If Satan can get you to believe the opposite, he has corrupted the core of your existence as the child of a loving Father.

THE DEVIL HAS A POKER TELL

Demonic forces frequently attack Christians in the area of their identity, but most of us are unaware of it. In the accounts of Adam and Jesus we just examined, there is an incredibly insightful clue. Like a poker player's "tell," Satan's subtle behavior is detectable if you watch for it, and it can alert you of his attack on your identity. When speaking to Adam, Jesus, and you, the demonic realm speaks in the second-person word *you*. To Adam and Eve, Satan said, "*You* will not surely die" and "*you* will be like God." When speaking to Jesus, Satan said twice, "If *you* are the Son of God."

When you speak of yourself, you use the first-person pronoun "I." When someone else speaks to you, they use the second-person pronoun "you." When a physical being talks to us in the second person, we easily recognize that we are being spoken to by someone else. But when a spiritual being talks to us in the second person, we have to decide if we are hearing from God or the devil and his demons. Sometimes when a demon does speak to us, we can easily overlook the fact that we are being spoken to by a demon because they are unseen.

Here are some common examples of Satan's attacks on the believer's identity:

- You are worthless.

- You are a failure.

- You got what you deserved.

- You will never change.

- You are hopeless.

- You are disgusting.

- You are not a real Christian.

- God is sick of you.

- If people knew what you were really like, they would all hate you.

- You are probably going to hell.

- You should kill yourself.

If any of this sounds familiar, you need to know it's demonic. These are counterfeit lies Satan tells to undermine the truth of what God says about His people. Our Father does not say things like this to any of His kids.

Tragically some people overlook the demonic and think they are saying awful things to themselves. They wrongly assume negative self-talk and a low self-image when the truth is they are under attack. This leads to self-contempt.

Even worse, some people confuse the demonic message as a word from God. Satan is so tricky that he will try to get you to believe that his attack is actually from your heavenly Father, which leads to God-contempt.

In more than two decades of leading churches, we have explained this countless times. When you receive a message regarding your identity in the second person, you need to test it by the Word of God. Jesus did this. When Satan attacked Jesus' identity, Jesus kept saying, "It is written..." and quoting Scripture, because truth casts out lies and light casts out darkness. Jesus did not get defensive or coerced into an argument. Jesus let the battle be between the enemy of God and the Word of God, because that's a battle that the Word always wins.

If you forget this when the enemy attacks your identity, you will end up like the sad story of Gladys. You will have a God who loves you and is present with you every day like a husband, but you will not remember who He is or who you are.

GENERATIONAL CURSES

Regarding identity, one of the most common questions Christians have is whether generational curses in their family extend to them. For unbelievers (people who do not belong to God) it is entirely possible for whole family lines to be cursed with what we often refer to as ancestral or generational bondage. For example, we have encountered some occult families who are so demonic that each generation is born into pure evil—repeated sexual assaults of one another starting in infancy and every kind of wickedness—extending back so many generations that no one can recall a time when the family was not demonic. Tragically it can seem normal rather than evil.

Starting in Genesis, the theme of cursed and blessed family lines appears repeatedly and carries forth throughout the Bible until the curse lifts.[a] From beginning to end the Bible speaks of generations of family lines being blessed or cursed. In Egypt people worshipped the entire family line of pharaohs as gods while generation after generation were involved in demonic spirituality and sought to curse the Hebrew people that God blessed. The Edomites, as another example throughout Scripture, continually tried to destroy the children of God, including King Herod killing baby boys in the days of Jesus and seeking to murder the Messiah.[1] God created His family, and Satan counterfeited them with evil families that attack God's family.

This helps explain why throughout the Old Testament, God commands that entire people groups be wiped from the earth. Deuteronomy 7 is a whole chapter devoted to God's people annihilating the seven nations of the "Hittites, the Girgashites, the Amorites, the Canaanites, the Perizzites, the Hivites, and the Jebusites" (v. 1). God commands, "You defeat them...devote them to complete destruction...show no mercy to them. You shall not intermarry with them, giving your daughters to their sons or taking their daughters for your sons, for they would turn away your sons from following me, to serve other gods" (vv. 2–4).

The issue is a family line blessed by God and cursed by Satan versus a family line cursed by God and blessed by Satan. So long as the demonic line remains, it will seek to destroy the godly line and also seduce those in the godly line into counterfeit and demonic sexuality and spirituality. Therefore, God commands, "Break down their altars and dash in pieces their pillars

---

a Rev. 22:3

and chop down their Asherim and burn their carved images with fire" (v. 5). Furthermore, you "shall not pity them, neither shall you serve their gods, for that would be a snare to you....The carved images of their gods you shall burn with fire....And you shall not bring an abominable thing into your house and become devoted to destruction like it. You shall utterly detest and abhor it, for it is devoted to destruction" (vv. 16, 25–26). The Bible includes numerous similar situations.[a]

Some families and entire nations that descend from or follow a family are demonic and therefore cursed. God alone knows these people will not be saved and are used by Satan to cause harm to God's people in any way they can. They are like the demons that sided with Satan and are never going to change. This is a bit like an intruder in your home who comes only to harm your family. He has no intention of stopping, cannot be reasoned with, and therefore must be prevented from doing great evil and harm. For those who like peace at all costs, understand there is no such thing as a negotiated peace treaty with the demonic; the only way peace comes is for the demonic to be defeated and destroyed.

For the Christian, this is why Jesus died. Jesus died to lift the curse against us and adopt us into God's family. This started with Abraham, our father in the faith: "Christ redeemed us from the curse of the law by becoming a curse for us—for it is written, 'Cursed is everyone who is hanged on a tree'—so that in Christ Jesus the blessing of Abraham might come to the Gentiles, so that we might receive the promised Spirit through faith."[b]

The blessing upon God's people is the opposite of the cursing upon God's enemies. God says, "I the LORD your God am a jealous God, visiting the iniquity of the fathers on the children to the third and the fourth generation of those who hate me, but showing steadfast love to thousands of those who love me and keep my commandments."[c] Those who hate God have that curse from generation to generation until they come to love God, at which time they are blessed from generation to generation.[d]

Some families pass demonic values from generation to generation and are cursed by God but "blessed" by Satan. However, these families can be radically changed by at least one person becoming a Christian and joining the

---

a Num. 21:2–3; Deut. 2:33–34; 3:6; 13:12–15; Josh. 6:21
b Gal. 3:13–14
c Exod. 20:5–6
d See also Exodus 34:7.

blessed family of God by faith. When this happens, a person is no longer under the curse of his family of birth physically because he was placed into God's family by virtue of his new birth spiritually.

Admittedly the position we hold on this issue is one that some other Bible-believing, Jesus-loving Christians would disagree with. They would encourage you to identify generational curses and break them. We would simply state that once Jesus saved you, He identified and broke all generational curses by adopting you into the family of God fully, completely, and instantly. We do not believe you need to do anything more since Jesus did all that could be done; faith is simply trusting that any ancestral or generational curses were broken when God became your Father, and living that new life as a new person. If you are a Christian with generational curses in your family line, God is now your Father, and you have been "ransomed from the futile ways inherited from your forefathers."[a] To be a Christian is to have a new Father and a new family that is blessed and not cursed. Therefore, be assured that your identity is totally new in Christ and you are blessed and not cursed. You may carry forth some bad concepts, habits, patterns, or problems from your family, but God is there to correct these things and not curse you for them. Sometimes this includes inner vows, which we examine next.

---

a 1 Pet. 1:18–20

CHAPTER 10

WIN YOUR WAR AGAINST INNER VOWS

Don't make any vows!
—MATTHEW 5:34, TLB

O N OUR FIRST date, I (Mark) was nervous. We were teenagers in high school, and I was smitten with Grace and knew her dad was a pastor. Driving in my first car, a 1956 Chevy I bought with money I earned at my first job, I had to work up the courage to park the car and meet her parents. Grace's family lived on a cul-de-sac, and I drove the loop many times until I finally mustered up some courage and pulled into their driveway.

Years later, after we had been married and had a few children, I got stuck on yet another cul-de-sac. I had not forgiven something in our past. Grace had apologized and repented, but I nursed my pain and continued to hold a grudge. Years had passed, but I continued to pull the painful past into the present. Like a relational archaeologist I would dig up the issue over and over, revealing that I had not forgiven her nor buried it with Jesus' death for our sin. As a result our disagreements fell into a well-worn groove with both of us driving in circles until we were exasperated.

Before Grace and I met, we both had unhealthy, unholy, and unhappy dating experiences. As a result, when we started building a relationship in high school, we were both a bit beat up. I did not fully realize it at the time, but I made an inner vow to myself as a non-Christian. Grace also had made inner vows that the enemy used to form a wedge between us.

Within a few years I came to Christ and we were getting married as Christians while still in college. The first years of our marriage were fun. We were broke but glad to be together. Before long we had planted a church and welcomed our first child into the world. Soon the other kids came as well.

We loved each other, but there was something between us. We were faithful to one another, studied the Bible, served in ministry, and tried to grow in our relationship with Christ, but we would very quickly get stuck. This happened numerous times, and when it did, we would go to the same place emotionally over and over and over. Resentment continued to build and cause hurt.

When we were kids, Grace had unknowingly violated that inner vow I had made as a non-Christian. As adults that vow from years prior was causing pain and problems for us both. God helped us work through this challenge, and we'll share how later in this chapter.

INNER VOWS DEFINED

An inner vow is a typical response to pain. Someone or something hurt us, and we want to ensure that we never experience that pain again. Rather than forgiving the people involved and trusting the Lord to be our shield of protection, we make an inner vow. Generally speaking, an inner vow is a "never again" promise we make to ourselves. "Never again will someone say, do, see, or cause this pain I have endured." Here are a few examples:

People who have been cheated on in a dating or marriage relationship might make an inner vow never to allow anyone close enough to hurt them again.

People with a domineering, overbearing, abusive parent might make an inner vow never to submit to any authority again.

Sexually abused people might make an inner vow never to enjoy sexual pleasure again, even with their spouses.

People shamed in their past might make an inner vow never to allow themselves to be in any situation where they can be made fun of again.

People who have been picked on and bullied might make an inner vow to be the aggressor no one wants to mess with.

People who have been hurt or traumatized might make an inner vow never to forgive their offenders.

People from a controlling relationship might make an inner vow to be the controlling one so they are not controlled in future relationships.

People with overly strict, rule-making parents might make an inner vow that they deserve to sin and have some fun for a change.

TEN INSIGHTS ON INNER VOWS

Making a vow with yourself is the counterfeit of making a covenant with God. An inner vow is a promise to live by a law that you make regardless of what God's law says. Here are ten more insights we've learned about inner vows.

1. We make inner vows rashly amidst pain.

When we are hurting deeply, we are often not thinking deeply. In those moments, the devil has a foothold to whisper in our ear and encourage an inner vow. Proverbs 20:25 warns, "It is a snare to say rashly...and to reflect only after making vows."

2. Some of us make inner vows at a very young age.

Inner vows made at a young age become part of how we see and deal with life. We carry them from childhood to adulthood, where they become habits that we are partially unaware of until truth shines a light on this darkness.

3. Some inner vows become entrenched as generational behaviors.

Some of us make inner vows into family laws that govern generations. For example, we know many men who do not hug their children or say, "I love you," to their wives because those were the inner vows that some man generations prior handed down to his family.

4. Inner vows can take God's place.

God is no longer Lord over that area we've vowed to protect. Instead, the inner vow rules in God's place. We cannot be led by the Spirit or free to walk in God's will. Conversely, we are led by the vow and walk in the will of the vow.

5. We become loyal to the inner vow instead of the Lord.

When our loyalty is tested, we remain devoted to our inner vow, even if it means we cannot be close to God or the people who are supposed to be the most important in our lives. We will protect the vow at all costs rather than trusting the Lord to protect us.

6. We often make inner vows without deep conscious awareness.

At the time of pain or trouble in the present, we can simply come to a decision intended to protect us in the future that seems reasonable without much thought. We often remain unaware that we have an inner vow until someone violates it and triggers us. When someone violates our vow, we are often shocked that they do not immediately see what an awful thing they have done, because for us, they have crossed a sacred line.

7. Violating an inner vow often triggers an overreaction.

When our inner vow is violated, we become more emotional than the situation would typically cause. Our passions rise quickly as our inner vow is under attack because it has become for us a place that we falsely think is protecting us from hurt. If the vow is violated, then we fear we will suffer the same kind of great pain that we created the vow to prevent in the first place.

8. We have a hard time not seeing our vows as equal to God's laws.

Everyone should submit to God's laws, but no one is obligated to submit to our vows. We are not God and are urged, "Do not add to his words, or he may rebuke."[a] When we elevate our vow alongside God's Word, we demand that other people obey us like God.

9. We punish people who break our inner vows.

Disobedience to our inner vow unleashes some sort of punishment on others to make them pay. In abusive relationships this can be cultlike, where one person takes the role of cruel god and rules over another with vows that are demonic strongholds.

---

a Prov. 30:6, NLT

10. An inner vow opens the door to the enemy.

The inner vow is an entry point for demonic harm because the vow is in some form or fashion a lie. The Bible is clear that just like a dad has kids, Satan is the "father of lies."[a] The lie under an inner vow is that it will protect you. Like all lies, this is demonic and delivers the opposite of what it promises.

In light of the demonic danger of inner vows, it is not surprising that the Bible warns against them. Jesus says, "I say to you, Do not take an oath at all....Do not take an oath....Let what you say be simply 'Yes' or 'No'; anything more than this comes from evil."[b] Echoing his big brother, James says, "Do not swear, either by heaven or by earth or by any other oath, but let your 'yes' be yes and your 'no' be no, so that you may not fall under condemnation."[c]

Inner vows create a heart of stone. The pain of our past, if not rightly grieved, and wrongs of our past, if not fully forgiven, leave an opportunity for the devil to encourage us to make an inner vow. The vow is intended to provide a hard layer of protection over our wounded heart. Tragically it becomes a tomb in which we slowly die.

Satan made the first inner vow: "You said in your heart, 'I will ascend to heaven; above the stars of God I will set my throne on high; I will sit on the mount of assembly...I will ascend above the heights of the clouds; I will make myself like the Most High.'"[d] The entire war between God and Satan started when Satan made an inner vow that he would supplant God as ruler of all. God created Satan to live in covenant to God, and Satan counterfeited with an inner vow to himself. Satan then invited Adam and Eve to adopt his inner vow and also become "like god." To this day Satan remains loyal to his inner vow, which he has used to replace God as the highest authority in his life. Many people have wrongly adopted his inner vow and caused harm. From the beginning inner vows have been demonic strongholds.

Has someone deeply hurt you, and rather than forgiving that person and handing that hurt to the Lord to be healed, you too sinned by making an inner vow and hardening your heart? If so, this inner vow gives the devil access to your thinking, feeling, and decision-making.

Think long and hard about your inner vows. Are they so familiar to you

---

a John 8:44
b Matt. 5:34–37
c Jas. 5:12
d Isa. 14:13–14

that you are no longer aware of them? Have you asked the Holy Spirit to bring to your mind any inner vow you might have? Have you invited godly people in your life to point out any inner vows that you might be unaware of because they are blind spots?

The best thing to do with an inner vow is to kill it before it kills you and your relationship with God and others. Breaking your inner vow invites the Holy Spirit to rule over you, lead you, and guide you. By renouncing your vow, you invite the Holy Spirit to heal your hurting heart of stone, making it tender toward God and others and open to healthy relationships. God promises, "I will give you a new heart, and a new spirit I will put within you. And I will remove the heart of stone from your flesh and give you a heart of flesh. And I will put my Spirit within you...and you shall be my people, and I will be your God. And I will deliver you."[a]

How do we know? As we shared at the beginning of this chapter, we've lived the pain of this problem. Thankfully, God showed me (Mark) how to forgive Grace for what she did, she forgave me for being unforgiving, and God forgave me for making an inner vow. Grace's inner vow of not wanting to be harmed, as she had been in previous relationships, and a false identity of not having value we both revealed and then healed as we worked together to respond with the kindness of Christ. We experienced spiritual deliverance, emotional healing, and relational warmth. Ever since then God has continually sent His Spirit to give us loving, tender hearts for a relationship with Himself and one another. Had this change not occurred, who knows where we would be today. We would likely not be writing a book about winning your war, because we'd still be losing our war. We've all lost a few fights and need to be cleaned up from the past, which we will study next.

---

a Ezek. 36:26–29

CHAPTER 11

WIN YOUR WAR AGAINST DEFILEMENT

You will be clean from all your sins before the LORD.

—LEVITICUS 16:30, HCSB

HERE IS A portion of a letter we received a while back that represents so many people who reach out to us in their struggle to win the war against defilement. We pray that you are encouraged by Grace's answer to this letter and you find hope through the teaching in this chapter. If you find yourself relating to this letter, we encourage you to not only read this chapter but also search the Scriptures, find a trustworthy Christian counselor, and begin that process of healing.

> Dear Pastor Mark and Grace,
>
> I really hope you answer my question. I have had this question in my mind since I was very young. I was abused sexually....I have no one to talk to about it, and I have prayed and seen your videos since I was fourteen. In your videos you say we can get cleansed by Jesus, but something I feel very guilty for is not only that I have never been a virgin, but that I had sex after my abuse, so I feel that any chance of being clean with my body was sabotaged because of it. I don't feel good enough for a man or God, and as much as I want to believe that Jesus doesn't judge me harshly for it, I just

can't. What do I do? I know there are other women who are pure and I am just not, or ever was. How do I cleanse myself through Jesus? How do I take all this feeling of not being good enough for anyone because I'm so impure? I have cried so much about this over the years, and I don't know how to deal with it. I hope you answer my question. God bless you and your family! It makes me happy to see how you talk about your daughters, and they are so blessed to have a father involved in their lives! Your wife is so beautiful, and I am glad she shared her story and it makes me happy she is blessed with a beautiful family now!

P.S.: How should I live my life from now on if I want to be seen pure through God's eyes?

Dear Dinah,

As a mother of two daughters, this story brought tears and deep grief to my heart as I [Grace] read it. It's wrong, and it's not what God wants to happen to sweet young girls. It's evil, it's hard to forgive, it's scarring to your soul as a young woman, it's something you can't erase. I'm so very sorry. Though it requires grieving and working through these wounds, the other part of your story can include healing and forgiveness and purity in God's eyes! You've been courageous to share what happened and how you're feeling now. God doesn't want you to live under the shame and condemnation the enemy continually uses to haunt you. Though your earthly father perhaps didn't protect you, your heavenly Father wants you to experience freedom from the shame of both the sins against you and the sins you committed later. You are loved, valuable, and precious to the Father!

As I worked through my own abuse, I wept, got angry, and shared with people I trusted, including Christian counselors. Then I wept some more and asked God to heal me in ways only He could. I wrote a processing letter (*not* to be shared with others) to vent all the hurt, anger, and pain I was feeling. At the end of the letter, I asked the Lord to help me forgive my abuser and take the burden of shame and impurity from me. It wasn't the last time I had to forgive because there were times I was reminded of the horror and had to forgive again. Forgiveness doesn't require you to reconcile with your abuser; it just means you've handed it over to God, and you trust Him to deal with it.

Over time, I felt the burden lift and a freedom replace it. Eventually, after God helped me see myself through His eyes (a redeemed, pure, loved daughter because of Jesus' death on the cross), I was able to share my story without vengeful desires, and help others get free from the bondage of Satan's condemnation. I wouldn't be writing this now if God was anything other than faithful in healing me. I've seen Him bring about freedom in so many women's lives, which is the opposite of what the enemy wants. Be encouraged that the moment you accepted Jesus, God saw you as clean because of what Jesus did *for* you, not dirty because of what was done *to* you. I'm so glad you wrote to us, and we are praying for you.

—GRACE

IT'S TIME TO CHANGE YOUR CLOTHES

Every day we wake up and decide what we will wear. What we wear says something about how we perceive ourselves and present ourselves to others. What do you like to wear? What style do you have?

Did you know that the devil and his demons also like to dress people and are trying to dress you? Satan wants to take the filth of sin—both the sins you have committed and those committed against you—and cause you to wear that guilt and shame. This is pictured in Zechariah 3:1–5. In a heavenly scene of the unseen realm we find "Joshua the high priest," who intercedes on behalf of sinners in the presence of God.

In the revelation Joshua, representing you and all of God's people, is standing between two people. One is "the angel of the Lord," who is Jesus Christ. The word for *angel* is a broad one that generally means messenger. And the Old Testament distinguishes between "an angel of the Lord," which refers to one of God's created angels, and "the angel of the Lord," which is often God Himself coming down.[1]

In keeping with the revelation of Zechariah 3, picture Jesus on one side. On the other side picture Satan standing ready to accuse. Put yourself in the picture. Hear Satan bringing up all the sins you have ever committed. Hear all of the filthy, naughty, disgusting, horrible, awful things you have ever said or done. Confronting you with your guilt, he now adds all the vile evil that has been done to you by others such as abuse (verbal, physical, mental, spiritual, or sexual), name-calling, abandonment, and rejection. Imagine that as Satan heaps verbal disgust upon you, with every statement he reaches into a large bucket filled with mud and feces and throws it on you one handful at a time. When Satan finishes, you are standing there wearing all of your sin and shame as "filthy garments." Demons mock you as you look at the ground defeated, disgraced, and defiled.

Imagine then hearing the voice of Jesus rising in righteous anger to declare with full authority, "The LORD rebuke you, O Satan! The LORD...rebuke you! Is not this a brand plucked from the fire?"[a] Unable to defend yourself, you suddenly realize that Jesus is standing with you and standing up for you. You then hear Jesus give an order to an angelic soldier standing at the ready: "Remove the filthy garments...I have taken your iniquity away from you, and I will clothe you with pure vestments."[b] With tears of joy in your eyes and a smile on your face you look up to see the loving face of Jesus as He puts His arm around you.

On the cross Jesus spiritually wore your filthy garments. To remind you of this, when Jesus walked away from the grave, He left His graveclothes. Once you were forgiven, no one—including you or Jesus—ever needed to wear them again. Theologians like to call this *double imputation*. On the cross Jesus traded clothes with you. He wore your filthy clothes of sin and placed upon you His clean clothes of righteousness: "For our sake he made him to be sin who knew no sin, so that in him we might become the righteousness of God."[c] Martin Luther fondly called this "the great exchange." Jesus took your place and wore your clothes, and Jesus put you in His place to wear His clothes.

Sadly, confused Christians continue to wear their old spiritual garments of sin and shame, disgust and defilement, filth and failure. They are a bit like Lazarus in John 11. Lazarus was one of Jesus' best friends. When Lazarus died, Jesus wept and traveled to His friend's grave. Dead four days, the King James Version said of Lazarus, "He stinketh" (v. 39).

Standing graveside, Jesus called, "Lazarus, come out" (v. 43). One old

---

a Zech. 3:2
b Zech. 3:4
c 2 Cor. 5:21

British preacher said it was a good thing Jesus said Lazarus' name, otherwise He would have emptied the entire graveyard. Lazarus, who was dead, was made alive! However, he was still wearing his old clothes, which friends had to help take off him.

Many Christians are like Lazarus. Satan buried them in filthy grave-clothes, but Jesus brought them forth and has fresh, clean clothes for them to wear. Like Lazarus, godly friends help us take off our old, filthy garments so we stop wearing them and start wearing the clean robe of righteousness Jesus has for us. The old clothes are Satan's counterfeit to the new clothes Jesus has for you.

GOOD NEWS FOR THE GUILTY

Not only do you commit sin, but sins are also committed against you. Not only does sin make you guilty, but it also makes you filthy.

Roughly a dozen Bible words speak of sin in terms of staining our souls, defiling us, and causing us to be filthy or unclean.[a] The effect of sin, particularly sexual sin committed against us, is that we feel dirty. This explains why victims of sexual assault often take a shower after their abuse, seeking to cleanse both the body and the soul from being defiled. The Bible uses the word *defiled* in reference to sexual sin such as rape, incest, and adultery.[b] Beyond sexual sin there are innumerable other causes for our defilement, including demonic involvement with the occult and false religion as well as violence and trauma.[c]

The Bible mentions three categories of defilement:

1. **Places can be defiled**.[d] We tend to avoid locations where something demonic and traumatic happens, thinking of them as haunted or unholy. What defiled places are you avoiding whenever possible?

---

a Ps. 106:39; Prov. 30:11–12; Mark 7:20
b Gen. 34:5; 1 Chron. 5:1; Num. 5:27; Lev. 21:14
c Lev. 19:31; Ezek. 14:11; Lam. 4:14
d Lev. 18:24–30; Num. 35:34

2. **Objects, such as the marriage bed, can be defiled.**[a] For some people their own body or home might feel defiled. What things feel defiled to you?

3. **People can be defiled**. The Old Testament and the Gospels record the lives of many people who were ritually unclean and not to be associated with or even touched. The ceremonial washings and such throughout the Old Testament foreshadow the cleansing power of the death and resurrection of Jesus. Do you consider yourself or anyone else (e.g., spouse, parent, former friend) defiled and unclean?

SHAME CAUSES SUFFERING

The predictable result of defilement is shame, including the fear of being found out and known, having our deep, dark secret revealed. God created our first parents to be naked together as a married couple, which displayed complete intimacy and oneness without any shame. Once Satan showed up, sin happened, and our first parents experienced shame for the first time, covering themselves with fig leaves, trying to hide their defilement. They hid from God and one another, afraid of being truly known. As guilty and dirty people do, they could not look God or other people in the eye.

Thankfully, God came and clothed them as a foreshadowing of what Jesus would do for us on the cross. God took off their garments of shame and replaced them with garments of grace, and He does the same for you.

We must no longer wear what was done *by* us or done *to* us. Instead we must wear what Jesus has done *for* us! On the cross Jesus dealt with the sin that has stained your soul. On the cross Jesus both forgave and cleansed all sins committed by you, and cleansed all sins committed against you. Jesus went to the cross to take not only your sin but also your shame: "Jesus, the founder and perfecter of our faith, who for the joy that was set before him endured the cross, despising the *shame*, and is seated at the right hand of the throne of God."[b] What was the joy on the other side of the cross for Jesus? Glorifying God by clothing *you* in glory.

---

a Heb. 13:4
b Heb. 12:1–3, emphasis added

WALKING IN THE LIGHT

Taking off your filthy clothes begins with confessing what you have been wearing. This is the process of coming to grips with the brokenness, regrets, abuses, sins, and pains you have been wearing so that you can take them off. Practically, this means prayerfully and carefully choosing a safe person who can be wise counsel and a confidant for you. This can be a spouse, counselor, pastor, ministry leader, or close friend. This should be done privately with the goal to have someone help you take off the graveclothes you have been wearing. They need to know that their role is to help you see the demonic counterfeit you have been wearing, and help you remove it and replace it with the righteousness created for you by Jesus Christ.

Jesus wants all filth off of you, all old clothes removed from you, and all burdens lifted from you and replaced with His righteousness, His holiness, and His joyfulness. Parts of life feel so dirty that they seem impossible to clean. In response we either hide them in shame or accept them as our identity. We are not to be ashamed or proud of sin but rather cleansed from all sin. As you continue to believe these truths, the lies will fall as your faith rises.

Sometimes God has His people go through physical rituals to remind them of spiritual truths. Every time you do a load of laundry, clean your dishes, wash your hands or face, take a shower, or brush your teeth, stop and remind yourself that God has also made you clean in His sight. Even when you sin, He cleans you up just as you clean things up in your life.

Lastly, at least once in a while, wear something white. When God's people prepare to worship Him, they put on fresh, clean, white clothes in the Bible. Jesus not only forgives, but He also makes clean. The church of Jesus Christ is His bride, and we all know that the church is a bride with a lot of faults and failures. Nonetheless to "his Bride...it was granted her to clothe herself with fine linen, bright and pure."[a] As a Christian you are clean thanks to Christ, which is why the New Testament often tells you to take off the old and put on the new just like you would dirty clothes. The Holy Spirit is ready right now to help you do this very thing. As you do, you might even experience supernatural healing, which we will study next.

---

a Rev. 19:7–8

CHAPTER 12

WIN YOUR WAR AGAINST DEMONIC SICKNESS

Surely our griefs He Himself bore, and our sorrows He car-
ried; Yet we ourselves esteemed Him stricken, smitten of God,
and afflicted. But He was pierced through for our transgres-
sions, He was crushed for our iniquities; the chastening for our well-
being fell upon Him, and by His scourging we are healed.

—ISAIAH 53:4–5, NASB

IT SEEMED LIKE a typical Saturday family night. We snuggled in our pajamas, ate licorice and popcorn, and watched a movie together. Then we prayed with the kids and tucked them in bed before turning in early ourselves in anticipation of a long day the next day serving at church.

During the night, while we were both sound asleep, I (Mark) felt like someone or something large and heavy fell on my chest, knocking the wind out of me. Grace was unaware of what was happening, but I was struggling. I thought maybe a tree had fallen on our house and crashed in on my chest. At the same time it felt like someone had his hands around my throat and I could not breathe.

Opening my eyes, I could see no one and nothing. I was pressed down into the bed, unable to move with the heavy weight of something or someone on my chest, and felt like I was going to pass out, unable to breathe.

I tried to call out to Grace but could not speak. I also tried to cry out to

God in prayer with no success. I began to panic. I remembered that when we pray, we do not need to pray aloud. Satan and demons can hear our words but cannot know our thoughts. Only God knows our thoughts. Even though I could not verbally command whatever was on me, I could call out to God in the silence of my mind and invite Him to deliver me. As soon as I began praying in my mind, the battle ended, and everything lifted.

Since it was the middle of the night and I had been fast asleep, I was unsure if it was a demonic attack or a bad dream. Eventually my adrenaline slowed down, and some hours later I was able to fall back asleep and get a bit of rest before preaching. In the morning I told Grace about the strange night and went in to preach. Sometime the next day, when I took off my shirt in the bathroom and looked in the mirror, I had bruises across my chest, which told me this was not a dream. A spiritual attack from the unseen realm harmed my physical body, which can happen with both injury and sickness.

God made you as one person in two parts. Part of you is immaterial and spiritual—your soul. Part of you is material and physical—your body. You are one whole person, and your spiritual and physical aspects affect one another. It is the same for all of us: sin has infected and affected every dimension of who we are.

Sin has brought suffering to the body. Every one of us is either battling an injury or illness or walking with someone who is. Consider for a moment how much money and energy we spend on the war against physical suffering—ambulances and hospitals, doctors and nurses, medical devices and medications.

Thankfully the God who made us also sent His Son to heal us, both body and soul with outer and inner healing: "He was pierced for our transgressions; he was crushed for our iniquities; upon him was the chastisement that brought us peace, and with his wounds we are healed."[a] Jesus died for both our sin and our suffering. Importantly this promise of physical healing does not come with a time frame. Some of God's people will experience bodily healing in this life; all of God's people will experience total healing in their resurrection bodies in the eternal life. In the rest of this chapter we will examine sickness and healing according to the Bible.

---

a Isa. 53:5

WHY IS THERE SICKNESS AND INJURY?

When God finished making the world, everything was "very good" and alive; sin made everything very bad and brought death. There are at least three reasons why people suffer sickness and injury. These categories are not mutually exclusive, and sometimes all three work together, which requires multiple levels of care to help a person experience total healing.

One, the fall of humanity has infected and affected all of creation. Therefore, not every person who is sick or injured has a direct cause of personal sin. Sometimes suffering results from being in a broken, fallen, dying world. "Sin came into the world through one man, and death through sin, and so death spread to all men."[a] Suffering is something we experience personally, but the cause can be general rather than personal. In instances like this, spiritual responses such as prayer and physical responses such as a doctor's visit are the steps to take on the path to wellness.

Two, not only is the world fallen, so is each person on the planet. Not only are sin and its effects a general problem *around* us, but they are also a specific problem *in* us. Sometimes our sinning directly causes our suffering. One of the most rebellious and ungodly churches in the New Testament was in the Vegas-like city of Corinth, with everything from homosexuality to drunkenness and prostitution at church. Some church members were dying because God got sick of watching them do sick things: "That is why many of you are weak and ill, and some have died."[b] God can see the future and knows when sin will continue without repentance. In instances like this, repentance of personal sin and inviting of the Holy Spirit to empower a new lifestyle are the keys to healing.

Three, sometimes the sin behind the suffering is not general sin from Adam or specific sin from the victim, but demonic sin, where spirits who hate God attack the people God loves. This is the case in the story of Job. Job was a godly man who endured a vicious season of injury and sickness solely because of satanic attack. Not understanding this third category, his "friends" kept trying to get him to come clean about any personal or secret sin that was causing his suffering. They only had category two (personal sin causing suffering) and did not understand category three (demonic

---

a Rom. 5:12
b 1 Cor. 11:30

suffering). This case study is important because it shows us that to help the whole person, we need to understand the whole Bible.

Many times in Jesus' ministry people were healed through deliverance. The demon brought the sickness or injury, and once the demon was gone, so was the sickness.[a]

DOES HEALING REPLACE TRADITIONAL MEDICINE?

A doctor named Luke wrote more of the New Testament than anyone. His concurring books, Luke and Acts, record verified healings by the Holy Spirit's power operating through Christ and Christians. Luke was also the personal physician to Paul and traveled on various mission trips, bandaging him up after beatings, riots, or imprisonments. Paul and Luke had a close friendship and ministry partnership. Setting an example for all Christians and caregivers, Paul had a doctor who cared for his body and soul: "Luke the beloved physician."[b]

God can and does heal. Sometimes God does this naturally through a physician. Sometimes God does this supernaturally as the Great Physician. Therefore, healing does not replace traditional medicine. As we see in Doctor Luke, it is biblical to believe in both medical science and faith-filled prayer. We know many medical professionals who went to college for a degree and also go to the Spirit for power. They minister to not only the bodies of their patients but also their souls. This is the example of Doctor Luke, which helps prevent the either/or thinking that someone needs to be healed either only through prayer or only through a doctor.

DOES GOD HEAL TODAY?

Jesus began His public ministry reading from Isaiah 61: "The Spirit of the Lord is upon me, because he has anointed me to proclaim good news to the poor. He has sent me to proclaim liberty to the captives and recovering of sight to the blind, to set at liberty those who are oppressed, to proclaim the year of the Lord's favor" (Luke 4:18–19). Jesus declared His entire ministry would be done by the power of God the Holy Spirit. He could have healed people out of His divinity, but much if not most of the time He

---

a Matt. 4:23–25; 8:16; 9:32–33; 12:22–23
b Col. 4:14

did so by the power of the Spirit to set an example for us. Many scholars believe Luke's Gospel is the only one written chronologically. Chapter 4 includes a reference to Jesus as "Physician"[a] and records the way He healed a man from sickness by casting out the demon that was harming him.[b] The remainder of Doctor Luke's Gospel records other healings Jesus performed.

One Christian teaching says in effect that God worked in supernatural ways in the early church but those ways have largely ceased in our day. There are nuances to this position, but it is referred commonly to as cessationism. Both the Bible and church history refute this false teaching. Furthermore we cannot simply dismiss the testimony of saints around the globe who report divine healing because it does not fit a flawed theological paradigm.[2]

To begin with, Jesus was healed. He suffered and died on the cross and then rose to conquer sin, sickness, and death. When Jesus rose from death, some dead people also rose as a foreshadowing of the healing power of God's kingdom. Jesus also healed others. Roughly twenty-seven times in the Gospels we see Jesus heal an individual. Roughly ten times we see Jesus heal entire groups of people.[c] Jesus performed other verified healings not recorded in the Bible.[d] Specific deliverance miracles Jesus performed through the Holy Spirit include healings from bleeding, epilepsy, deafness, muteness, and blindness.[e]

Once Jesus returned to heaven following His healing from death, some wondered if God would continue to heal people. Doctor Luke wrote his follow-up book, Acts, which reports the supernatural acts of the Holy Spirit through Christians who continued the Spirit-filled ministry of Christ. Just as the Holy Spirit descended upon Christ at His baptism, the Holy Spirit then descended upon Christians so that they could live by His power and continue His kingdom ministry.

The Book of Acts records roughly fourteen healing miracles. Twelve of the twenty-eight chapters in Acts record a miraculous healing reported by Doctor Luke. This was to be expected as it's what Jesus promised His first followers: "Heal the sick, raise the dead, cleanse lepers, cast out demons."[f] In obedience we read of the early church, "Now those who were scattered

---

a Luke 4:23
b Luke 4:31–37
c Matt. 4:23–25; 8:16; 12:15; 14:14, 34–36; 15:30; 19:2; 21:14; Luke 6:17–19
d John 20:30
e Luke 13:11–16; Matt. 17:14–18; Mark 7:35; Matt 9:22–23; 12:22
f Matt. 10:8

went about preaching the word. Philip went down to the city of Samaria and proclaimed to them the Christ…they heard him and saw the signs that he did. For unclean spirits, crying out with a loud voice, came out of many who had them, and many who were paralyzed or lame were healed. So there was much joy in that city."[a] Simply stated, the miraculous is part of ministry.

It is also important to note that problems arise when people seek the miraculous rather than the God who does the miraculous. Jesus warned of this tendency: "An evil and adulterous generation seeks for a sign."[b] God's people are not to chase after signs and wonders but rather to use their energy to pursue God. As we follow God, signs and wonders will follow us.

WHY DOES GOD HEAL?

We know of at least five reasons God heals. These reasons are not mutually exclusive, and in His loving creativity God often heals people for more than one reason.

One, healing reveals God's love and mercy to the afflicted person.

Two, healing validates someone as a chosen servant of God.

Three, healing reveals the kingdom of God.

Four, healing motivates Christians to increase faith and worship. When God does something wonderful, it encourages His people to be worshipful. On the very day that we are writing this chapter, a young couple introduced themselves to us at church to share their testimony to increase our faith. They live out of state but one week a year are in Arizona for work. One year prior they had faced sickness that had prevented them from having children. As I (Mark) was preaching on healing, the wife reported that for the only time in her life, God spoke to her promising she would be healed and have a baby. One year after that encounter with God they were back in town for their annual visit, and with tears in their eyes and smiles on their faces they testified to their divine healing and introduced me to their beautiful newborn baby girl! We hope that kind of testimony increases your faith in and worship of God as it does ours.

Five, healing evangelizes non-Christians. Some people come to Christ by persuasion, and some people come to Christ by power. Those who come to

---

a Acts 8:4–8
b Matt. 16:4

Christ by persuasion have a lot of questions and objections that they need a thoughtful, researched, and learned person to answer before they cross the line of belief. Those who come to Christ by power see God show up in a supernatural way and trust in the reality of their experience. This was the case with my (Mark's) mom. She was healed at a prayer meeting, which caused her to commit to a personal relationship with Jesus as the first believer in our family.

FOUR WAYS TO MINISTER TO THE SICK

To follow in the footsteps of Jesus, we must minister to the sick. We know of at least four ways to do so.

1. Pray from a distance.

Jesus healed from a distance at least three times in the Gospels.[a] Sometimes Jesus would travel to be present to heal someone. Other times He would pray from a distance, and the person would be healed. This just goes to show that whether we are present or not, so long as the Holy Spirit is present with the suffering person, there is a possibility of healing.

2. Lay hands on people and pray.

Laying hands on sick people to pray for them was part of Jesus' earthly ministry,[b] and it is part of local church ministry.[c] The laying on of hands is foundational doctrine to Christian ministry,[d] and it is relational in that it brings comfort and friendship to the hurting person. The laying on of hands is part of the ministry of presence. Having a loving person present with us in our suffering is a tremendous ministry. Laying hands on someone can include spiritual transference, where the presence and power of God are released. One deliverance manual says, "Just as power lies in the hand of God (Hab. 3:4), it also lies in the hands of His servants (Acts 5:12; 19:11). There is tremendous power released through anointed, holy hands."[3]

3. Anoint people with oil.

Jesus anointed people with oil and expects the church to do the same.[e] Oil is symbolic of the Holy Spirit, who anoints us for ministry. By praying

---

a Mark 7:24–30, cf. Matt. 15:21–28; Matt. 8:5–13, cf. Luke 7:1–10; John 4:46–54
b Luke 4:40; Matt. 9:18
c Jas. 5:14
d Heb. 6:1–2
e Mark 6:13; Jas. 5:14–15

and anointing with oil, we are showing with our words and works that we invite God's presence into the situation to minister to the hurting person.

4. Minister in faith.

If Jesus were walking on earth today, hurting people would flock to Him. Just because Jesus is in the kingdom does not mean we cannot approach Him, since by faith we can and do approach Him to heal in our realm from His realm. "Let us then with confidence draw near to the throne of grace, that we may receive mercy and find grace to help in time of need."[a]

IS ALL HEALING FROM GOD?

Hurting people are vulnerable people. When you or someone you love is struggling with chronic pain, suffering, or is in the process of dying, the grief and fear can be overwhelming. This compels us to try most anything to bring health and stop suffering, including spending large sums on medical treatments or taking risks on experimental medicine.

The demonic realm is so evil that demons look for opportunities to exploit hurting people. The devil and his demons will even heal someone if it is a way to lead them away from the Lord. This is Satan's counterfeit to God's healing. Think of it like an evil doctor infecting a patient without his knowledge with the intent of making him sick, and then charging him an exorbitant fee for the antidote. Jesus warned of this very thing: "For false christs and false prophets will arise and perform great signs and wonders, so as to lead astray, if possible, even the elect."[b]

Why would Satan do this? He is willing to trade short-term physical suffering on the earth for long-term spiritual suffering in hell. If it takes a healing miracle to get someone to worship a guru, false god, or spiritual deception, then he will heal someone to lead them astray. This explains the occurrence of real healing miracles in false religions and spiritualities—demonic forces bring sickness and relieve that suffering in exchange for powerful and delusional deception. It is better to suffer in this life and be healed in eternity than to be healed in this life and suffer for eternity.

a Heb. 4:16
b Matt. 24:24

CAN EVERYONE RECEIVE HEALING IN THIS LIFE?

God can heal people in this life, and God will completely heal all of His people in eternity. At times the kingdom of God shows up in power, and the supernatural power of God invades the natural realm. These are occasions of signs, wonders, and miracles, including healing. This leads to a reasonable question as to whether everyone who seeks healing from God receives healing in this life.

In surveying all of the New Testament occurrences of divine healing, sometimes the person's faith does play a role, and their faith somehow helps unlock God's power to bring supernatural healing to the natural realm. Sometimes, however, the healed person evidences no faith at all. They do not seek or ask for healing and instead are entirely passive and not in any way active in the healing process.

One example is in John 5. A man who could not walk for thirty-eight years sat day after day at a place in the temple where God would on occasion provide healing. Jesus arrived asking, "Do you want to be healed?" (v. 6). Without demonstrating any faith in any way, the sick man answered him, "Sir, I have no one to put me into the pool when the water is stirred up, and while I am going another steps down before me" (v. 7). Despite the man not exercising any faith, Jesus said to him, "'Get up, take up your bed, and walk.' And at once the man was healed, and he took up his bed and walked" (v. 9).

God is free to do whatever He chooses for whatever reasons He chooses. This is one of the primary differences between paganism and biblical belief. In pagan belief across various belief systems their god, gods, and/or goddesses are not entirely free and can be manipulated. Paganism teaches that the seen natural realm can manipulate the unseen spiritual realm.

We've ministered to numerous former practitioners of Wicca as well as converts from various pagan beliefs over the years. During that time, we have seen a unifying common belief that the unseen realm is not good, sovereign, or free and must be manipulated by people engaging in some sort of activity that forces the spiritual realm to give the person what they want. Spells, incantations, sacrifices, oaths and vows, offerings, and the like are used to force the demonic realm to unleash some desired blessing or outcome, such as healing or prosperity. God is not like demons. The Creator is not like the counterfeit.

According to the New Testament, there are times we can contribute to our healing. If the problem is unrepentant habitual sin, we can repent and cancel the stronghold we have given the demonic realm, which can bring physical healing. If the problem is unbelief, we can pray and act in faith to welcome the power of God to work in our life. But being a godly and faith-filled person does not guarantee that a person can unlock the power of God and unleash healing in his or her life. This is because we can cooperate with God, but we cannot control God.

To start, we need to look to the Lord Jesus. In the Garden of Gethsemane on the eve of His crucifixion, Jesus was suffering, unable to sleep from stress, and His sweat was like drops of blood. Jesus, of course, did not have sin but did have perfect faith. Knowing that enduring the wrath of God on the cross was before Him, Jesus in earnest prayed all night asking that the suffering would end before His life was poured out. In the end He surrendered, saying, "My Father...your will be done."[a]

God answers every prayer in one of three ways. Yes now; no, never; or later, as I have better timing planned. The answer to the faith-filled prayer of Jesus was no. His pain continued and escalated until He endured the greatest possible suffering—separation from the Father and Spirit, taking our place, enduring the wrath of God until He died.

Similarly Paul "left Trophimus, who was ill, at Miletus."[b] Trophimus was a godly man. This section of Scripture mentions people who have betrayed and abandoned Paul in his time of trial and trouble. Thankfully Trophimus was a trophy of loyalty who walked with Paul when others walked away. He faithfully carried money for the ministry to the saints in Jerusalem.[c] Unlike Judas, Trophimus was tested, tried, and true but became too ill to travel with Paul. Despite being godly, faith-filled, and seeing numerous other people healed, Trophimus was not healed.

Paul was even unable to heal himself: "A thorn was given me in the flesh, a messenger of Satan to harass me, to keep me from becoming conceited. Three times I pleaded with the Lord about this, that it should leave me. But he said to me, 'My grace is sufficient for you, for my power is made perfect

---

a Matt. 26:42
b 2 Tim. 4:20
c Acts 20:4–6; 21:29

in weakness."[a] Paul had some sort of physical suffering that had a demonic cause, but he had to learn to live with it rather than be delivered from it.

Paul wrote at least thirteen books of the Bible (fourteen if he is the author of Hebrews) and is the central human figure in the Book of Acts recording his conversion and expansion of the Christian church through his missionary journeys. Paul had faith through beatings, shipwrecks, imprisonments, floggings, mobs, and riots that he gladly endured until he was put to death—the only way to silence him. For those who love Jesus, you may suffer for Jesus and suffer like Jesus, not because you lack faith but because you have enough faith to love Christ more than your own comfort.

WHEN WILL ALL OF GOD'S PEOPLE RECEIVE HEALING?

When God made the world, there was no sin, sickness, or suffering. When sin entered the world, it unleashed the demonic, difficulty, and death.

Christians are residents of an earthly nation but citizens of God's kingdom. We Christians ought to see ourselves as "sojourners and exiles."[b] An exile is someone who is away from his homeland, and a sojourner is someone who sees himself as a missionary passing through a foreign land until he returns home.

The Bible often repeats this because we are prone to forget it. Paul writes, "To all the saints in Christ Jesus who are at Philippi."[c] They live in the city of Philippi, their temporary home. These Christians are then reminded "our citizenship is in heaven."[d] Though they live in Philippi, it does not feel like home because their home is in heaven with God. One day, however, the next verse says, "from it we await a Savior, the Lord Jesus Christ, who will transform our lowly body to be like his glorious body, by the power that enables him even to subject all things to himself."[e]

This is our tension—we are already citizens of the kingdom but not yet residents of the kingdom. Some Christians relieve this tension with something called an *underrealized eschatology*. The big idea is that the kingdom exists in heaven and does not show up until it comes with King Jesus.

---

a 2 Cor. 12:7–9
b 1 Pet. 2:11
c Phil. 1:1
d Phil. 3:20
e Phil. 3:20–21

Therefore, we should not expect much in the way of the supernatural or miraculous, such as healing.

Other Christians relieve this tension with something called *overrealized eschatology.* Those big words mean some believers think that since our citizenship is in heaven, all of the power and prosperity of our eternal kingdom life is ours to enjoy in this life. Both of Paul's letters to the Thessalonians were written to Christians who erred in this way, telling them that the work of God was not completed until Jesus returned a second time and the dead were raised.

Every Christian will be fully, totally, completely, and eternally healed forever. This will happen upon the second coming of Jesus Christ and the resurrection of the dead. On that day the curse will be fully lifted, death will be defeated, and Jesus "will wipe away every tear from their eyes, and death shall be no more, neither shall there be mourning, nor crying, nor pain anymore, for the former things have passed away."[a]

Until the day of Jesus' return, the resurrection of the dead, the removal of the curse, the ruin of Satan and demons, and the re-creation of the world, we are in the time between the times. The kingdom of God does show up in power at times, bringing revivals, awakenings, healings, and outpourings of God's presence that are sneak previews, glimpses, and dress rehearsals for the coming of King Jesus and the kingdom of God. Until that day of sight the righteous live by faith and forgiveness, which we study next.

a Rev. 21:4

YOUR RELATIONSHIP WITH
OTHERS

CHAPTER 13

WIN YOUR WAR AGAINST UNFORGIVENESS

Be angry and do not sin; do not let the sun go down on your anger, and give no opportunity to the devil. . . . Let all bitterness and wrath and anger and clamor and slander be put away from you, along with all malice. Be kind to one another, tenderhearted, forgiving one another, as God in Christ forgave you.

—Ephesians 4:26–27, 31–32

H
AVE YOU EVER been part of a family feud? If so, then you know that they can drag on forever and get demonic, escalating until everyone is losing and no one is winning. One family feud made it all the way to the US Supreme Court. The legendary Hatfields and McCoys were rugged Appalachian mountain families in the 1800s. The patriarch of the Hatfield family was William Anderson, whom they referred to as "Devil Anse." His counterpart in the feud was Randolph McCoy. Each man fathered at least thirteen children. The families lived across a stream from one another with the water serving as the dividing line.[1]

The two families had occasional fights, but things took a turn for the worse when the McCoys shot Ellison Hatfield. In retaliation the Hatfields kidnapped and murdered three McCoy men. From that point on the bitterness battle raged as the two families abducted one another, stole from one another, killed one another, and burned down homes, apparently even taking the lives of women and children.[2]

What caused the war? That is a great mystery for the ages. No one really knows. It just goes to show that sometimes we get so bitter and ready for a battle that we can no longer even recall what the problem was in the first place. We've all been there, and if we don't watch our flesh, we can let our hurt turn into hate as well.

Unforgiveness has many names—hurt, disappointment, woundedness, grudge, beef, ax to grind, resentment, bitterness, brokenness, and carrying an offense. Unforgiveness is the opposite of love. When we keep a record of wrongs, we are acting as an accountant and keeping score of the spiritual debt others have accrued to us. This is why unforgiving people say things such as, "They owe me," "I will make them pay," and "I will get even."

Jesus teaches us that when we forgive someone, we are canceling whatever debt they owe us. History's most famous prayer is the Lord's Prayer. There are two versions in the Bible. In one Jesus teaches us to pray, "forgive us our debts, as we also have forgiven our debtors."[a] Perhaps teaching it on a different occasion, Jesus makes a slight modification: "forgive us our sins, as we forgive those who sin against us."[b] Did you catch the difference? Jesus uses the words "debts" and "sins" synonymously.

When someone sins against us, they accrue a debt to us. Who will pay their debt? If you make them pay, that is vengeance. Vengeance is something that we need to trust God for and not take into our own hands. God said, "Vengeance is mine, I will repay."[c]

If you absorb the loss and pay for them, that is forgiveness. In forgiving someone, you choose not to sit as a judge and render a sentence on someone else. Instead you are sending that case to God's higher court, which will result in them either being sentenced to the eternal debtors' prison of hell or having their debt paid by Jesus on the cross.

JESUS PAID OUR DEBT

Our relationship with God is only possible because Jesus paid our debt to God. God is the biggest victim in all of history. Everyone has sinned against

a Matt. 6:12
b Luke 11:4, NLT
c Rom. 12:19

God, and God has sinned against no one. Rather than making us pay, God sent His Son Jesus Christ to pay our debt to God. This was necessary because the debt (or wage) owed to God for sin is payable only by death: "For the wages of sin is death."[a] The Bible uses the financial term *ransom* to explain our spiritual debt to God. Jesus says, "The Son of Man came...to give his life as a ransom for many."[b]

Most religions have some concept of human failure and a debt to be paid. This is because God made us with a conscience, and even if we do not know how good God is, we do know how bad we are. In basically every religion except Christianity you have to pay back your debt. Hinduism wrongly teaches that you need to reincarnate and suffer to pay off your debt to karma. In works-based religions like Islam, your good works need to outweigh your bad works so that you can pay off your debt to God.

The only person who has ever walked the earth that has never sinned or accrued any spiritual debt is Jesus Christ. He lived a life we have not lived, died the death we should have died, and paid the price we could not pay. We responded by attacking, slandering, arresting, and murdering Him. At the cross of Jesus both the goodness of God and the badness of man were revealed. While hanging on the cross, Jesus' first words were, "Father, forgive them."[c] Jesus starts with forgiveness.

Hating what Jesus was saying, Roman soldiers shoved a sponge in His mouth. That sponge was likely part of their field kit and what they used as toilet paper to scrub themselves after going to the bathroom. With the taste of a bowel movement on His lips, our God and Savior then answered His own prayer and died in our place to pay the price for our sins. If you belong to Jesus Christ, you are totally, completely, and eternally forgiven for all of your sin in the past, present, and future. Jesus paid the highest price for you and forgives your debt to God as a free gift called grace.

FORGIVENESS IS A GIFT TO SHARE

Not only are you a sinner, but you are also a victim of sinners. Just as you have done evil that pains God, others have done evil that pains you. Who

---

a Rom. 6:23
b Mark 10:45, cf. 1 Tim. 2:5–6
c Luke 23:34, NIV

owes you? Who has done the greatest damage, caused the deepest pain, and left the ugliest scar?

Forgiveness is not only a gift we receive from God but also a gift God requires us to share. Forgiven people should be forgiving people. "Put on then, as God's chosen ones, holy and beloved, compassionate hearts, kindness, humility, meekness, and patience, bearing with one another and, if one has a complaint against another, forgiving each other; as the Lord has forgiven you, so you also must forgive."[a]

When you forgive someone, you treat your enemy as God treated you when you were His enemy. When you forgive someone, you leave the matter in God's hands and move on with your life. Forgiveness does not require trust; forgiveness is free, but trust is earned. Neither does forgiveness require reconciling the relationship. Forgiving is the first step in blessing someone. In fact blessing your enemy is the test of whether you have actually forgiven them, as Jesus says, "from your heart."[b] Until you can in some way bless them, you have not truly forgiven them. Why? Because God has not only forgiven you but also blessed you, and how you treat others should reflect, or glorify, how God in Christ has treated you.

DEMONS TRANSPORT IN BITTERNESS

In the physical realm different modes of transportation (e.g., an automobile or airplane) carry humans from one place to another. In the spiritual realm various modes of transportation carry demonic persons. Bitterness, or unforgiveness, is a vehicle by which demonic forces travel into your life and relationships. James says that what bitter people are doing "is not the wisdom that comes down from above, but is earthly, unspiritual, demonic."[c]

You live on earth, the battleground between heaven and hell. Hell is the place of unforgiveness; when you do not forgive, you are pulling hell up into your life. Heaven is the place of forgiveness; when you forgive, you are inviting heaven down into your life.

To help us understand this, Jesus tells a parable in which someone owes a great financial debt[d]—let's say a million dollars for the sake of simplicity.

a Col. 3:12–13
b Matt. 18:35
c Jas. 3:14–15
d Matt. 18:21–35

Unable to pay, he goes to his lender begging not to be sold as a slave, along with his wife and children. Graciously the lender forgives the man's entire debt by paying it himself. This picture of the gospel of forgiveness is how Jesus treats us. Overjoyed, the exonerated man rushes home to share the good news with his family.

Before long the man forgiven of a great debt confronts another man who owes him a much smaller debt—we will call it a thousand dollars. Rather than forgiving the man of his minor debt in the same way he had been forgiven of his major debt, Jesus says he seized the man and "began to choke him, saying, 'Pay what you owe.' So his fellow servant fell down and pleaded with him, 'Have patience with me, and I will pay you.' He refused and went and put him in prison until he should pay the debt."[a]

Witnesses of this awful scene rush to report the unforgiving person to the person who forgave him. His response is, "'I forgave you all that debt because you pleaded with me. And should not you have had mercy on your fellow servant, as I had mercy on you?' And in anger his master delivered him to the jailers, until he should pay all his debt. So also my heavenly Father will do to every one of you, if you do not forgive your brother from your heart."[b]

Jesus' point is that when you allow your hurt to turn into hate, you invite demonic torment into your life, causing it to feel like you are serving a jail sentence in a dark and despairing dungeon. The image of the jailer in Jesus' teaching is Satan and the demonic realm. Satan and his demons condemn you, haunt you, and torment you. They encourage you to respond to your hurt by hurting others and to your torment by tormenting others. God creates forgiveness, and Satan counterfeits it with bitterness.

Satan and demons are never forgiven for anything and never forgive anyone for anything. When you choose not to forgive, you are choosing to welcome the demonic and satanic into your life.

In the most brutal season of our life and ministry, as we were under an overwhelming avalanche of external attack, we met with a godly older pastor and licensed counselor to help us process, learn, unburden, repent, and forgive. During that season we also studied forgiveness and unforgiveness in the Bible at a very deep level. We learned that the Bible often speaks of unforgiveness and the demonic together.

---

a Matt. 18:28–30
b Matt. 18:32–35

Many of those sections are written by Paul, who previously worked for the devil, persecuting Christians and murdering the early church leader Stephen. While dying, Stephen echoed Jesus and prayed for his murderers, "Lord, do not hold this sin against them."[a] Stephen's prayer was answered. Paul was saved, forgiven of his debt to God by Jesus Christ, and he stopped serving Satan and started serving his Savior by preaching forgiveness. It just goes to show, if you forgive your enemies and pray for them, you may be used of God to help unleash the next apostle Paul on the earth.

Who has caused you pain? The Holy Spirit through Paul, who is writing on pages wet with "many tears," begs that those who were hurt "forgive and comfort him." He then teaches that when we are hurt, Satan seeks access to us, our family, and our church family when he writes to ensure "that Satan will not outsmart us. For we are familiar with his evil schemes."[b] What is Satan's battle plan? To find a hurt person and encourage him not to forgive, so he can add to his pain by haunting, embittering, and tormenting him.

Is there anyone you have not fully forgiven from the heart? How has the demonic used your hurt to cause you more hurt?

You can disarm and defeat the demonic through the weapon of forgiveness, according to Colossians 2:13–15. There was a "record of debt that stood against us with its legal demands." Consider for a moment what the complete record of all your sins would be. Don't overlook any thought you have had, deed you have done, word you have said, or motive you have hidden. Don't just consider your sins of commission, where you have done wrong, but also recount your sins of omission, where you have failed to do right. How many pages long would all of the debts from your life be?

Now, believe by faith that when the soldiers drove the nails into Jesus' hands and feet, they were in the spirit realm also "nailing it [the record of your sinful debts] to the cross." When Jesus died, the result was "canceling the record of debt," "having forgiven us all our trespasses." In forgiving you, Jesus conquered the demonic as "He disarmed the rulers and authorities and put them to open shame, by triumphing over them in him."[c] How did Jesus defeat and disarm the demonic? By paying the price of death for your debt to God to be forgiven.

---

a Acts 7:60
b 2 Cor. 2:1–11, NLT
c 2 Cor. 2:13–15

To defeat and disarm the demonic, you must forgive as you have been forgiven. If you do not forgive, you may be forgiven by God but still be haunted, tormented, and broken until you do forgive.

FORGIVENESS INVITES THE HOLY SPIRIT TO DEFEAT THE UNHOLY SPIRIT

In our few decades in ministry together we have heard hurt, wounded, and offended people say over and over, "I cannot forgive them." We agree. We cannot, on our own, forgive someone. To truly forgive from the heart, as Jesus says, is a miracle. A miracle is something supernatural that could not occur apart from God's power at work in an unusual way.

The Holy Spirit through Paul speaks of the miracle of forgiveness: "Be angry and do not sin; do not let the sun go down on your anger, and give no opportunity to the devil."[a] Anger is not a sin, as God Himself gets angry, such as when Jesus made a whip and drove corrupt religious businessmen from the temple. Anger, however, can lead us to sin if we are not careful. As we've heard Pastor Jimmy Evans say many times, "Today's anger is not a problem, but yesterday's anger is a problem."

In the Jewish world a day begins at sundown, so to carry anger from the daytime into the nighttime was dragging yesterday's anger into today. That unforgiving, smoldering, fiery anger is a bit like hell, and the kind of place where the devil is happy to reside. You know that old anger is still with you when the words you say violate the command to "let no corrupting talk come out of your mouths, but only such as is good for building up, as fits the occasion, that it may give grace to those who hear."[b]

This is doubly true when Christians war with Christians in front of non-Christians, because the only person who wins that war is the devil. To defeat and disarm the demonic, the Bible commands us to "be kind to one another, tenderhearted, forgiving one another, as God in Christ forgave you."[c] This kind of forgiveness is not natural but rather supernatural. Thankfully, the same Holy Spirit who empowered Jesus to pay your debt and forgive your sin is also standing at the ready to empower you to forgive

---

a Eph. 4:26–27
b Eph. 4:29
c Eph. 4:32

as you have been forgiven. When we do not invite His presence and power into our hurt, we "grieve the Holy Spirit of God."[a]

The Holy Spirit wants to help you forgive those who have wronged you so the demonic forces causing you harm can be defeated, disarmed, and dismissed, replaced by His hope, help, and healing. If you turn your enemies and the harm they have caused over to the Holy Spirit, you can then, by God's power, "let all bitterness and wrath and anger and clamor and slander be put away from you, along with all malice."[b] When you focus on the one who hurt you, you ignore the One who can heal you.

When you forgive, you stop focusing on winning and start focusing on worshipping. When you forgive, you do not let those who wrong you get away *with* anything but rather let yourself get away *from* everything. When you forgive, you not only bless them, but you also bless yourself. When you forgive, you trade the haunting of unholy spirits for the healing of the Holy Spirit.

We love you, and we want good for you. We would urge you to schedule a meeting with God and write out the list of debts the person(s) you need to forgive has accrued to you. Then, as you have what we call a "heart funeral" with God, we want you to do as Jesus did for you, "canceling the record of debt."[c] Burn your list to remind yourself of the flames of hell from which Jesus saved you, or bury it to remind yourself that Jesus was buried for your sin. In this way you are making a record of wrong and forgiving that total debt but not *keeping* that record of debt, as "love…doesn't keep a record of wrongs that others do."[d] I (Grace) have done this during the most challenging betrayals in my life. A wise counselor told me to write processing letters (not to be shared with others or posted publicly but only for my personal healing) that allowed me to purge my hurt, anger, and frustration and truly unburden through forgiveness. As I did this, I felt a weight lift and the person (or people) no longer held control over my life. I released them to God and experienced profound personal freedom.

As you forgive, something breaks in the unseen realm. When the first Christian martyr, Stephen, was dying at the hands of his enemies and praying for their forgiveness, he got a supernatural glimpse into heaven and

a Eph. 4:30
b Eph. 4:31
c Col. 2:14
d 1 Cor. 13:5, CEV

saw Jesus standing.[a] As you forgive your enemies, imagine Jesus Christ getting up off His throne to cheer for you while the devil flees from you. As light casts out darkness, so forgiveness casts out the demonic.

Not only does forgiving someone cause Jesus to stand and cheer in the divine council, but it also makes the opportunity easier for the person who sinned against you to repent to God and you, because kindness leads to repentance.[b] When you forgive others, you get out of the way and let God deal with them directly. Sometimes they then repent, which also breaks something in the unseen realm and causes an explosion of celebration in the divine council. People commonly say that when a sinner repents, there is rejoicing in the presence of God. That is almost true, but the Bible specifically says of the divine council that when we forgive on earth, God rejoices in the throne room as the angels watch Him cheer. "There is joy before the angels of God over one sinner who repents."[c]

Think of the possibility that you could forgive someone right now, and Jesus would jump off His throne to celebrate like a rabid sports fan at a game with the angels joining in. Then the person who sinned against you one day repents, and Jesus jumps up to lead the angels in yet another all-out victory celebration, as everyone is a winner when there is forgiveness!

On the other hand, if we do not forgive, we become evil people, and Satan brings other evil people into our lives to form unholy alliances or soul ties, and we all do evil together. Often this comes in the form of a common enemy or common cause to harm in the name of vengeance. We see examples of these unholy alliances among evil people throughout the Bible including Jannes and Jambres, who opposed Moses; Sanballat and Tobiah, who opposed Nehemiah; Ananias and Sapphira, who opposed Peter; and Hymenaeus and Alexander, whom Paul "handed over to Satan."[d] Have you ever wondered how bitter, evil people who do not know one another end up becoming allies? The secret is simple. Even though the people do not know one another, their demons do and make the introduction. This often begins with lies, which we will explore next.

---

a Acts 7
b Rom. 2:4
c Luke 15:10
d 1 Tim. 1:20

CHAPTER 14

WIN YOUR WAR AGAINST LIES

You are of your father the devil, and your will is to do your father's desires.
He…does not stand in the truth, because there is no truth in him. When he
lies, he speaks out of his own character, for he is a liar and the father of lies.

—John 8:44

WHEN WE PLANTED The Trinity Church in Scottsdale, Arizona, as a family project, God was gracious to provide a midcentury modern church building as our first home. In a series of miraculous provisions from God we were able to purchase it and renovate it before we even publicly launched the church. The dark blue carpet in the auditorium was likely the same kind used by Noah on the ark. As we rolled it up to toss it out, we discovered that the concrete floor under the carpet was cracked and crumbled in a large circle.

Evidently the old stained-glass ceiling dome had leaked for a long time. Year after year, when rare rain did come to the desert, it fell below, settling into the concrete beneath the carpet. Year after year, decade after decade, and drip after drip, the water found the low points, settled in until it caused cracking, and eventually eroded the concrete until it needed complete repair.

Lies are like those drops of water. Each one seems small and harmless, but over time they find the low points in lives, relationships, families, and nations where they settle in to cause deep erosion. This explains why God listed His prohibition against lying as His ninth commandment.

SIX WAYS WE LIE

Lying is either telling what is untrue or not telling all that is true, which is why a person placed under oath in court swears "to tell the *truth*, the *whole* truth, and *nothing but* the truth." Lying is demonic. God creates truth, and Satan counterfeits with lies.

In the kingdom of God there was and is only truth, because God never lies.[a] When the devil and his demons were cast down to the earth, they brought lies with them. Jesus says in John's Gospel roughly forty times, "I tell you the truth," or some variation of the phrase. In one heated debate with religious people Jesus says, "You belong to your father, the devil, and you want to carry out your father's desires.... When he lies, he speaks his native language, for he is a liar and the father of lies."[b]

When we lie, we are speaking for the devil even if we think we are serving the Lord. On earth many languages are spoken. In heaven there is a language called the "tongues of angels."[c] In hell the language is lying. In fact Satan and demons are so adept at lying that it is their "native language." When we choose to speak the language of lies, we quickly find ourselves outmatched, much like a person who travels to a foreign country knowing only a few words trying to negotiate a contract with the locals. When we lie, we enter into a demonic realm where we are incapable of escaping harm. This happens in six different ways.

1. Flattery

Singles use flattery to get a date or a mate. Kids use flattery to get dessert. Employees use flattery to land a raise. Sucking up and kissing up are not spiritual gifts.

Flattery can feel pretty good and yield some favorable results at the moment, but "everyone utters lies to his neighbor; with flattering lips and a double heart they speak."[d] You can have a double mind. You can have a

---

a Titus 1:2
b John 8:44, NIV
c 1 Cor. 13:1
d Ps. 12:2

double tongue. Flattery is a double heart. It is insincere and excessive praise intended to manipulate.

On this point it's essential to distinguish sinful flattery from the gift of encouragement. There's nothing wrong with being a happy person who helps people look on the bright side. The difference between encouragement and flattery is the motive of the heart. Encouragement is godly and intended to *build* you up to benefit *you*; flattery is demonic and intended to *butter* you up to benefit *me*.

2. Deception

Deception twists what was the truth into a weapon for harm and destruction—cheating in school; half-truths on a resume; falsifying reports at work; double-billing clients; reporters who have an agenda and write to fulfill it regardless of the facts; politicians skewing everything they have ever said or done positively while tilting everything regarding their opponents negatively. We all construct stories in such a way as to omit what makes us look bad and emphasize what makes others look bad at some point. Social media seems to be a breeding ground for deception, and who isn't sick of the constant flood of advertising that no one believes anymore because it's all half-truths?

Deception is demonic. In Genesis 3 God created our first parents and spoke the truth to them, and then Satan came and lied to them. They sinned against God. The Bible says on more than one occasion that Satan deceived them—Eve in particular. Like Adam and Eve, we're not only guilty of deceiving but also of being deceived.

Many of us like to think that we're too clever to be deceived, but this self-assurance can actually put us at risk. God is our Father, and the Bible often addresses us as His kids. You could fool a kid pretty easily, right? They're a little gullible and a little naïve, and sometimes we're like that. There's a difference between child*like* faith and child*ish* faith. Childlike faith takes God at His word. Childish means easily lured into danger by deception.

3. Slander/libel

Just as deception is demonic, slander is satanic. Malicious and often false information used to inflict harm is slander (spoken form) or libel (written form). God commands, "You shall not go around as a slanderer."[a]

Case builders collect information like stones to throw—just waiting for the right opportunity to impugn and attack someone. Case builders have decided that someone is their enemy and then justify gathering information the same way that an Old Testament mob gathered stones to throw.

Numerous lies were told about the Lord Jesus when He walked the earth, and numerous more lies are told about Him every day. False witnesses stepped forward to slander Jesus. To counteract counterfeits of the truth, after rising from death, Jesus commissioned us to be His "witnesses" testifying to the truth and against the lies of false witnesses.[b] Paul kept saying, "I am not lying."[c] Jesus' half-brother says, "Let your 'yes' be yes and your 'no' be no," which is a surefire way to reduce lying and bearing false witness.[d]

In our day we have an opportunity to slander people more immediately and effectively than ever through technology. In a conversation we had, Pastor Rick Warren said this type of communication is fourfold. It is:

1. Instant—we can now have our emotions push us to post something before we have the facts.

2. Constant—we can lie anytime from anywhere.

3. Global—once we post, our lie is available to the world.

4. Permanent—once online, our lie can live on and do damage forever.

Before you post, remember Jesus' words: "On the day of judgment, people will give account for every careless word they speak."[e] Did you know that today Jesus has internet access and sees our social media? Even if what you've communicated is factual truth, your motives are ungodly if the

---

a Lev. 19:16
b Acts 1:8; 5:32
c Rom. 9:1; 2 Cor. 11:31; Gal. 1:20; 1 Tim. 2:7
d Jas. 5:12
e Matt. 12:36

purpose in communicating is to harm your neighbor rather than to bring glory to God and good for your neighbor.

4. Condemnation

Condemnation is a bit like getting the flu. No matter how hard you try, at some point a cold or flu bug hits, and suddenly you feel like a shell of your normal self. You cannot usually predict when you will get hit with a bug, but you know that at some point it will happen.

In the same way, we can be doing just fine and suddenly get hit with condemnation out of nowhere. Spiritually it is discouraging, zaps your energy, and makes you feel not like yourself. Condemnation is a demonic counterfeit of conviction. Conviction comes from the Holy Spirit and is specific so that we know what to do to walk in God's will. Condemnation comes from the unholy spirit (Satan) in one of two ways:

1. Condemnation occurs when sin or shame from our past is brought up to make us feel bad all over again. Even though the issue is in the past, we feel the weight of it in the present. We know that Jesus forgave us, and we have repented, have moved on, and are not doing it anymore, but the past comes back to haunt us in the present. A person with a tender conscience can get stuck in a repeating cycle of reliving the past and repenting over and over. He or she remains unable to move on because it keeps resurfacing. In extreme circumstances some people wonder if they are saved and loved by God. The idea that the past is not forgiven in the present or the future is a lie.

2. Condemnation can also occur when we want to do what is right and are open to being corrected for any wrongdoing, but Satan uses our sincere heart to heap vague, general accusations that if not recognized, can propel us into deep introspection as we frantically search for sin. Satan counterfeits God and perverts His work. The Holy Spirit convicts us of specific sins so that with His compassionate help we can repent and move on to freedom and joy. The unholy spirit seeks to defeat and discourage us through guilt so general that we never know exactly

what to repent of and are thereby left in paralyzing bondage and despair.

Condemnation is a form of lying. The truth is, "There is therefore now no condemnation for those who are in Christ Jesus."[a]

5. Negative narrative

Our modern world gives us access to more information than any other generation, but that's not always a good thing. It has become commonplace to receive information framed in a negative narrative—everything from political campaigns to divorces and church fights. Sometimes the narrative is downright bitter and nasty, and more often than not it's false.

While our modern access to negative narratives may be unprecedented, the problem is certainly not new. Consider the life of Jesus, for example. The enemy worked through a variety of enemies, starting with religious and political leaders who formed an unholy alliance:

- They not only called Him a liar but also extended the negative narrative to discredit His mother, saying she was a sexually sinful woman and a liar like her son.[b]

- When Jesus cast out demons, the negative narrative was "He is possessed by Beelzebul," and "By the prince of demons he casts out the demons."[c]

- When Jesus hung out with people, the negative narrative reported Him as "a glutton and a drunkard, a friend of tax collectors and sinners!"[d]

- To continue carrying the negative narrative forward, as they sought to arrest and kill Jesus, "many false witnesses came forward."[e]

If social media, blogs, and skewed media had existed in Jesus' day, most would wrongly assume His mother was a lying con artist who raised a

a Rom. 8:1
b John 8:41
c Mark 3:22
d Matt. 11:19
e Matt. 26:60

demon-possessed, alcoholic son pretending to be spiritual as part of a great demonic deception. This same pattern continues in every age as the same demons encourage people to do the same things that were done to Jesus. Negative narratives are a demonic form of lying.

6. Gossip

In the age of social media and technology perhaps the most common form of lying and false witness is gossip. Tabloids make ad dollars by enticing people to click on the latest celebrity gossip. Social media exists in large part for us to act like God and peer in on the lives of other people. This is all the sin of being a gossiping busybody. Godless gossipers "learn to be idlers...and not only idlers, but also gossips and busybodies, saying what they should not" and in so doing "give the adversary...occasion for slander. For some have already strayed after Satan."[a]

Gossip is telling news that is not ours to tell; it is talking *about* people rather than talking *to* them. Gossip is involving people who are not part of the problem or the solution. If everybody comes to you for disclosing secrets, that's not necessarily a good thing. You might be the spiritual equivalent of a toilet that flushes everything into the pipelines. Calling it a prayer request does not sanitize the sewage.

Sometimes gossips say things that are not true, but more often they simply say things they should not say. Telling people about somebody else's business is no way to love your neighbor. In fact gossips often intentionally share damaging information. Murder kills a person's body; gossip kills a person's reputation.

Websites and magazines have turned celebrity gossip into a business model. Just because someone is famous doesn't mean you need to know what they eat, where they live, or what their kids look like. That's actually stalking, eavesdropping, and being a busybody, and it's unspiritual. Whom do you need to stop following? The information you're getting might be true, but what is your motive in hearing or reading it? Do you like peering into the lives of others so you can pass judgment?

---

a 1 Tim. 5:13–15

SIX REASONS WE LIE

If the Spirit of God lives in you, then you have to agree that we are all guilty of lying. If we know lying is wrong, why do we do it? Here are six reasons:

1. We lie to avoid negative consequences.

2. We lie to create or protect an illusion of who we are.

3. We lie to get what we want.

4. We lie to remain in control of a situation.

5. We lie to punish others.

6. We lie about someone else to be accepted by others who despise them.

In short, we lie because we want to be like God, which was the very first lie Satan ever told. We want to establish our own standard of truth. We want to control our lives and their outcomes. We want to look good. We want to judge and sentence others.

Our hearts are saturated with this, which is why we can't stop lying—at least not without God's help. We need a new heart through Jesus by the power of the Holy Spirit if we ever hope to escape the power and consequences of our past, present, and future lies.

ONE BIG, IMPORTANT QUESTION

If you now desire to be a truth teller, obeying the ninth commandment, here is a helpful series of checkpoints to ask yourself within an overall question:

Does this exact information...
    need to be communicated...
    by me...
    to this person (or these people)...
    at this time...
    with this motive...
    through this medium?

If any of the above checkpoints results in a no, we don't need to share what we were going to share. If we regularly ask ourselves this big, important question, we will significantly reduce the number of times we violate the ninth commandment.

Couples especially need to guard against lies. The first lie ever told to humans was when Satan lied to a married couple, our first parents. This is why we encourage couples to remain vigilant regarding this tactic of the enemy. The devil and his demons are highly skilled at getting us to believe that telling a lie will make things better. When this happens, they convince us that telling another lie will help make up for the failure of the first lie. Of course this is just their way of lying about lying.

Some people lie so much that they lose sight of reality and the truth. An old Jewish proverb tells the story of a visitor who walked into town carrying a pillow with a hole in it. One after another the feathers fell out of the pillow and scattered in the breeze. Eventually the person recognized that the pillowcase was nearly empty and sought in vain to collect all of the feathers he had dropped. Lies are like those feathers. Once dropped and scattered, it becomes virtually impossible to make right all that has gone wrong.

FOUR TROUBLE SPOTS FOR TRUTH

In closing, when the subject of lying comes up, some reasonable questions arise. There are at least four scenarios where the issue of truth telling versus lying can be difficult to differentiate.

1. Secrets and surprises

In raising our five children, we taught them that keeping secrets—choosing not to tell about bad things that are true—is wrong. For example, when children are abused, they are often told to keep the secret, which stops them from getting the help they need. We wanted to prevent this kind of opportunity for the enemy by teaching our kids about the sin of keeping secrets. One of our children, however, was a strict rule keeper and very literal. So we had to teach our kids the difference between a secret and a surprise. A secret is a bad thing that someone doesn't want anyone to know. A surprise is a good thing that we *do* want known at the appropriate time. So if we were throwing a surprise birthday party for one of the children, for example, we would ask the other children to help plan it but not tell their sibling in advance, keeping it a surprise.

2. Exaggerations

There are times when a joke contains embellished details for the sake of making a funny point. Those who hear the joke know it is not entirely true but also not a lie. Jesus had a sense of humor and did this very thing. Some scholars say, "If there is a single person within the pages of the Bible that we can consider to be a humorist, it is without a doubt Jesus....Jesus was a master of wordplay, irony and satire, often with an element of humor intermixed."[1] Examples would include shoving a camel through the eye of a sewing needle, or pointing out the sawdust in someone else's eye while ignoring the giant beam sticking out of your own head. Usually this kind of communication is understood by the hearer as a fun way of making a point without intent to deceive.

However, there are times when we exaggerate the truth in an effort to make a dishonest misrepresentation. For example, if a single guy who makes a modest income tells a woman he is interested in that his income is south of a million dollars a year, he is technically telling the truth but exaggerating in hope of impressing her.

3. When telling the truth would be slander

We can face a dilemma when we are forced to either lie or slander someone. For example, in John 8 in the Bible there is a story where a woman caught in adultery was brought to Jesus by religious leaders for public shaming and condemnation. Rather than saying anything, Jesus wrote something on the ground that remains a mystery to us, and this caused her accusers to flee once they read it. In this instance Jesus did not publicly slander the woman or her accusers, although both the woman and the accusers were acting shamefully. In these kinds of sticky situations it is often best to remain silent. Proverbs tells us, "It is foolish to belittle one's neighbor; a sensible person keeps quiet. A gossip goes around telling secrets, but those who are trustworthy can keep a confidence."[a] Modeling this very thing, many times "Jesus remained silent."[b] When your momma said, "If you can't say something nice, then don't say anything at all," she was onto something.

a Prov. 11:12–13, NLT
b Matt. 26:63; 27:12; Acts 8:32

4. When telling the truth would cause incredible harm

These are admittedly uncommon ethical dilemmas. An example of this type of situation is found in Exodus chapter 1 when the government told the Hebrew midwives to kill all the Hebrew baby boys they delivered. Torn between lying to a godless political leader or murdering countless innocent babies, the midwives rightly chose to disobey ungodly demonic authority, save innocent lives, and avoid a genocide. Moses' parents did the same: "By faith Moses, when he was born, was hidden for three months by his parents, because they saw that the child was beautiful, and they were not afraid of the king's edict."[a]

On another occasion, in Joshua 2, Rahab helped to keep God's servants from being murdered. When their ungodly enemies arrived, she lied to preserve the innocent lives of the godly. On rare occasions revealing the full truth empowers the demonic to bring devastation, death, and destruction. We should not allow the truth to be abused in that way, and so we keep it to ourselves rather than handing it as a weapon to the enemy, which is why Rahab is a model of faith.[b]

Admittedly, in a fallen and evil world with demonic powers at work, there are rare and complex ethical situations. One example would be Corrie ten Boom's family hiding Jews from Nazis who wanted to murder them during World War II. However, most of the time lying is not motivated to glorify God and save innocent lives but rather to benefit ourselves.

Other times we lie to harm someone else. This is the case with a woman who was married to a powerful man named Potiphar. She repeatedly sought to seduce Joseph, and out of loyalty to God and the woman's husband, Joseph repeatedly refused her advances. Angry, she falsely accused Joseph of rape.[c] Innocent, Joseph was then arrested, convicted, and thrown in prison all because of a lie.

When all is said and done, lies come up from hell, and truth comes down from heaven. There was no lie in heaven until the great war, and today and forever there will be no lying in God's kingdom. Hell is where all the lies and liars go. When we choose lies, we pull hell up into our lives.

---

a Heb. 11:23
b Heb. 11:31
c Gen. 39

When we choose truth, we invite heaven down into our lives and push the lies back down to hell where they belong.

Lastly, regarding spiritual warfare, sometimes when we are working with someone who is possessed or oppressed by a demon, that spirit can communicate through them or reveal information to them. If this happens, we need to remember demons are liars. Any information revealed by a demon should be taken with incredible suspicion. A demon being interviewed by a Christian is like an enemy captured in war who lies to interrogators and as a general rule is not to be trusted. One goal of demonic lying is to cause us to be covetous, as we will examine next.

CHAPTER 15

WIN YOUR WAR AGAINST COVETING

If you harbor bitter envy and selfish ambition in your hearts, do not boast about it or deny the truth. Such "wisdom" does not come down from heaven but is earthly, unspiritual, demonic.

—JAMES 3:14–15, NIV

THE NEXT TIME you are in a store gazing upon all of the products displayed for sale, consider for a moment how recent this phenomenon is. One of the first American department stores to put all of the products out on the floor was Woolworth's. Before that, stores stocked all items for sale behind the counter, and if you wanted something, you would ask a salesperson to get it for you or simply hand them a list of what you wanted to buy.

Once all of the items for sale were able to be touched and selected by the consumer, people started coveting more and therefore buying more. How many of us have done this very thing? We go to the store to buy something and end up buying other things we did not even know existed until we got to the store. We bring them home, pay for extra storage units to stow them away, and later throw them out because we had no need of them after all. Yes, we pay to take the item home, pay to store it, and then pay the sanitation workers to take the item to the dump. That's the power of coveting.

It seems we have based our economy on getting people to break the tenth and final commandment. Advertising and marketing awaken in you a desire to spend money you don't have on something you don't need to impress someone you don't know. Add to this the spiritual gravity of the world that pulls you toward being jealous and covetous of what others have, and the constant onslaught of social media where it seems everyone is showing off the stuff they have, places they go, and luxuries they enjoy. The stage is set for coveting.

COVETING DEFINED

Coveting is ungodly and discontented desire, passion, envy, craving, greed, jealousy, obsession, longing, or lust for someone or something that is not supposed to be yours. In short, coveting is when you aren't content with what God wants for you, and instead you want something He has not chosen for you.

Coveting is a sin that starts with our eyes. Satan tempted our first parents according to a pattern that he later used on Jesus Christ[a] and uses on us today. "For everything in the world—the lust of the flesh, the lust of the eyes, and the pride of life—comes not from the Father but from the world."[b]

1. The lust of the eyes happened when our first parents "saw the fruit."

2. The lust of the bodily flesh happened when they realized it was "good for food."

3. The pride of life happened when they wrongly believed it was "desirable for gaining wisdom."

It is curious that of all the things God could have possibly listed in the Ten Commandments, coveting made the list. Perhaps this is because you cannot simultaneously love your neighbor and covet your neighbor's things. When we covet what someone else has, we cannot be happy for whatever blessing is in that person's life. Instead we become bitter that it's not in our life. Even worse, we might seek to steal it for ourselves or at least cause the person to lose it so that neither of us can enjoy it. Ultimately, coveting creates a mind-set of greed and selfishness that leads to sinful actions.

The most interesting thing about the Ten Commandments from a

---

a Matt. 4:3, 5–9
b 1 John 2:16, NIV

historical perspective is not that God made a list of rules for the Israelites to follow. Many ancient cultures followed clear public moral codes and lists of virtues. However, most only covered external things, such as stealing, murder, or lying. It is incredibly rare to find any ancient moral code that includes the inner life of motive, desire, and thought as do the Ten Commandments. This is because God alone sees, knows, and judges the heart and mind. Therefore, God's list includes coveting because it is the root of other sins.

Consider it this way: The first two commandments teach there is only one God and we should not covet Him but rather worship Him. The seventh commandment is not to commit adultery, and when you covet someone else in your heart, it is only a matter of time before you commit adultery with your hands. In the eighth commandment we are told not to steal, but when we covet things in our hearts, eventually we steal. Yes, without coveting we would have no idolatry, no adultery, and no stealing. Many of the world's problems would go away if coveting were no more. Consider these questions for a moment:

1. Have you ever seen a car that you deeply wished you could own and drive?

2. Have you ever seen a home that was so great that you deeply wanted to have it for yourself?

3. Is there a person whose abilities (mental, physical, spiritual, etc.) you wish you could have?

4. Whom do you honestly wish you looked like?

5. What things do other people have that you really want for yourself?

6. Whose spouse have you met that you secretly wished you were married to?

7. What is the one experience that someone else has had that you wished you had instead of that person?

8. Whom would you trade lives with if you could swap your life with someone else's?

Did answers to any of these questions readily come to mind as you read them? If so, you likely sinned against God in your heart and fell for the demonic trick of coveting.

The last of the Ten Commandments warns us against the demonic deception that enticed even the angels to align with Satan's scheme by coveting God's glory. God says, "You shall not covet your neighbor's house; you shall not covet your neighbor's wife, or his male servant, or his female servant, or his ox, or his donkey, or anything that is your neighbor's."[a] To put it in modern terms—stop looking up the square footage, sale price, and interior design of other homes; stop comparing the age, beauty, and allure of someone you are not married to with your spouse. Don't worry about the new car and fancy vacation your friends just posted online; instead be content with what God has given you.

God wants us to be content with what He's given us, and Satan counterfeits contentment with coveting to make us want what God has *not* given us. Coveting damages our relationships, starting with our relationship with God.

COVETING HURTS YOUR RELATIONSHIP WITH GOD

God is a Father. Like any good parent, God knows what His kids need and does not give them things that will harm them. For example, we have five kids, and although some would have liked us to buy them a car at age six, we waited until age sixteen. Our withholding from them was an act of love for them. So it is with God. When there is something we want, the Father sometimes says "no," and at other times says "later" for when we are ready.

We knew a child who had generous parents. At a birthday party the child was given numerous presents by family and friends. After opening all of the gifts, the child grew furious because there was apparently one present that he wanted most but didn't receive. The child proceeded to throw a fit and push all of the presents onto the floor as an act of rejection and stomped away angry. The parent said, "This is exactly why we did not buy the present. The present was fine, but his heart was not ready to receive it." God often feels like the parents at that birthday party, since "every good gift and every perfect gift is from above, coming down from the Father."[b]

a Exod. 20:17
b Jas. 1:17

Coveting makes us forget that we are, in fact, rich. Most people reading this book live at a quality of life that people in the past couldn't even imagine. Furthermore, with much of the world in poverty, those of us with electricity, central heating, and a fridge and pantry to hold our extra food qualify as "the rich" in this scripture: "As for the rich... charge them not to be haughty, nor to set their hopes on the uncertainty of riches, but on God, who richly provides us with everything to enjoy."[a]

Coveting is deep dissatisfaction with what the Father has given. God is a generous Father who wants us to enjoy the gifts He gives. When God the Father says no, it is to protect us, not punish us.

COVETING HURTS YOU

Why do we care whose name is on our pants? Why does it matter if our car was made in Korea or Germany? Why do people fret over the latest generation of technology when the old one does pretty much the same thing for a third of the price?

Consumerism has become a religion. It's how we gain social status and prestige in the eyes of others. Malls are churches, and online shopping carts are prayers sent to the retail gods who answer by sending us what we want. Sociologist Thorstein Veblen, who coined the phrase *conspicuous consumption*, articulated this idea at the turn of the last century. Veblen argued that the chief way we obtain social prestige and power is through conspicuous displays of leisure and consumption. Social prestige is connected to wealth, and we demonstrate our wealth by flaunting it.

Other sociologists have used the phrase *competitive consumption* to explain this sacrament of consumerism. We work ourselves to death and spend ourselves into debt because we wrongly think our self-worth is tied to our net worth. This explains why even teens will sometimes murder one another for a pair of vintage retro Jordans but not do the same thing for a pair of dollar-store flip-flops.

The problem is not in the stuff that we hold but in the stuff that holds us. The issue is not in our hands but in our hearts. "Take care, and be on your guard against all covetousness, for one's life does not consist in the abundance of his possessions."[b]

a 1 Tim. 6:17
b Luke 12:15

COVETING HURTS PEOPLE YOU LOVE

Have you ever noticed that someone had a beef with you and you didn't know why, and you later learned that you had not done anything and the person was simply jealous of you?

Now let's put the shoe on the other foot and wear it for a while. Who makes you jealous? Who annoys you because of his or her beauty, income, humor, intellect, popularity, success, health, marriage, children, and so on? How is your relationship with that person? Do you criticize the person behind his or her back? Do you wish the person would suffer or lose what he or she has? Do you wish you could trade places with the person?

God did nothing wrong to Satan. Satan simply coveted the glory God received. As a result their relationship was destroyed. This demonic deception continues in human relationships today, which is why God's Word admonishes, "What causes quarrels and what causes fights among you? Is it not this, that your passions are at war within you? You desire and do not have, so you murder. You covet and cannot obtain, so you fight and quarrel. You do not have, because you do not ask."[a]

When we covet someone and feed our jealousy, the issue is not really between us and the person; it's between us and God. God invites us to replace coveting with praying. In prayer we can ask God for what we need rather than seeking to have what He has already given others. When we take our requests to God, it reveals our heart. If we are honest, we all covet things that we'd never ask God for because we know the desire is ungodly or unhealthy. As we bring what we think we need to God, we invite God to show us the difference between our need and our greed. Sometimes God graciously gives us the thing we ask for, just as He has graciously provided it for the person we envied.

COVETING ROBS YOU OF BLESSING

As parents, the Christmas season holds some of our favorite memories. The kids were always faithful to give us gifts, often homemade cards and crafts that we kept as sacred memories. It was fun to open these gifts from the kids. What was even more fun, however, was watching the kids open *their* presents.

There's a little line with big implications tucked away in Acts 20:35. It is

---

a Jas. 4:1–2

the only place in the Bible you can find the "words of the Lord Jesus, how he himself said, 'It is more blessed to give than to receive.'"

There is a false teaching, commonly referred to as prosperity, that says we give to get a blessing. The truth is that *giving is the blessing*. God is the most generous person and is, therefore, the most blessed. The apostle Paul describes a giver as cheerful because when we give, we are blessed to share in God's joy.

The opposite of giving is coveting. Coveting leads to hoarding, where we keep it all and do not share. Coveting leads to stealing, where we do not allow others to enjoy what God has given them and take it for ourselves. Coveting leads to not giving, which is not loving. Out of love God "gave his only Son."[a] Giving is love in action. Coveting also leads to bad stewardship, where we spend more than we should to give to ourselves rather than also giving to God and others, which contributes to our debt. For these reasons, coveting is not just a personal problem. Coveting ruins relationship with people we could be loving if we were not so consumed with coveting.

COVETING INVITES THE DEMONIC INTO YOUR DESIRES

Have you ever stopped to ponder where this spirit of discontent and coveting began? According to the Bible, the first person to covet and get jealous of someone else was Satan. In heaven Satan got jealous of God's place in authority and coveted the glory that belonged to God alone. Unwilling to remain content with who God made him to be, the role God made him to play, and the position God intended for him to occupy, Satan got greedy, jealous, and covetous. The angels who aligned with him became demons. The difference between an angel and a demon is that an angel is content, while a demon covets. We see this battle in heaven continue on the earth. As they were seeking to have Jesus crucified, we learn the motive of the religious leaders leading the mob: "It was out of envy that they had delivered him up."[b]

Once Satan and his covetous demons were cast down to the earth, they brought coveting with them. To covet is to invite the demonic into your desires: "If you have bitter jealousy and selfish ambition in your hearts, do not boast and be false to the truth. This is not the wisdom that comes down from above, but is earthly, unspiritual, demonic. For where jealousy and selfish ambition

---

a John 3:16
b Matt. 27:18

exist, there will be disorder and every vile practice."[a] Satan has always tried to sow discontent—from the war in heaven, to Eve in the garden, to Jesus in the desert, and to this day in every culture. The entire world is caught in the grip of demonic desires. Think of it this way: If you covet, you are pulling that spirit up from hell, and it is "earthly, unspiritual, demonic." If you pull contentment down into your life instead, you are welcoming the Spirit down from heaven with "wisdom that comes down from above."

CRUSHING COVETING WITH CONTENTMENT

Jesus was teaching the principle of replacement when He said that if a demon were cast out but the Holy Spirit did not take its place, then seven more demons would fill the gap. This is why Paul tells us not only to "take off" certain mind-sets and desires but also to "put on" others.

It is not enough to simply cast out or take off coveting. It's not enough to give away everything that doesn't "spark joy" or to move into a tiny home. In every generation some people think that if they had more stuff, they would have more contentment. So they get a big home and fill it up with stuff. Eventually they become unhappy and sell all their stuff to people who are sick of not having lots of stuff and hoping the stuff that failed to make someone else happy somehow makes them happy. Contentment has nothing to do with your stuff and everything to do with your soul. Like Jesus, who was equally content whether rich in heaven or poor on earth, we have to welcome in and put on contentment. Just as light drives out darkness, so contentment drives out coveting. Paul said, "I have learned in whatever situation I am to be content. I know how to be brought low, and I know how to abound. In any and every circumstance, I have learned the secret of facing plenty and hunger, abundance and need."[b]

Contentment is not based upon what we have in this world but rather what we have in our relationship with God, because He meets our deepest needs and is our greatest treasure. A content person can be ruling from a lofty position or serving from a lowly position with an equal amount of peace in his or her soul. This is the example of our Lord, who was content to sit on a throne and be worshipped by angels as well as to hang on a cross and be mocked by enemies. A content person can be rich in possessions or reeling in poverty

a Jas. 3:14–16
b Phil. 4:11–12

while having the same quality of character and life of love as Jesus. This is the example of our Lord, who is today bountiful and blessed in the kingdom and was equally content while homeless and hungry on the earth. The key to contentment is trusting the Father heart of God, which we will study next.

CHAPTER 16

WIN YOUR WAR AGAINST A FATHER WOUND

*You have received the Spirit of adoption as sons, by whom
we cry, "Abba! Father!" The Spirit himself bears witness with our spirit that we are children of God.*

—ROMANS 8:15–16

A MIXED MARTIAL ARTS fighter named Jens Pulver became a Christian later in life and wrote an autobiography. The 5-foot, 7-inch lightweight known as "Lil' Evil" was a lefty who fought his way through the inaugural Ultimate Fighting Championship to win his weight class.

This brutal fighter had grown up under the worst of circumstances, including an incident where his dad put a gun in seven-year-old Jens' mouth but then pulled it away, saying "You aren't worth the bullets."[1]

Pulver was fighting his dad every time he climbed in the ring. He explains his father wound, saying, "When I was 15 I made myself a promise. My dad had just beaten me and my mom, and we were huddled in the bathroom, crying. It was a horrible situation. But I made myself a promise—one day I'm going to get so famous that I'm going to tell everybody about him. I'm going to get so famous that they are going to listen. It took me 20 years, but it kept me out there chasing the dream until I became a world champion."[2]

FIVE KINDS OF FATHERS

Everyone is marked, positively or negatively, by their earthly father. Although everyone's family experience is unique, we have identified five general categories of fathers.

1. Tragic dad—this father isn't in the picture for some tragic reason (i.e., death, permanent debilitating medical problem).

2. Terrible dad—this father is absent for no good reason (i.e., runs off either before or after kids are born, shows little to no interest in being a parent).

3. Tough dad—this father is overbearing, dominating, and intimidating (i.e., threatens like a drill sergeant, pushes like a bad boss, or yells like an awful coach). The tough dad abuses his family.

4. Tender dad—this father is kind, sweet, and nice but fails to protect his family (i.e., gets run over by tough guys, allows his kids to get bullied and pushed around, and watches his daughter end up with an abusive boyfriend because he won't step in the middle). This family is often financially broke because strong guys beat weak dad in business. The tender dad lets other people abuse his family.

5. Terrific dad—this dad isn't perfect, but he is godly, relational, wise, healthy, present, and knows how to be both tough *for* the family and tender *with* the family (i.e., their dad provided for *all* of the family's needs). Financially, he makes good money. Spiritually, he leads in the worship of God. Relationally, he is encouraging, warm, and connected. Socially, he nurtures healthy relationships with other families to provide community for his family. Humbly he owns his mistakes and apologizes when he is wrong.

How about you? What kind of father do you have? If you are a father, what kind of dad are you?

The father wound is an unhealed hurt from a physical or spiritual father or father figure in our lives. Fathers fail us, and unless we forgive them and invite God the Father to heal our father wound, we remain burdened instead of unburdened, broken instead of healed, and made bitter instead of made better. It leaves people open to the demonic through hurt and bitterness.

The father wound shows up early in human history and continues to this day. In Genesis we see in generation after generation a father who plays favorites and sets rivalry and ungodliness in motion among the family members. The unchosen and unloved are wounded by their fathers and open to evil.

Before Jacob favored Joseph and Isaac favored Esau, the pattern began with Abraham, who took two wives (Sarah and Hagar) and had two sons (Isaac and Ishmael). God had promised that Abraham's "seed" would be the chosen son through whom the nations would be blessed and to whom the Promised Land would belong. Abraham should have never slept with Hagar the Egyptian or fathered Ishmael. Once Abraham chose Isaac and rejected Ishmael, the father wound created two people groups who have been at war ever since—the Jews and the Arabs.

To this day many Arabs are Muslim and have retold their version of the story of Abraham, making themselves the chosen son and Isaac the rejected son. In part because of their father wound, they deny that Jesus is the Son of God and worship a demon god named Allah. The entire geopolitical crisis over the nation of Israel and battle between the physical and spiritual "sons" of Abraham (Judaism and Christianity) versus global Islam is largely the result of a father wound. It has opened the door to demonic forces to cause those who were wounded to be at war and create a counterfeit religion. God created one family line, and Satan counterfeited it with another from the same father.

In addition to physical parents the Bible teaches that we also have spiritual parents. This explains why we ought "not rebuke an older man but encourage him as you would a father" and to treat "older women as mothers."[a]

Paul was a spiritual father himself, even though there is no indication that he had any biological children: "For though you have countless guides in Christ, you do not have many fathers. For I became your father in Christ Jesus through the gospel."[b] Paul also refers to Timothy, Titus, and Onesimus as "sons" and calls the Christians in Galatia "my little children."[c]

---

a 1 Tim. 5:1–2
b 1 Cor. 4:15
c Gal. 4:19

In addition to wounds from our biological fathers, we can receive wounds from our spiritual fathers. Sometimes this pain cuts doubly deep. If someone has a failed father and then comes into the church family only to have a failed spiritual father, they have the painful double portion of a father wound.

So how do you recognize someone with a father wound? We have identified at least six ways to spot it, and we'll take a look at them now.

SIX WAYS TO IDENTIFY A FATHER WOUND

1. Fear

People with father wounds often have great fears about getting married and having children. Unhealed from the failure of their father and family, the fears from their past counteract faith for their future. Some people are reticent to marry and start a family despite wanting to move into that next life stage. Fathers both give us an example to follow and help when tough times come. People who fear becoming like their fathers and causing the kind of pain for their children that they experienced as a child become gripped by that fear.

2. Immaturity

People with father wounds often deal with immaturity. Good fathers help us to grow up, take responsibility, and make the move from child to adult. Speaking as a spiritual father, Paul says, "When I was a child, I spoke like a child, I thought like a child, I reasoned like a child. When I became a man, I gave up childish ways."[a] This explains why men are taking longer to grow up and are less likely than their female counterparts to be in college, have a job, attend church, or even have a driver's license. Today they live with their parents and wait longer to get married than at any other point in history.

3. Rebellion

People with father wounds often have a rebellious spirit. Because fathers provide authority and structure, a father wound causes a person to see authority as dangerous, unsafe, and untrustworthy. As a result they rebel against it. In more moderate forms the father wound causes people to be suspicious of leadership and prefer governance structures in the home or church where there is no leader rather than a team of fully equal leaders. This violates the principle of singular headship and plural leadership

---

a 1 Cor. 13:11

established by the Trinity. This error started with the war in heaven when Satan would not recognize the Father as the singular head and as a result inflicted the first father wound on himself with no one else to blame. Rather than accepting the Father as his Maker and head, Satan declared war on the Father, seeking to overthrow Him. This was the beginning of the demonic pattern of the father wound.

4. Selfishness

People with father wounds are often selfish. In a healthy home with godly parents the center of the home is God, followed by the marital relationship of mom and dad, then followed by the children. Children who grow up with a healthy father in a healthy family know they are not the center of the universe. Children who grow up in an unhealthy family because of the failure of the father often have their mothers treat them as the center of the universe, which causes them to be over-mothered, under-fathered, and selfish.

5. Warped view of God

People with unhealed father wounds have a wrong and warped view of God. Our view of God is often a projection or rejection of our imperfect earthly dad onto God. The following sampling of belief systems shows what we mean.

- Atheism says I have no Father.

- Agnosticism says I may or may not have a Father, but I've never met Him, I don't know who or where He is, and I don't really care to find out.

- Deism says I have a Father, but like my dad who abandoned me when I was little, He lives far away and we don't have a relationship.

- Reformed theology says I have a Father who is distant, controlling, and not very relational (like the domineering dad we discussed earlier).

- Arminian theology says I have a Father who is passive and lets me make my own decisions and do whatever I want, like my earthly dad, who stayed out of my affairs.

- Liberal theology says I have a Father who acts more like an enabling older sibling and does not tell me what to do but helps me do whatever I want, even if it's foolish or rebellious.

- Feminist theology says I don't need a Father, since men are dangerous and harmful, so I should instead move on and be happy to be spiritually raised by a single parent and worship God as Mother.

6. Lack of real-life mentors

We all need godly mentors, especially if we do ministry. But people with father wounds have a hard time connecting to wise, older men or women who can train them. They avoid this type of relationship. If young people look to the living at all, it often goes no further than leaning on older leaders through books and podcasts, making distant spiritual heroes like their own distant dad, an absentee parent they know *about* but don't actually *know*.

People in ministry with untended father wounds are a massive generational issue for the whole church. They avoid real-life mentors and instead are enamored with dead mentors. Countless angry brothers look to John Calvin, Martin Luther, Charles Spurgeon, and Jonathan Edwards as their spiritual fathers, but dead men can't speak into their lives to affirm their faithfulness or correct their foolishness. Not to mention the best of men are still men at best:

- John Calvin had a guy murdered.[3]

- Martin Luther drank a lot, had a foul mouth, and smuggled a young nun out of a convent to marry her.[4]

- The emotional Charles Spurgeon struggled with depression over being publicly maligned in the press, was kicked out of his denomination, and smoked cigars.[5]

- Jonathan Edwards was fired by his church.[6]

Catholics venerate saints by rewriting their stories to present them as nearly perfect, barely mortals. In Protestantism, folks with father wounds and a "Spurgeon is my homeboy" shirt just have different saints.

Time magazine wrote about a "young, restless, and reformed" trend and mentioned me (Mark) in it.[7] This trend is in large part the world I would call the "immature, hurt, and father wounded." The trend toward Reformed theology is driven in large part by a generational father wound with brothers fighting on blogs and social media over how to make their new family, a church family, ideal by doing things just the right way—or more specifically, *their* way. Rather than joining a family with an older spiritual mother and father, they plant their own churches to have their own families, where they lead as brothers who join networks also led by brothers, with rarely a true spiritual father in sight. They band together over their hurt rather than under the loving hand of the Father who can heal them and make them men like Jesus.

This also explains the prevalence of Son theology over Father theology—and if they have to pick a second favorite, it's always the Spirit. These sons with father wounds don't talk as much about God the Father as they do Jesus the Son. They get very excited to preach the Son as the hero, Savior, and liberator. Technically this is true. The key to understanding the whole Bible is the person and work of Jesus Christ. In the same way, Jesus was clear that He came to reveal the Father, submitted to the Father, did the Father's will, and as the Bible says, Jesus is the image of the invisible God who is our Father. If you only love the Son of God because you are a son, you are missing the Father and unable to grow into being a father.

When the Bible talks about older leaders laying on hands to anoint and appoint younger leaders, that means ministry transfers relationally. You cannot lay hands on anyone through the internet—you have to do life with them. Laying your hands on yet another book is not the same as someone laying their hands on you. One godly and wise real-life mentor is worth more than a thousand books and downloaded sermons because he or she knows you personally. If you don't let godly leaders into the down and dirty of your day to day, that's a problem. The result is knowledge, which *puffs* up, and not love, which *builds* up. You can become an emotionally unhealthy person who thinks God provided Bible verses to beat people up rather than build people up.

In the most difficult season of our life this point was revealed in a spontaneous prophetic word from a pastor we did not really yet know at a conference with around five thousand ministry leaders in attendance. Pastor Jimmy Evans later became one of our overseers and a founding board member at

The Trinity Church. But at that conference, which was in the middle of our war, God spoke to him during the worship time at the beginning of his session. Taking the platform, he asked me to stand in front of everyone and said:

> I've got something to say before I preach…As I was sitting over there, I heard the Lord speaking something that I wanted to say to you, and I wanted to say it publicly. You lead a great movement of young people, and you lead them as an older brother, and you'll return as a father, and it'll be a greater movement, Mark. Your scars will heal millions, and the transition that you are going through in your life right now is very important for what God is going to do in the next season. Your latter years will be greater than your former years. Man looks on the outside, Mark, but God looks at the heart, and God sees integrity in your heart, Mark. You have a heart of integrity. And you're here because of your integrity. You're gonna make it through this process because of your integrity. God wants you to know and God wants these people to know that He has a plan for you, He has a future and a hope for you, and His plan for your future is good.

This man had no idea how precise his words were or how deeply they penetrated. When I was a young new Christian in college, God spoke to me at a men's retreat, telling me to marry Grace, preach the Bible, train men, and plant churches—a testimony I have shared repeatedly in more than two decades as a senior pastor. But God also said, "Mark, I have called you out from among many to lead men." Jimmy's prophecy confirmed and clarified my calling as a young man. Through Jimmy, God also spoke one more thing to me, and the words brought me to tears. In an ensuing private conversation he explained that I attracted a generation of young men with father wounds, and I was part of a fatherless movement, which was all in fact true. I was a big brother. I was becoming a father. This was a revelation from God for me, and I pray it helps and heals you. Today Grace and I are grateful to have had not only fathers who loved the Lord but also older godly pastors who are there for us.

Protestants need to understand that our birth came through protest—in fact the root word of Protestant is *protest*. However, at some point, if we do not move from protesting what we are against to proclaiming who we are for, we are carrying forth a demonic spirit of rebellion instead of a godly spirit of redemption.

Aligning yourself with dead guys is no substitute for dealing with the haunting pains of your past. Latching on to distant mentors isn't in the same universe as the presence of nearby men and women investing in your life, guiding your ministry, and leading you to maturity. No beard is big enough to cover the father wound of the little boy behind it.

The father wound is a form of bitterness that opens the demonic door for the Absalom spirit, which rebels against authority, especially fatherly authority in the home or church. This is driven by a proud belief that the son is better able to lead the family than the father and the subordinate is more capable of leading the organization than the leader. This is a demonic trap and the same thing Satan thought in heaven.

Absalom was one of the many sons of King David.[a] He was noted for being handsome.[b] Absalom had a beautiful sister named Tamar, who was sexually assaulted by their half-brother Amnon, who further dishonored her by rejecting her. To care for his sister, Absalom had his sister live with him while expecting their father, David, to care for and protect his daughter. For two years David did nothing for Tamar, and Absalom seethed with bitterness against David and Amnon. The bitterness resulted in a plot whereby Absalom got his half-brother drunk and murdered him. Fearing that his father would punish him, Absalom fled and lived in exile for three years. Then he was brought back to Jerusalem, summoned by David to be his military general commanding the warriors.

With the father wound unhealed, Absalom began a covert campaign to undermine his father, David, usurp him, and take the throne. Absalom secretly built a rebellion coalition intent on a coup against David, as the governance war in heaven was playing out on earth. God is a Father who creates a kingdom, and Satan counterfeits with father-wounded sons who seek to overthrow their fathers and rule in their place. Absalom would take those who were bitter against David and assure them that if he were king, he would serve them better. He strategically positioned himself where he was well-known by others and spent day after day at the city gate making himself more relational

a 2 Sam. 13–15; 18–19; 1 Kings 15
b 2 Sam. 14:25

and accessible to people than King David. He would befriend them, "put out his hand," and (like Judas with Jesus) take hold of them and kiss them.[a]

Over time "Absalom stole the hearts of the men of Israel."[b] Absalom succeeded in overthrowing his father, which forced King David to flee, literally running for his life. Absalom overtook Jerusalem without any resistance, as he had turned the hearts of the warriors from their king to himself. This was a copy of what Satan had done with the angels who became demons in the heavenly coup attempt.

Advisors recommended that Absalom send twelve thousand troops to destroy David, but Absalom was so bitter that he personally led the charge to kill his father. This bitterness and pride would lead to Absalom's downfall, as it gave David time to prepare and rout Absalom's forces. In great irony, Absalom's beauty led to his demise. (Like Satan, he was noted for his beauty.[c]) While fleeing the battle on a mule, Absalom's long hair got caught in some oak tree branches, which killed him. This was not what David wanted, because he still loved his son, and David grieved the death of Absalom.

Speaking of the Absalom spirit and providing a summary of his life, Francis Schaeffer says, "Absalom was a man of anti-law in the same spirit as the coming Antichrist."[8]

An unhealed father wound that invites the Absalom spirit compels men (and sometimes women) to believe that if they were in the position of highest leadership, they would do a better job of defending the hurting and caring for the needy. As a result they seek to form unholy alliances and overthrow established governance. This can be a son overtaking a father in the home, a spiritual son overtaking a spiritual father in a church, or a team member overtaking a leader in an organization. Though evil and proud, it is done in the name of love, care, and protection, much like Satan, who felt he could do a better job than God and had angels who felt the same.

IF YOU GET THE MEN, YOU WIN THE WAR

We are all familiar with the power of a grand finale. At the end of a concert, the band saves the best for last. When watching a firework display on a holiday, you need to make sure to stick around for the end. The final words

---

a 2 Sam. 15:5
b 2 Sam. 15:6
c Ezek. 28:11–19

of the Old Testament are about John the Baptizer: "His preaching will turn the hearts of fathers to their children, and the hearts of children to their fathers. Otherwise I will come and strike the land with a curse."[a]

God is identifying two kinds of people: those who are cursed and those who are blessed.

How do we know that a people group is cursed? When fathers do not have a heart for their children, and as a result the children do not have a heart for their fathers. Practically this looks like men who love sex but not God, marriage, or children. So they worship sex as their god, use and abuse women, and murder their children. If their children live, they live without their father involved or invested in their life. This is why Jesus told some men, "You are of your father the devil, and your will is to do your father's desires. He was a murderer from the beginning."[b] The adage is true, "Like father, like son," and the devil's boys look like their dad. Make no mistake, many if not most of our social problems would be solved by dads living, loving, and leading with the Father heart of God.

How do we know that a people group is blessed? When fathers have met God the Father, received a new heart (the Father heart of God), and love their children the same way their Father loves them. This is the miracle that God performs in the hearts of men. As men learn to become sons of the Father, they learn to father others, starting with their own children.

When it comes to war, both physical and spiritual, if you can get the men to fight for the right side, you win the war, because they are the heads of homes. If you lose the men, you lose the war. Men either war against the enemy and for women and children, or the enemy gets men to war against women and children.

God ends the Old Testament with men because change starts with men. God starts with men's hearts because the want-to precedes the how-to. When a man *wants* to be godly, he can apply the principles of *how* to live, love, and lead like his Father.

After those final words from Malachi, the next stage of human history was set. God would not inspire the writing of another book of the Bible for four hundred years, as people waited for the Father to send the Son. Jesus Christ is the Son of God and the revelation of the Father heart of

---

a Mal. 4:6, NLT
b John 8:44

God. Jesus turns our hearts toward the Father and gives men new hearts to love the Father and live in love like the Father. When this happens, the kingdom of God begins to overtake the death of this world, starting with blessing at home, flowing out to the church, and from there out to transform the culture that is cursed.

HEALING THE FATHER WOUND

God the Father is largely forgotten. In Evangelical, Reformed, and Bible churches the focus is on Jesus Christ, the Son of God. In Pentecostal and Charismatic churches the focus is on God the Holy Spirit. Books are written on the Son and Spirit, but hardly anything is written on the Father. Sadly the Mormons and Muslims are the ones filling the gap and talking a lot about their demonic, counterfeit views of god as father. This might explain the growth of the Mormon cult and allure of Islam to young men around the world.

According to the Bible, when we look at Jesus, we see God the Father. Jesus says, "Whoever has seen me has seen the Father."[a] When the Bible says that people, including Jesus, are God's image bearers, it means that people are made to mirror. A mirror's only job is to reflect accurately. A mirror does not exist to create any images but only to reflect. When the Bible says Jesus "is the image of the invisible God,"[b] it means that the character of the Father is reflected perfectly in the life of the Son. Those who love Jesus need to know that in Jesus they are seeing the Father heart of God.

To heal the father wound, you need to forgive the earthly father(s) who failed you. This forgiveness will remove the demonic foothold that bitterness brings. Jesus promised, "I will not leave you as orphans."[c] The orphan heart is the result of the father wound. Once you forgive your earthly father, your heart will be opened to receive the relationship you need with your heavenly Father.

To heal the father wound, you also need to deepen your relationship with God the Father. To be a Christian is to experience the fullness of "adoption as sons."[d]

When a child gets adopted, he needs to get used to having a father

---

a John 14:9
b Col. 1:15
c John 14:18
d Gal. 4:5

and spend time getting to know his new father and family. To become a Christian is to get a new family (the church), a new big brother (Jesus), and a new Father (God).

The Old Testament talks a lot about fathers and even includes genealogies listing generations of dads. God is referred to as Father roughly fifteen times, and those few occasions are in reference to God's relationship with the nation of Israel, not warm and personal communication to an individual. Everything changes with the coming of Jesus Christ. Jesus' favorite title for God is "Father"—and in the four Gospels alone He calls God His Father roughly 165 times, specifically using the word *abba*, translated in most Bibles as "Father."

A theological dictionary says that "the uniqueness of Jesus' teaching on this subject is evident for several reasons. For one, the rarity of this designation for God is striking. There is no evidence in pre-Christian Jewish literature that Jews addressed God as '*Abba*.' A second unique feature about Jesus' use of *Abba* as a designation for God involves the intimacy of the term...*Abba* was a term not only that small children used to address their fathers; it was also a term that older children and adults used. As a result, it is best to understand *Abba* as the equivalent of 'Father' rather than 'Daddy.'"[9]

The father wound leaves people open to the demonic spirits of slavery and fear. Healing from the father wound leaves people open to the Holy Spirit of adoption and sonship. "For all who are led by the Spirit of God are sons of God. For you did not receive the spirit of slavery to fall back into fear, but you have received the Spirit of adoption as sons, by whom we cry, 'Abba! Father!' The Spirit himself bears witness with our spirit that we are children of God, and if children, then heirs—heirs of God and fellow heirs with Christ."[a]

As you walk away from the demonic spirits of the father wound and by the Spirit walk with the Father, you will experience radical life change. Although you may be a Christian, even a devout and seasoned Christian, you may have not yet made the full journey from Jesus to the Father. Jesus said, "I am the way, and the truth, and the life. No one comes to the Father except through me."[b] The Holy Spirit brings you to Jesus. Then Jesus brings you to the Father. The Spirit convicts you of sin and brings you to Jesus for the forgiveness of sin. Jesus forgives your sin and then brings you to the Father for

a Rom. 8:14–17
b John 14:6

healing. Many Christians understand conviction and forgiveness but have not yet experienced the Father's healing because of their father wounds.

The good news is that on the cross, Jesus Christ took our place and endured a Father wound so that ours could be healed. On the cross, when Jesus asked the Father, "Why have you forsaken me?"[a] He was wounded by the Father. At that moment, the Father turned His back on the Son as Jesus was wounded and forsaken in our place. When Jesus endured the Father wound, He broke a spiritual curse and reconciled us back to our Father so that we would not experience the forsaking that He did.

THE FATHER AND HIS CHURCH FAMILY

Among our peers we have a generation of sons with father wounds preaching a Son-centered theology, leading churches as brothers rather than fathers, lacking spiritual moms and dads, and attracting people who bring their own family wounds and who want the church to be family minus the presence of any kind of older fatherly or motherly leadership. Add to that a lack of wise governance, and the pin is pulled from the grenade.

Bringing healing to this issue might just be the key for an entire generation, removing the demonic foothold brought by bitterness instigated by brokenness. Healing will only happen when sons and daughters can forgive failed fathers. Add to that an openhearted anticipation of the good things that can happen when we choose to become good sons and daughters rather than simply demanding that others be perfect parents, whether biological or spiritual.

Healing also requires the participation of godly older leaders who understand the unique needs of this generation. Many weren't parented, leaving gaps in their life learning. The biggest thing they can give hurting younger men and women is relentlessly patient love. However, if elders force this approach on the next generation, more damage will inevitably ensue because the young will misinterpret the forced intervention as abusive spiritual parenting. Younger brothers and sisters need space to invite spiritual fathering and mothering if and when they are ready to heal. We all bring hurt, either big or small, into our relationships with our families and church families if we do not allow the Father to heal our father wounds. When we parent at

---

a Matt. 27:46

home or minister at church out of our own hurt, we are more likely to cause the people we care about pain. It is vital that if you have a father wound, you take the time to heal so God can change your life and legacy.

We believe the Western church is on the brink of a third turning. The baby boomer generation wanted to take the church from their parents and make it more practical and accessible. Generation X wanted to plant their own churches and set up their own families due to their father wounds and unwillingness to have healthy older spiritual fathers and mothers in their midst. The Millennial generation is most concerned about marriage and parenting, according to a national research group. They do not want to take the church away from older people or leave the church to form a church with younger people but instead to have an intergenerational church that functions as a healthy family. This could lead to a strengthening of struggling churches and allow the church of Jesus Christ to fill the needs left by divorce and broken homes where generations no longer do life together.

We believe this insight might be crucial for the next season of church life. Older generations have an opportunity to be life-giving sources for emerging leaders who have a hunger where our generation had a hurt. Our church plant is an attempt to discover a healthy way to walk in this revelation as we serve there in the role of a mother and father with our children, loving and leading our spiritual church family of all life stages and ages. We also know that all efforts at healthy families and ministries face attempts at demonic fear, which we will study next.

CHAPTER 17

WIN YOUR WAR AGAINST FEAR

God has not given us a spirit of fear...
—2 Timothy 1:7, nkjv

WE WERE SPENDING our family vacation tucked away in a remote cabin surrounded by barren dirt hills and jagged rocks where we could breathe fresh air, splash in a lake, and do our best to grab some family time. Mark had barely stepped in the front door when our kids clamored for his attention.

"Dad—where were you?"

"Out in the car," Mark said. "Taking a call."

"But Dad—you promised you would drag us around the lake on the inner tubes!"

Our five kids were all there, waiting in swimsuits in the front room of the cabin. Mark and I (Grace) had hoped that a break would bring calm, but our time away was actually the most intense point of our life and ministry. Crisis-level problems hit every day. Our phones buzzed constantly. Our black Jeep was parked in a carport alongside a windowless wall of the cabin, so we took calls out in the car. We didn't want our kids looking on. We didn't want them to overhear hard conversations or be overcome with fear. We wanted them to feel like life was normal even though we were in a war. We needed to process things so we could then share with them in a healthy way.

We spent hours every day in that car while on vacation. Often as we talked, we stared at a wall. Sometimes calls broke up, so we left the kids behind, drove up a hill, pulled off the road, and parked alongside a dumpster because that location had better reception.

That day, Mark made the call from the carport, just a few feet outside the front door. He couldn't understand why the kids were exasperated.

Kids: "We've been waiting forever!"

Mark: "Well, I'm sorry. I had to take a call."

Kids: "Why did it take so long?"

Mark: "It didn't. I was only gone a few minutes."

Kids: "We've been sitting here in our swimsuits for hours."

That made no sense to Mark, and he said so. "It was just a couple-minute call!"

Kids: "No, Dad—that was like four hours ago."

The news he got was so wrong that he was apparently in shock and sat in our hot, parked car for four hours staring at the dash, overwhelmed at the anxiety of what it all meant. He was fraught with fear.

SHOVELING OUT FROM AN AVALANCHE

In the scene we just described, one of the worst seasons of our life, we felt as if an avalanche hit us. One thing after another collapsed, and it felt like we were going to be overtaken and overcome by everything falling down around us. We are sure you can relate, as we've all had avalanches in our lives. You may be in the middle of one right now.

What is the first thing on your mind in the morning, or the last thing on your mind at night? Is there a future event you are frantically seeking to prevent from happening?

What sign is your body giving you that you are living in a state of fear? Do you have a nervous twitch, any brain fog, trouble sleeping, high blood pressure, stomach problems, tension headaches, chronic sickness, moments of unexpected anxiety, panic attacks, sadness, or anger? Have you found yourself fantasizing about death or suicide? Are you overly interested in end-times theology, hoping you will soon be able to leave this life?

During our avalanche, we experienced great fear. Some of the concern was legitimate—based on actual negative things happening in the present that we needed to deal with. This kind of fear can be life-saving, much like the adrenaline that kicks in when your life is in danger and you need to survive. Some of the concern was illegitimate—based on possible negative things in the future, many of which did not happen. This kind of fear can be life-taking, diverting our precious life energy from investing in real people and things and wasting it on a mirage. God creates faith, and Satan counteracts that faith with his counterfeit of fear.

Fear is one of the major topics of the Bible. Guilty of sin and hiding from God and his wife, Adam said, "I was afraid."ᵃ Though hard to imagine, this was the first time that anyone ever felt fear. Since that day everyone has felt fear.

A traumatic experience can push us from fear to anxiety or even phobia. Sometimes triggers can bring us back to a moment of trauma, and the Bible calls these "strongholds."ᵇ You know that you have a stronghold when something from your past is ruling your decision-making for your present and future. You know that you have a stronghold when a trigger brings you back to relive a past trauma as if it were happening all over again in the present, when in fact it is not.

EIGHT REASONS FEAR IS A FRAUD

Most fears are frauds. They are not based upon reality and cause us to make unhealthy, unwise, and often unholy decisions, which in turn make us unhappy. We know of at least eight reasons why a spirit of fear is a fraud.

1. Fear is godless.

A spirit of fear is hopeless because it is godless. A spirit of fear compels us to look into the future and see only the worst possible outcome, ignoring that God will be there and likely has a different plan for our good. This is what Jesus was driving at when He said, "Do not be anxious about your life.... Which of you by being anxious can add a single hour to his span of life?... Why are you anxious?... O you of little faith!... Do not... be worried."ᶜ

2. Fear is a false prophecy.

A false prophet is a person who predicts a future that never happens. When we are ruled by fear rather than faith, we become false prophets in our own lives, predicting a hopeless, apocalyptic future that does not come to pass.

a Gen. 3:10
b 2 Cor. 10:3–5
c Luke 12:22–29

3. Fear makes us selfish.

When fear grips us, we think solely of ourselves in the same way that a person running out of a burning building is not concerned about whatever trouble a friend a hundred miles away might be going through at that same moment.

4. Fear makes us ineffective.

When fear drives us, we can be so scared of failing that we become paralyzed and do not do the things that God asks of us. For example, Jesus talks about a man who was given a bit of money to invest but did nothing with it, saying, "I was afraid."[a]

5. Fear causes us to lose touch with reality.

Like binoculars, fear becomes the lens through which we magnify and enlarge all the negative data we focus on in our lives. Eventually we start imagining things that aren't real and let the fears drive us to a life of isolation and pointless worry.

In Proverbs 22:13 we read about a fearful person who cannot leave his home for the unfounded reason that "there is a lion outside! I shall be killed in the streets!" His fears may seem silly to us, but our fears likely also seem silly to him.

6. Fear causes us to seek to be God.

The devil's first temptation was for us to "be like God."[b] We become obsessed with information in an effort to be all-knowing like God and predict the future. We can also become obsessed with controlling the future to get the results we want and avoid the results we do not want rather than accepting God's will for our lives. This is an attempt at sovereignty.

7. Fear robs us.

Jesus spoke of the thief who "comes only to steal and kill and destroy."[c] Fear is a thief. Fear steals your joy, hope, and health. Fear kills your heart, soul, mind, and strength. Fear destroys your relationship with God, yourself, and others.

---

a Matt. 25:24–26
b Gen. 3:5
c John 10:10

8. Fear makes us double-minded and unstable.

"The one who doubts is like a wave of the sea that is driven and tossed by the wind. . . . He is a double-minded man, unstable in all his ways."[a] When God tells us to do something, we are to obey Him as an act of faith. However, when fear grips us, we are often torn between obeying the spirit of fear and obeying the Spirit of God.

The ongoing feeding of unfounded fear starves our faith and causes us to become ungodly. One Bible dictionary references:

> An array of people . . . are plagued with deep-reaching anxiety (e.g., Cain, Saul, Ahaz, and Pilate). Anxious fear seizes the wicked (Job 15:24), surprises the hypocrite (Isa. 33:14), and consumes evildoers (Ps. 73:19), whose faithless lives are characterized by fear (Rev. 21:8). Pharaoh's mighty host was virtually paralyzed by fear as God moved against them (Exod. 15:16), and Job's associate Bildad spoke of men driven to their knees by the judgments of God (Job 18:11).[1]

How do we feed our faith and starve our fear? One particular section of Scripture is perhaps most helpful, and it happens to be my (Grace's) life verse:

> Rejoice in the Lord always; again I will say, rejoice. Let your reasonableness be known to everyone. The Lord is at hand; do not be anxious about anything, but in everything by prayer and supplication with thanksgiving let your requests be made known to God. And the peace of God, which surpasses all understanding, will guard your hearts and your minds in Christ Jesus.[b]

FIVE WAYS TO FEED YOUR FAITH AND STARVE YOUR FEARS

In the remainder of this chapter you will learn five ways to feed your faith and starve your fears based upon Philippians 4:4–7.

1. Focus one eye on each track.

Some years ago while driving in his truck, Pastor Rick Warren said something to me (Mark) that has stuck with us ever since. He said most people think of life as being a series of good and bad seasons, but he felt

---

a Jas. 1:5–8
b Phil. 4:4–7

that every season of life was more like train tracks with good and bad happening constantly and congruently. He was right.

When troubles, temptations, and trials come, we tend to see only the bad track. This makes us like Puddleglum in the Narnia series or Winnie-the-Pooh's friend Eeyore. Puddleglum the pessimist had a dour disposition. He expected the worst in every situation and assumed the worst in every person. Eeyore is always in a gloomy mood and is famous for saying things such as, "It's all for naught," and "It'll never work."

When the bad comes to feed our fear, we need to practice the discipline of also seeing the good track where good things are happening in life at the same time to starve our fear and feed our faith. This is why Philippians instructs us to "rejoice in the Lord always; again I will say, rejoice" (4:4) and to respond with thanksgiving (4:6). There is always something to be fearful of and always something to be thankful for.

2. Make your will your rudder.

Fear stirs up emotions. Fear in the mind causes a multitude of systems to fire in the body. Fear causes blood pressure to rise, adrenaline to flow, and senses to heighten, making you feel alert and on guard. This is a good thing when you have an actual threat to your life; it is why people tend to run faster when there is danger. However, when people live in an ongoing state of fear for a prolonged time, they can have a hard time turning it off. This can cause people to self-medicate with things such as drugs, alcohol, sex, food, or shopping.

Think of it this way: Your emotions are like a sail. They are big, powerful, and drive your life. When filled with fear, your emotions are like a sail in a hurricane. Imagine a sailboat in a hurricane with no rudder. When filled with fear, many people are like that.

Instead, when anxious and fearful, "Let your reasonableness be known to everyone."[a] *Reasonableness* means to use mental reasoning to make wise, faith-filled decisions that drive you forward into God's will. This is the opposite of being unreasonable and allowing your emotions and circumstances to steer you toward rocks that will sink you. Your mind must be your rudder.

---

a Phil. 4:5

3. Replace panic with prayer.

When a spirit of fear comes over us, our first response is often panic. Some people even experience panic attacks. Our mind races with all of the possible dangers. Sometimes these fears are legitimate, but often they are lies. Rather than panic, we should pray. Freaking out is not a spiritual gift; faith is. Panic helps nothing, but prayer helps everything.

To remind us to replace panic with prayer, Philippians tells us, "Do not be anxious about anything, but in everything by prayer and supplication..."[a] When we pray instead of panic, at least three things happen:

First, praying transfers the burden to God.

In the midst of our avalanche one of our pastors asked how our prayer life was going. I (Mark) said it was going well. Our pastor then asked if the burden we were carrying remained, to which I said, "Yes, I'm carrying a heavy burden." With a bit of humor our pastor then said that until the burden was transferred to God, we were not really praying, rather just complaining to God. When something is out of our hands, we need to leave it in His hands. If someone needs to worry, let it be God. The Protestant Reformer Martin Luther was fond of saying, "Pray, and let God worry."[2]

Second, praying allows God to be our lightning rod.

We minister in the desert around Scottsdale, Arizona. Every year, monsoon season comes, and lightning explodes across the valley, lighting up the night in glorious fashion. Lightning rods are set up to harness the energy and ground out the storm to prevent significant damage. When a storm rolls into your life and the lightning bolt of fear hits you, prayer is the lightning rod to have God ground out your storm. As you read books of the Bible such as Psalms, Lamentations, or Ecclesiastes, you will quickly see how other saints used God as their lightning rod.

Third, praying allows you to process verbally but privately.

When a spirit of fear overcomes us, we often need to express what we are feeling to help make some sense of our inner life. This can lead to us scaring other people, burdening and wearing out those who care about us, or harshly lashing out at others because we are not in a good place emotionally. Making matters worse is social media, where we can post things we later regret and

---

a Phil. 4:5–6

get drawn into arguments that escalate quickly and serve no useful purpose. Praying allows us to privately process what we are feeling in relationship with God. Before we talk to anyone, we should talk to God alone.

4. Tell the Father what you want.

When a spirit of fear comes upon us, it reveals what we love and hate. Like a coin, fear has two sides. On one side is the fear you will experience something bad. On the other side is the fear you will lose something good. What terrible thing are you afraid is coming? What precious thing are you afraid of losing?

After a few decades in pastoral ministry we have seen one thing repeatedly: people who love God and want to walk in His will get anxious when God does not speak to them in some way and direct their next season of life. When God is silent, it may be because He wants to hear from you. God is a Father, and we are His kids. With our five kids, we tell them some things because we need them to listen and obey, but on many other occasions we ask the kids what they want. So long as their request is reasonable, we are prone to say yes.

God's will is less like a tightrope and more like a highway. So long as we are going the direction God wants, we can drive in a few different lanes to get there. If none of the lanes is sin or folly, God is often happy to let us pick a lane and drive in it.

For example, God was clear that we needed to be loving, serving, trusting, obeying, and enjoying Him wherever we landed—so God set the direction. In the end we wanted to move to Arizona, and God said yes in ways He confirmed by godly, wise counsel. Through a series of supernatural events God gave us an amazing season of healthy life and ministry, and He let us pick where we lived.

Sometimes we ask God, "What do You want?" and God replies, "I was going to ask you the same question." In a season of fear when what we want and don't want needs to be clarified, it is reasonable to tell God what we want and see what He says. "Let your requests be made known to God."[a] Jesus does the same thing when He asks someone, "What do

---

a Phil. 4:6

you want me to do for you?"[a] Sometimes God's will is to ask you for the desires of your heart.

5. Enjoy God's presence and peace.

When we sense a spirit of fear coming over us, it can cause us to feel overwhelmed. Fear is such a common experience that the most frequent command in the Bible is "Fear not," which appears roughly a few hundred times. God has to remind us continually to "fear not" in some form or fashion because we forget.

When some of our kids were little, they had bad dreams that caused them to wake up crying at night. We would walk into their room and encourage them not to be afraid because we were present to hold them, rub their back, pray for them, and comfort them. Eventually their fear would subside, and they would return to sleep. God is a Father, we are His kids, and this is how it works.

Curiously, we also find it common that when God says fear not, He then tells us in some way, "for I am with you." Examples include Abraham, Moses, Elijah, King Jehoshaphat, Israel, Jeremiah, and many others.[b] Before returning to heaven, Jesus said, "Do not be afraid," because "I am with you always, to the end of the age."[c]

Returning to Philippians 4:5–7, we were told, "Do not be anxious about anything" because "the Lord is at hand." For those who choose faith over fear, "the peace of God, which surpasses all understanding, will guard your hearts and your minds in Christ Jesus." Like a soldier God will guard the emotional life of our hearts and the thought life of our minds if we stand with Him against the spirit of fear, which is an act of spiritual warfare.

It is not the absence of trouble that brings peace but the presence of God. Consider you are walking through a dangerous neighborhood and feeling fearful. Now consider going on that same walk with a platoon of armed guards surrounding you. God and His angelic army are much like that. The presence of the help is more powerful than the presence of the harm.

The presence of God brings the peace of God. This is the ministry of the

---

a Mark 10:51
b Gen. 15:1, 24, 26; Exod. 33:14; 2 Kings 1:15; 2 Chron. 20:17; Isa. 41:14; Jer. 1:8
c Matt. 28:20

Holy Spirit. Light drives out darkness, truth drives out lies, and the Spirit of God drives out the spirit of fear.

THE SPIRIT OF FEAR

One of the most powerful cessationist Christian leaders we have personally met oversees an entire denomination of churches that adamantly denies that such things as supernatural spiritual gifts exist in this era. Tragically, he is reacting to deep pain in his own life. In a conversation over lunch he said that when he was a boy, a guest preacher at their church told him he would be dead by a specific age in his teenage years. This word, which was demonic, caused this man gripping fear until the age passed that he was told he would die, proving the man was a false prophet. It seems likely that the counterfeit prophet with the counterfeit prophecy put a counterfeit spirit of fear on this boy. Ever since, he has devoted his life to preventing others being harmed, which may mean the spirit of fear continues to drive him. But the abusive counterfeit of a genuine spiritual gift does not negate the genuine gift of God. After all, the world is filled with false teachers, but the answer is not to deny that the gift of teaching exists but rather for genuine Bible teachers to use their gift to drive out darkness with the light of God's Word.

Sometimes professional help and medication can help with fear and anxiety. Sometimes the problem is more physical than spiritual and requires medical attention. Sometimes fear and anxiety are at least in part spiritual. If a demonic spirit is behind the fear, then the answer to the problem is spiritual: "For God has not given us a spirit of fear, but of power and of love and of a sound mind."[a]

The Bible speaks on occasion of various demonic spirits of fear.

> Apollyon—ruling spirit of fear (Rev. 9:11). Scorpion spirits of fear that cause torment (Rev. 9:1–11; 1 John 4:18). Perfect love casts out fear. People raised in an atmosphere without love (i.e., rejection, strife, violence, etc.) usually have many spirits of fear...[including] Enim (Deut. 2:10–11)—the giants meaning the terrible, formidable, terrors, objects of terror.[3]

---

a 2 Tim. 1:7, NKJV

The way to deal with a demon spirit is to cast it out and replace it with the love of God. This is why replacing worry with worship, fear with faith, and panic with prayer drives out the spirit of fear. "There is no fear in love, but perfect love casts out fear. For fear has to do with punishment, and whoever fears has not been perfected in love."[a]

We find the peace, presence, love, and life of God in our Helper, the Holy Spirit. Jesus promised, "The Helper, the Holy Spirit, whom the Father will send in my name, he will teach you all things....Peace I leave with you; my peace I give to you. Not as the world gives do I give to you. Let not your hearts be troubled, neither let them be afraid."[b] Paul confirms, "For you did not receive the spirit of slavery to fall back into fear, but you have received the Spirit of adoption as sons, by whom we cry, 'Abba! Father!' The Spirit himself bears witness with our spirit that we are children of God."[c]

Jesus models how to overcome fear with faith. In the Garden of Gethsemane, with the cross only hours away, Jesus experienced fear and anxiety. Unable to sleep, His sweat like drops of blood, spending the entire night in prayer, He was honest with God the Father about His struggles. He asked if there were any way to save sinners without having to suffer. In the end Jesus surrendered in faith to the Father, saying, "Your will be done." On the cross Jesus was no longer fearful or anxious but instead had the peace that surpasses understanding, saying with His final breath, "Father, into Your hands I commit My spirit."

DEATH IS GAIN

Perhaps the strongest spirit of fear is the fear of death. Having preached in a bulletproof vest at our church and having experienced security issues at our home from critics, we understand this fear for oneself and one's family.

Admittedly, if we find ourselves in danger, making reasonable efforts to remain safe is wise. However, we can find ourselves moving down a sliding scale from prepared to paranoid for unhealthy reasons. In the end death will come for us all. None of us will live forever. An unhealthy fear of death can rob us of enjoying life. Faith pours courage for life into us, whereas fear drains courage for life out of us.

a 1 John 4:18
b John 14:25–27
c Rom. 8:15–16

Someday death will defeat you. Thankfully, Jesus defeated death. Jesus' resurrection is the pattern and precedent for all of God's people. Death does not get the last word; the risen Jesus does. "When the perishable puts on the imperishable, and the mortal puts on immortality, then shall come to pass the saying that is written:... 'O death, where is your victory? O death, where is your sting?'"[a]

Faith in Jesus casts out the fear of death. Comforting a woman whose brother died, Jesus said, "I am the resurrection and the life. Whoever believes in me, though he die, yet shall he live, and everyone who lives and believes in me shall never die. Do you believe this?"[b] If you believe in Jesus' resurrection, the fact that you will die one day casts out the fear of death that can grip you on any day. Our faith says death is not to be feared because "to die is gain."[c]

Peter stands out as a glaring example of living by fear of death rather than faith in God. He pledged complete devotion to Jesus, only to have Jesus foretell that before a rooster crowed, he would deny the Lord three times.[d] Despite knowing this, Peter still failed. When Jesus suffered interrogation, He declared that He was God. Outside, when Peter was asked by a young girl, he denied that Jesus was his God.[e] Peter feared death, and that fear overrode his faith. Like Peter we all live either by faith or fear.

Often overlooked in the story of Peter's denials, however, is the work of Satan and the demonic. One of the disciples, Judas, betrayed Jesus because he welcomed Satan into his soul.[f] The governance war in heaven was again playing out between God and Satan, this time on the earth. In addition to Judas, Satan also wanted Peter. Jesus says, "Simon, Simon, behold, Satan demanded to have you, that he might sift you like wheat, but I have prayed for you that your faith may not fail. And when you have turned again, strengthen your brothers."[g]

Satan exploited Peter's fear of death so that he would deny Jesus. However, Jesus prayed for Peter, and at this moment He is praying for you so that failure would be overcome with faith.[h] History outside of the Bible reports that when

---

a 1 Cor. 15:54–55
b John 11:25–26
c Phil. 1:21
d John 13:37–38
e John 18:15–18
f John 13:27
g Luke 22:31–32
h Heb. 7:25

the Romans came to crucify Peter later in his life, he chose Spirit-filled faith rather than a spirit of fear, and he asked to be crucified upside down because he was unworthy to die like his Lord. He no longer had any fear of death. The same kind of faith is possible for you to overcome your fears.

Practically, how do you enjoy the presence of the Holy Spirit so that your fear is replaced with faith and the spirit of fear is cast out by the love of God? Stopping to sing aloud to God? Praying to God from the heart when things hurt? Journaling out your thoughts so that you come to grips with reality and trust God for your future? Bible reading to fill your mind with truth to push out any lies? Being part of a church family where the presence of God is enjoyed with brothers and sisters in the faith who help you grow in faith? Freedom from fear helps us live free of demonic division, as we will examine in the next chapter.

YOUR RELATIONSHIP WITH
CHURCH

CHAPTER 18

WIN YOUR WAR AGAINST DIVISION

Rebellion is as sinful as witchcraft.
—1 SAMUEL 15:23, NLT

A N EPIC SCENE in the classic movie *Rocky IV* provides an insight about vision. After being battered in the ring by the giant Russian boxer Ivan Drago (actor Dolph Lundgren), Rocky (actor Sylvester Stallone) had this conversation between rounds in his corner:

> Rocky: I see three of him out there.
>
> Paulie: Hit the one in the middle.
>
> Duke: Right! Hit the one in the middle.[1]

That legendary line is borrowed from boxing lore. Apparently, in the 1933 heavyweight fight between Max Baer and Max Schmeling, Baer got knocked senseless and staggered to his corner saying, "I see three of him." The ex-champ Jack Dempsey, who was one of his cornermen, replied, "Hit the one in the middle." Baer did just that and went on to win the fight via knockout.[2]

Have you ever had double vision? Maybe you were a kid and saw double after bonking your head. Anyone who has had trouble seeing, even for a short while, knows that it is nearly impossible to live without clear vision to see where you are going and what you are doing.

In the war with the devil and his demons, you will lose your vision at times. The key is not to allow the decline in your vision to lead to division. *Division* means two visions. When two or more people have differing visions for what should happen, division has begun. When other people line up behind the leaders with the differing visions, then factions have formed.

Division started in heaven long before it arrived on the earth. Satan had a different vision than God. Holy angels sided with God, and unholy angels created a faction siding with Satan and supporting his division. Today there is one vision and no division in heaven. The faction of demonic division is now present across the earth as Satan counterfeits what God creates to make confusion and division.

As we mentioned earlier, religious leaders made the incredulous false accusation of Jesus, "He is possessed by Beelzebul," and "by the prince of demons he casts out the demons."[a] Jesus responded by asking, "How can Satan cast out Satan?"[b] Satan and demons are often united, standing together with an allegiance that Christians do not have. Jesus goes on to say, "If a kingdom is divided against itself, that kingdom cannot stand. And if a house is divided against itself, that house will not be able to stand."[c] Jesus' point is startling. Demons sometimes have more unity, respect for authority, and obedience than the Christians they battle. The first division between human beings was between our first parents, which is why it is so important that a husband and wife share God's vision for their life.

REBELLION

Division leads to rebellion. Unfortunately rebellion is seen as a virtue and not a vice in our culture. It is viewed as inevitable between children and parents. Anyone in any leadership position can expect division, faction, and rebellion to roll in like a false trinity of trouble. The Bible says, "Rebellion is as sinful as witchcraft."[d] Witchcraft is how people actively invite demonic spirits into their lives, and this verse tells us that rebellion does the same thing. Referring to demons of rebellion, one deliverance manual says:

> The spirit of Jezebel causes wives to forsake the covering of their husbands. It is a Hebrew name meaning untouched, untouchable,

a Mark 3:22
b Mark 3:23
c Mark 3:24–25
d 1 Sam. 15:23, NLT

non-cohabiting, without husband, adulterous, base, licentious. This spirit is characterized by domination, control, and manipulation of the husband instead of submission to his authority. The spirit of Jezebel also operates in the church with spirits of seduction, fornication, and idolatry (Rev. 2:20). It works with the Ahab spirit in men but hates the Elijah spirit (Mal. 4:5–6). It is a very religious spirit and loves to operate in the church. This spirit has been known to operate in both males and females. Jezebel was very religious and a devout high priestess of Baal.

Athaliah (2 Kings 11:1)—daughter of Ahab and Jezebel who married into the royal family of Judah. She had the same spirit as her mother in usurping authority in the kingdom of Judah, an example of how this spirit is transferred from Jezebellic mothers to their daughters. These spirits also operate through curses of destruction of family priesthood, destruction of family, and Ahab and Jezebel.[3]

Adding the story of Ahab,[a] it goes on to explain he was a godless king who allowed Jezebel, his wife, to usurp his authority.

The Ahab spirit causes men to be weak as leaders in the home and church (Isa. 3:12). This spirit works with fear of Jezebel to prevent God's order in the home and the church. The result is the destruction of the family priesthood. This is a curse that must be broken before Ahab spirits can be driven out. The curse of Jezebel opens the door for these spirits to operate in a family.[4]

If this sounds like Adam and Eve, it is because the pattern that started with Satan attacking the first marriage continues through his demons attacking other marriages.

Just as division leads to rebellion, so too rebellion leads to a mob mentality. In the frenzy of a mob people behave completely out of character—looting, rioting, and engaging in criminal activity. It is as if demonic powers are leading the mob and causing chaos. A mob descended upon Jesus, and "a great multitude of people…came to hear him and to be healed of their diseases. And those who were troubled with unclean spirits were cured. And all the crowd sought to touch him, for power came out from him and

---

a 1 Kings 16:29–20:34; 21:1-29

healed them all.”ª Speaking of the mob, we learn that “the word *vexed* in this verse is the Greek word *ochleō*, which means to mob. A mob is a group of persons bent on riotous actions.”[5]

MOB MENTALITY

Jesus had to deal with mobs throughout His ministry. Possessed by Satan, Judas showed up to arrest Jesus with an armed mob.ᵇ Then a mob rose up demanding Jesus be put to death and Barabbas be released.ᶜ

Mobs were a problem for Paul in multiple cities:

- Acts 17:5 (NIV) reports that people “were jealous; so they rounded up some bad characters from the marketplace, formed a mob and started a riot in the city.”

- Acts 19:23 (NIV) says, “About that time there arose a great disturbance about the Way.”

- Acts 19:29 (NIV) says, “The whole city was in an uproar.”

- Acts 19:40 (NIV) says, “We are in danger of being charged with rioting because of what happened today. In that case we would not be able to account for this commotion, since there is no reason for it.”

- Acts 21:31 (NIV) says, “The whole city of Jerusalem was in an uproar.”

- Acts 21:35 (NIV) says, “When Paul reached the steps, the violence of the mob was so great he had to be carried by the soldiers.” In fact one of the chief accusations against Paul found in Acts 24:5 (NIV) was “We have found this man to be a troublemaker, stirring up riots.”

In Acts 19 “God was doing extraordinary miracles,” and for many tormented people, “their diseases left them and the evil spirits came out of

---

a Luke 6:17–19
b John 13:27; 18:1–4
c Mark 15:15

them."[a] Trying to cash in on the power and popularity of God, some free-lance, do-it-yourself, itinerant "Jewish exorcists undertook to invoke the name of the Lord Jesus over those who had evil spirits."[b] Things ended poorly when "the man in whom was the evil spirit leaped on them, mastered all of them and overpowered them, so that they fled out of that house naked and wounded."[c]

Scripture says when the residents in Ephesus saw the power of God at war with the power of the demonic, "fear fell upon them all, and the name of the Lord Jesus was extolled. Also many of those who were now believers came, confessing and divulging their practices. And a number of those who had practiced magic arts brought their books together and burned them in the sight of all. And they counted the value of them and found it came to fifty thousand pieces of silver. So the word of the Lord continued to increase and prevail mightily."[d]

When the kingdom of God advances, the kingdom of Satan shows up for the showdown. When God creates a revival, Satan counterfeits with a riot. In Ephesus there was a revival of sorts, and the demons were losing. So in the next verses we see that in the spiritual realm, for every action of God there is a reaction of the demonic. A man named Demetrius, who made a good living forging demonic idols of their highest-ranking demon goddess, Artemis, brought together a group of business leaders who profited from Ephesus being a demonic headquarters with visitors flooding in to worship at the temple of Artemis and to participate in many forms of ancient dark religion and magic.

The businessmen knew they were working with and for unclean demon spirits that were their gods. They were offended by newly converted Christians who were "saying that gods made with hands are not gods."[e] They rightly understood that their demonic religion and the income it provided could come crashing down if "the great goddess Artemis may be counted as nothing, and that she may even be deposed from her magnificence, she whom all Asia and the world worship."[f]

In response to the worship of Jesus they began crying out, "Great is

---

a Acts 19:11–12
b Acts 19:13
c Acts 19:16
d Acts 19:17–20
e Acts 19:26
f Acts 19:27

Artemis of the Ephesians!" and "the city was filled with the confusion, and they rushed together into the theater....Now some cried out one thing, some another, for the assembly was in confusion, and most of them did not know why they had come together." The impromptu demonic worship rally continued "for about two hours [as] they all cried out with one voice, 'Great is Artemis of the Ephesians!'"[a]

MOB MINISTRY 101

You won't find much pastoral training that includes mob ministry 101, but from the case study in Acts 19, as well as other mobs in the ministries of Jesus and Paul, we can learn some principles:

- When God creates a revival, Satan counterfeits with a riot. When a ministry is making headway and taking ground against the kingdom of darkness, you can bet that the backlash is coming.

- Attacks against ministries are often ultimately fueled by demonic forces with a visible human leader. Today, online, mobs can form almost instantly. Some critics specialize in gathering from the comfort of their phones.

- Once a demonic mob shows up, even online, a crowd stands around to watch and has no idea why: "The assembly was in confusion: Some were shouting one thing, some another. Most of the people did not even know why they were there."[b] In the age of income streams for clicks to websites and social media platforms, it is profitable to attack leaders, cause riots, and watch the masses stand by while the instigator enjoys the attention and money.

- Because it often has demonic elements, you cannot reason with a mob. Well-meaning people will say that we simply need to identify the problem and apologize, and then the mob will disperse. But the whole point of a mob is that it is not held together by any singular cause, and once in a frenzy it is not open to reason.

a Acts 19:28–29, 32, 34
b Acts 19:32, NIV

Even Jesus was crucified because a mob "uproar was starting."[a] The mob shouting, "Crucify Him!" would not be reasoned with. Online, if you try to be the adult in the conversation and reason with the mob, you quickly learn it's pointless.

- When people don't get the result they want from a real court, they can convene a court of public opinion to force the outcome they desire. This is how they got Jesus killed.

- Swarming can kill. A bee sting or two is annoying rather than deadly, but a swarm of hundreds can kill you. Likewise, an actual mob in the ancient world or a digital mob online has a swarming effect. The goal is to keep stinging until the result is killing or destroying.

The book *So You've Been Publicly Shamed* explains how the online world has revived an eons-old practice in which crowds of fellow citizens would gather around and say horrible things to individuals as a form of punishment. It makes you wonder if there isn't a demon out there called "trending" that found a way onto the internet.

Both Jesus and Paul had to leave cities because of mobs. Their safety was in danger, and their reputations were so wrecked that meaningful ministry was no longer possible.

Mobs did not form against Jesus or Paul until they were well-known public figures. Today we'd call them celebrities. This sooner or later leads to an idolize-and-demonize cycle where people are built up and then torn down. Our culture has a fascination with rooting for the nobody on the rise, ripping them down when they reach the top, and then cheering their comeback story.

Neither Jesus nor Paul got any legal protection from the mob. The same is often true today. This leaves opportunities for wolves to ravage flocks, as we will study next.

---

a Matt. 27:24, NIV

CHAPTER 19

WIN YOUR WAR AGAINST WOLVES

*Beware of false prophets, who come to you in sheep's
clothing but inwardly are ravenous wolves.*

—MATTHEW 7:15

IN A STORY about wolves, the British Broadcasting Corporation (BBC) interviewed a woman who is a sheep farmer in the French Alps. Following is an edited version of that conversation. Matthew Bannister (MB) started the conversation with Caroline Bourda (CB) and John Laurenson (JL).

> MB: ...what is it like when you stare into the eyes of a wolf? Caroline Bourda knows the feeling all too well. She's a sheep farmer in the French Alps, and in the last couple of years, she's been on the front line of a battle with the beasts. The wolf was hunted almost to extinction in France in the 1930s. But after being labeled an endangered species, it made a surprising comeback. With wolves now killing 6,000 sheep a year, the government is allowing some wolves to be shot. It's also advised, and paid for, sheep farmers to buy electric fences and huge protection dogs with spiked metal collars to stop the wolves sinking their fangs into their necks....Now, it has allowed wolf hunts around threatened sheep farms like Caroline's....The wolves are clever. They spend

long hours watching, watching, learning the flock's movements. They wait and attack.

CB: When they attack a flock, especially when they get inside an enclosure that's supposed to protect the flock, they go berserk. They won't stop killing as long as there is still a sheep or lamb still moving. In general, we have one ewe eaten, and several others that they've killed just for the sake of it. It's very upsetting. Often it's ewes that are pregnant. It's awful for us…we spend quite a bit of time making sure she's not in too much pain and that the birth goes well. When she's given birth, we are capable of getting up several times in the night to make sure everything's OK and that the lambs are feeling alright. So…to be eaten alive is terrible. I wish we could see one tonight so you could know what it feels like when a wolf looks at you. It's something completely primitive when you meet those ice-cold eyes. You understand the danger, but not in your head; in your gut. Last year, we had a lot of attacks at our night enclosure, where wolves try to get in under the fencing. I came face to face with one. The dogs pushed him back, and it slunk away into the shadows. I saw it sinking down to wait. I thought I could see it there, but in the darkness, I wasn't sure. We stayed like that, him and me, for two and a half hours, until I started to doze off leaning against a tree. As soon as I felt myself nodding off, I woke up and saw the wolf coming towards me. Directly and quickly towards me. Even if you've got a rifle in your hands, it's frightening. The thought that an animal can wait so long to get you out. I'm not sure what happened next. It all went so quickly, but suddenly my dog was there, attacking the wolf. It chased it away and came back to protect me.

JL: What's frightening, says Caroline, is the wolf's singularity of purpose. She spends a lot of time looking after her sheep, but people also do other things: send text messages, do homework with the kids, do the hoovering [vacuuming]. The wolf stays concentrated on how he's going to get to run amok in her flock.

CB: All the time, they are watching us.[1]

The Bible uses the metaphor of Jesus as our Chief or Good Shepherd, with Christian leaders as shepherds, people as vulnerable sheep, and the presence of wolves working for Satan—who is their alpha—leading the entire pack. Just as the devil and his demons attacked in heaven, so too they continue their attack on the earth. People who ignore or underestimate the presence of spiritual wolves put themselves in harm's way, which is why the Bible gives repeated warnings.

One shepherd who faithfully battled wolves into his old age was John. First John describes wolves as "antichrists," "liar," "trying to deceive," "law-lessness," "children of the devil," "like Cain," "the world," "false prophets," "the spirit of the antichrist," "the spirit of error," and "in the power of the evil one."[a] Like wolves among a flock of sheep, false teachers were confusing the Christians, especially those newest to the faith. Some even left the Christian churches and were waging a public relations war on John and other leaders in an effort to draw people to their newly formed pack.[b]

Wolves and shepherds are both powerful leaders. The only difference is that a wolf will destroy you and a shepherd will die for you. The problem with wolves is that they are deceptive and disguise themselves as harmless sheep or trustworthy shepherds. Jesus gives the sternest warning: "Beware of false prophets, who come to you in sheep's clothing but inwardly are ravenous wolves."[c] God creates shepherds, and Satan's counterfeits are wolves who pretend to be sheep or shepherds.

FALSE APOSTLES

For the sake of simplicity, there was an office of apostle reserved for the disciples Jesus Christ handpicked while on the earth. This is a closed group of twelve leaders who met two criteria: (1) they were eyewitnesses to the risen Jesus,[d] and (2) they were chosen directly by Jesus Christ.[e]

In addition to the office of apostle, a spiritual gift of apostleship exists throughout the New Testament and to this day. For example, Paul refers to apostleship as a spiritual gift, and the term also applies in a secondary sense to people such as Barnabas, Apollos, Sosthenes, Andronicus, Junia, James,

---

a 1 John 2:18, 22, 26; 3:4, 10, 12; 5:19; 4:1, 3, 6
b 1 John 2:19, 26; 4:1–3; 2 John 7
c Matt. 7:15
d Acts 1:22
e Acts 1:2–3; 4:33

Silas, and Timothy. They, like apostles today, moved from place to place to establish local churches and work across multiple churches, aiding shepherds and fighting wolves. Today this would include pastors of multisite churches or networks of churches, denominational leaders, pastors of pastors, and those who spiritually parent the next generation of church leaders.

False apostles attack, criticize, and malign real apostles. They promote false teaching, spread slander and division, and lead people astray. They often have big personalities and tremendous spiritual power given them by demonic forces. They lead churches astray and sometimes start cults disguised as churches. The apostle Paul battled wolves, saying, "Such men are false apostles, deceitful workmen, disguising themselves as apostles of Christ. Even Satan disguises himself as an angel of light. So it is no surprise if his servants, also, disguise themselves as servants of righteousness. Their end will correspond to their deeds."[a] Jesus is an apostle[b] who calls out false apostles, commending a church for having "tested those who call themselves apostles and are not, and found them to be false."[c]

FALSE TEACHERS

Since God creates true teachers and Satan counterfeits with false teachers, the goals of godly teachers are twofold: first, to teach truth consistent with the Bible; second, to refute error contrary to the Bible.

In Christianity there are two kinds of issues: closed-handed and open-handed. Closed-handed issues are those that the church around the world since the beginning has agreed are essential and central issues for what it means to be Christian. Such matters would include:

- the Trinity;

- God as Creator;

- males and females as God's image bearers;

- the fall of humanity into sin;

---

a 2 Cor. 11:13–15
b Heb. 3:1
c Rev. 2:2–5

- Jesus as fully God and fully man, who lived without sin, died for our sin, and rose as our Savior;

- the necessity to turn from sin and trust in Jesus for salvation;

- eternal life beyond the grave for all people in heaven or hell; and

- the Bible as the Word of God.

If we give up on closed-handed issues such as these, we are no longer Christian and are instead in a cult, other religion, spirituality, or ideology.

Open-handed issues are matters that Bible-believing, Jesus-loving Christians can debate and disagree about without dividing over them. Since we will all be together forever in heaven, we should start to get along here on earth. Open-handed issues include:

- the age of the earth;

- speaking in tongues and other supernatural spiritual gifts;

- modes of worship and baptism;

- the role of women in specific church leadership roles; and

- particular details regarding the second coming such as the rapture or tribulation.

False teaching happens in two ways: One, we take what should be in the closed hand and put it in the open hand. Two, we take what should be in the open hand and put it in the closed hand. This is precisely what false-teaching wolves do. These wolves ravage churches, teach heresy, offend Jesus, lead people into sexual sin, make a good living, and are tour guides to hell.

> False prophets also arose among the people, just as there will be false teachers among you, who will secretly bring in destructive heresies, even denying the Master who bought them, bringing upon themselves swift destruction. And many will follow their sensuality, and because of them the way of truth will be blasphemed. And in their greed they will exploit you with false words....For if God did not spare angels when they sinned, but cast them into hell and committed them to chains of gloomy darkness to be kept until the judgment;...then the

Lord knows how to rescue the godly from trials, and to keep the unrighteous under punishment until the day of judgment.[a]

The mention of fallen demonic angels is God's way of reminding us that the false teaching started in heaven with Satan and demons and has made a pit stop on the earth before it is sent to hell forever. The key is to run from the wolf, not join that pack, and stick with your church flock.

FALSE DOCTRINES

False-teaching wolves labor to get false doctrines into churches. Sometimes they are popular because what they present seems new, and something in our pride wants to believe the evolutionary myth that "new is better" because we are smarter than those who came before us. Sometimes they are popular because they preach against repenting of sin and in the name of love and tolerance support people who are sinning; this often results in great popularity and pay, but it is an offense to God.

We are warned, "Now the Spirit expressly says that in later times some will depart from the faith by devoting themselves to deceitful spirits and teachings of demons, through the insincerity of liars whose consciences are seared."[b] False-teaching wolves will echo demonic spirits rather than God's Spirit, putting things in the closed hand that should be in the open hand and putting things in the open hand that should be in the closed hand.

Religious wolves tend to come in two breeds: liberals and legalists. Perhaps the most liberal church in the New Testament was in Corinth. After planting the church and volunteer pastoring for eighteen months, Paul left Corinth to advance the gospel in Ephesus.[c] People in the small church of perhaps fifty people quickly proceeded to deny the resurrection of Jesus, get naked and have sex, support the alternative lifestyle of some guy living and sleeping with his stepmother, swap genders, sue each other for money, and even get drunk at Communion in what could have only looked like a pilot episode of *Jerry Springer*. Visitors to the church were so distressed that they pulled the fire alarm and contacted Paul.[d]

The Corinthian church also sent Paul a letter with a number of their

a 2 Pet. 2:1–9
b 1 Tim. 4:1–2
c Acts 18:1–19:10
d Acts 16:17; 1 Cor. 1:11; 8:1; 11:18

questions.[a] The situation at Corinth had so escalated that Paul had Timothy deliver his stern letter and investigate the church on his behalf.[b] He says they brought demons into their Communion time by combining biblical spirituality with pagan ritual: "What pagans sacrifice they offer to demons and not to God. I do not want you to be participants with demons. You cannot drink the cup of the Lord and the cup of demons. You cannot partake of the table of the Lord and the table of demons."[c] Liberalism leads to demonism.

Legalism, on the other hand, promotes a different breed of false doctrines. In Jesus' day the Pharisees were the wolves who kept harassing and hounding Him, trying to kill God for breaking their rules as they were more conservative than God. The Pharisees started pretty well—they wanted to bring the Word of God back into the center of all of life. Eventually they started mixing up which issues went in open or closed hands and confused principles and methods, which is what legalists do. The Bible gives many principles that we would be wise to follow, but we are free to choose various methods. Examples would include the order of a church service to worship God or ways to educate and parent our kids. God gives principles, and we have a variety of methods by which to honor each principle.

Legalists think that only their method is faithful to God's principle, and unless you do things exactly how they do them, you are in sin and need to be hammered like a crooked nail to get straightened out. This is exactly how the Pharisees treated Christ and how their spiritual offspring treat Christians. Jesus was clear that legalism is demonic when He told the legalistic leaders amidst the heated exchange, "You are of your father the devil, and your will is to do your father's desires" and concluded, "Whoever is of God hears the words of God. The reason why you do not hear them is that you are not of God."[d] Rather than repenting, they rebuked Jesus, saying, "'Are we not right in saying that you...have a demon?' Jesus answered, 'I do not have a demon, but I honor my Father, and you dishonor me.'... [They] said to him, 'Now we know that you have a demon!...Who do you make yourself out to be?'...So they picked up stones to throw at him, but Jesus hid himself and went out of

a 1 Cor. 7–8
b 1 Cor. 4:17; 16:10
c 1 Cor. 10:20–21
d John 8:44, 47

the temple."[a] If Jesus were walking the earth today, He'd still get in lots of trouble for breaking religious rules wrongly made in His name.

Likely the most legalistic church in the New Testament was in Galatia. Behind their legalism, Paul said, were demonic forces at work causing pride and division in the false name of being holy, including an "accursed" fallen "angel from heaven" who came to "preach to you a gospel contrary to the one we preached," and a demon spirit who "has bewitched you."[b] A Bible commentary says, "The term translated 'bewitched' refers to the evil impact of spells."[2]

When our family visited Galatia, we learned with the help of a history professor that it was a headquarters for demonic worship to a female false god with a large pagan temple. The concept of being bewitched involved spells cast by the enemies of the gospel, which allowed demons to work through their legalistic doctrines. Today this phenomenon is much like Wicca, which is growing in popularity, with the worship of creation, a female deity, and the casting of curse spells and dark magic. The spiritual driving force behind the legalism in Galatia was demonic. Legalism leads to demonism.

START AND STAY WITH JESUS

Good doctrine starts with Jesus as your compass and cornerstone. In the Bible, Jesus is the compass that points north. Like setting the cornerstone on a building, once you get Jesus right, the rest falls into place. False teachers always try to create some false view of Jesus so that people are deceived into thinking they are learning about and walking with the real Jesus when they are not. Paul, the shepherd, was battling the wolves who decided he was merely an apostle and they were "super apostles." He said, "If someone comes and proclaims another Jesus than the one we proclaimed, or if you receive a different spirit from the one you received, or if you accept a different gospel from the one you accepted, you put up with it readily enough."[c]

Sometimes a counterfeit Christ is taught by ignoring parts of the Bible. Today false teachers commonly manipulate by only promoting "God is love" rather than teaching all of God's attributes. Love is then interpreted to mean tolerance, which falsely says Jesus is fine with whatever you do; there is no

---

a John 8:48–59
b Gal. 1:8; 3:1
c 2 Cor. 11:4

such thing as sin, repentance, or holiness; and no one is going to hell. This turns the truth that *God is love* into the lie that *love is God*. Love is *not* God; Jesus is God, and Jesus is love. Therefore, when Jesus talks about sin and hell (more than anyone else in the Bible), what He is doing is loving because God is also just, righteous, and holy (the most common attribute of God in all the Bible).

A counterfeit Christ is demonic. Nearly all false religions and spiritualities seek a way to include their fake version of Jesus in their false teaching, often by claiming Jesus was a good man but not the God-man.

- Jehovah's Witnesses say Jesus was merely Michael the arch-angel, a created being that became a man.

- Mormonism teaches Jesus was not God, but only a man who became one of many gods; it furthermore teaches that He was a half-brother of Lucifer.[3]

- Unitarian Universalism says Jesus was not God but rather a great man to be respected solely for His teaching, love, justice, and healing.

- New Age gurus see Jesus as yet another guru and not God.

- According to Scientology, Jesus is an implant forced upon a thetan about a million years ago.

- Freemasonry, or the Masons, include the reading of Scripture at lodge meetings but intentionally omit the name "Jesus" in their occult ceremonies.

- Bahá'ís say Jesus was a manifestation of God and a prophet but inferior to Muhammad and Bahá'u'lláh.

- Buddhism believes Jesus was not God but rather an enlight-ened man like Buddha.

- Hinduism has many views of Jesus (not the only God) but believe He was most likely a wise man or incarnation of God, much like Krishna.

- Islam says Jesus was merely a man and a prophet who was inferior to Muhammad.

There is only one real Jesus among many counterfeit christs. This includes demons who use the name "Jesus" to deceive people. Early in our ministry a young woman who was deeply involved in the occult had been visiting the church with a friend. During counseling sessions in our church office with this woman, sometimes her entire body would contort, her voice would change, and she would take on a fully different personality with a male voice. When asked, "Who are you?" the demon speaking through her said, "Don't worry; I'm Jesus." When asked, "Are you Jesus of Nazareth, God in the flesh, who was born of Mary?" with an eerie laugh it said through the young woman, "No, I'm not *that* Jesus." Counterfeit christs are demonic deceptions. These include false prophets, false elders, and evil people, all of which contribute to church hurt, which we will now examine.

FALSE PROPHETS

We want to now focus on true and false prophets, because this is a point about which there is great trepidation among many Christians. Some Christians fear that if we accept revelation beyond the Bible, we are open to false prophets. This is a valid concern, but we hope that some examples will help give some context for real versus counterfeit words from God.

After God spoke to me (Mark) audibly and called me into ministry at nineteen, my family was concerned. Being devout Catholics, they feared I'd joined a cult and was not in God's will. So my grandmother flew out to speak with me. She joined an order of nuns after my grandfather died and was in church praying so often that two Catholic churches gave her a set of keys to let herself in and out. We spoke at length about my salvation experience, my calling into ministry, and what I was learning in the Bible. My devout grandmother prayed earnestly all night for a word from God and emerged forth in the morning to tell the family that I did not need to be a priest or Catholic, I was walking in God's will, and there was a call on my life that the family needed to support. Her prophetic word was confirming for me and my family.

More recently, a few years ago during a time when we chose to take a break from ministry to heal, I embarked on a week of critical travel and meetings. I would first spend a few days in Florida with a church-planting network simply learning and building relationships. I would next travel to Arizona for a meeting with pastors in Phoenix, connecting with these godly leaders as a group and as individuals to build friendships and invite them to speak into a possible move to start our life and ministry over in Phoenix. Finally Grace and the kids would join me to see what they each thought of the city as our next possible home.

During a break at the Florida conference, God urged me to take time with Him to listen and process what I was learning. I got lost on my way to a coffee shop, so I pulled over for lunch at a random Mexican restaurant I spotted when my phone app took me down the wrong road. When I told the hostess I was going to wash up and be back to my table, a patron recognized my voice. As I walked back to my table, he stopped me and introduced himself as a pastor. He was also attending the conference and was surprised our paths had crossed, because he assumed I was at home in Seattle.

This pastor mentioned that for some time God had burdened him to pray for me and my family, and he had talked to God about us that very morning. We sat down to visit, and he asked if he could pray for all of us right then. As we bowed our heads over chips and salsa, God gave him a vision. He said he saw us packing up, moving to a sunny place, and writing a book about what God was teaching us—leadership lessons for the next generation of pastors. He had no idea what was going on in my life, but God knew and revealed it to him to share with me.

I was stunned, because a few hours later I boarded that plane to Phoenix to connect with fellow pastors, meet my family, and explore the city. The Phoenix pastors confirmed the prophetic word we received from a stranger at a Mexican restaurant days before on the opposite end of the country.

Once we moved to Phoenix, we weren't sure what was next. After some months the kids called a family meeting saying they wanted to plant a church together as a family ministry. So we did. The kids chose the name The Trinity Church in honor of their deceased grandpa and living grandma on Grace's side who planted a church of the same name and led it for more than forty years. Needing a building, we prayed as a family for God to do something supernatural. One of our overseeing pastors told us that God spoke to him and we were going to be able to buy an eight hundred–seat church building off Route 101, which connects much of the Phoenix valley.

I called a realtor, who said that church did not exist and one fitting that description had never been on the market to his knowledge. Then we got a call that a building off Route 101 might become available, so we met with the pastors who were renting the old building for their church. They prayed, felt God spoke to them, and vacated so we could occupy the building. We got the keys and had our first informational meeting on Easter 2016, the fiftieth anniversary of the first public church service in the historic mid-century modern church building. Shortly thereafter, through a series of miracles, the building was put up for sale. We needed a large sum of money to execute the purchase, but the church did not yet exist, and we did not have the money. So we prayed as a family, and soon after, the phone rang. An out-of-town friend called to say God told him to call and offer to help us. He did not know about the financial need, and we did not know he had the means to fulfill it. But God quickly worked it all out, and our friend wired us exactly what we needed. God answered our prayer to the dollar.

On Easter 2019 the church was filled for two services, and we put out every chair we could fit into the room—793 of them. I then remembered we had seven more chairs in the audio booth—the prophecy came true to the chair. This has been our experience throughout ministry. We do not come from Charismatic or Pentecostal backgrounds. But we walk in the supernatural without trying. And whenever a prophetic word has come up, it has pretty much always been confirmed by godly leaders and come to pass. We have been largely in functionally cessationist Christian groups that are very fearful of false prophecy, but honestly this has not been our experience.

The primary job of a true prophet is to prepare God's people for the real future. God knows and rules the future, and at times He chooses to reveal it to His people so they can prepare for it. Roughly one-quarter of the Bible was prophetic in nature, revealing the future to God's people. Here are five key ways to recognize false prophets.

1. False prophets are wolves who lie about the future.

Sometimes false prophets prophesy that good times are coming when they are not. God says that false prophets "have misled my people, saying, 'Peace,' when there is no peace."[a] False prophets only say things people want to hear, ignore personal sin, and like to say that everyone is going to

---

a Ezek. 13:10

heaven. Of false prophets we are told, "Woe to those who call evil good and good evil, who put darkness for light and light for darkness, who put bitter for sweet and sweet for bitter!"[a]

2. False prophets prey on people's fears.

Some people worry about a catastrophic future and are susceptible to scare tactics from wolves disguised as prophets. Sometimes wolves cause people to distrust everyone but them, and they rule out of fear and control. Jesus warns that "many false prophets will arise and lead many astray."[b]

3. False prophets are often flatterers.

They puff people up with praise, only saying what people want to hear rather than what God wants said. Jesus warns, "Woe to you, when all people speak well of you, for so their fathers did to the false prophets."[c] As demonic deception increases in the last days, "the time is coming when people will not endure sound teaching, but having itching ears they will accumulate for themselves teachers to suit their own passions, and will turn away from listening to the truth and wander off into myths."[d]

4. False prophets often work with demonic power that makes them seem like God's anointed.

Counterfeiting the kingdom of God, they lead people astray with clairvoyance, healing, revelations, visions, and other demonstrations of unusual supernatural power. But it is all demonic. "For false christs and false prophets will arise and perform great signs and wonders, so as to lead astray, if possible, even the elect."[e]

5. False prophets are wolves who wear the sheep's clothing until the Good Shepherd, Jesus Christ, exposes them.

Sometimes these people claim to love Jesus, prophesy at church, cast out demons, and see people they anoint with oil healed. But they have no relationship with the Shepherd because they are not among the sheep. "Not everyone who says to me, 'Lord, Lord,' will enter the kingdom of heaven....On that day many will say to me, 'Lord, Lord, did we not prophesy in your name,

a Isa. 5:20
b Matt. 24:11
c Luke 6:26
d 2 Tim. 4:3–4
e Matt. 24:24

and cast out demons in your name, and do many mighty works in your name?' And then will I declare to them, 'I never knew you; depart from me, you workers of lawlessness.'"[a]

FALSE ELDERS

In the church God appoints leaders in the church as shepherds who care for the flock. Just as wolves like to get into sheep pens so they can attack shepherds and devour sheep, so too Satan's wolves want to get into ministry leadership counterfeiting shepherds. The pattern, of course, was set by Satan, who was a leader in heaven and later, after being cast down, entered Judas, who was a leader on earth. Like Judas, wolves are covert and not overt. They do not let you know what they are plotting or planning until they attack suddenly.

One of the most emotional sections of the New Testament reports Paul's farewell address to the elders of the church in Ephesus before he leaves them in Acts 20:17–38. Luke records in Acts that Paul sent to Ephesus and called the elders of the church to come to him. Once the elders gathered, Paul reminds them of his hard work and sound doctrine as examples to follow upon his departure. Saying his last goodbyes until heaven, he says, "I am going to Jerusalem, constrained by the Spirit, not knowing what will happen to me there, except that the Holy Spirit testifies to me in every city that imprisonment and afflictions await me....I know that none of you among whom I have gone about proclaiming the kingdom will see my face again."[b]

Likely with tears in the eyes of those gathered for this farewell, Paul then prophetically warns the church leaders/elders of wolves in their midst who will rise and ravage the church once his strong leadership is gone: "I know that after my departure fierce wolves will come in among you, not sparing the flock; and *from among your own selves* will arise men speaking twisted things, to draw away the disciples after them. Therefore be alert, remembering that for three years I did not cease night or day to admonish every one with tears."[c]

Did you catch that? Some of the elders were the wolves. When this happens, churches are wrecked from the inside out, the sheep are devoured

a Matt. 7:21–23
b Acts 20:22–23, 25
c Acts 20:29–31, emphasis added

and the survivors scatter, and many Christians become bitter against the church. This is Satan's demonic plan to get wolves jobs as shepherds *in the church*.

God experienced this in heaven with Satan, Jesus experienced this with Judas, Paul had it in Ephesus, and your church will have it too. We then read, "When he had said these things, he knelt down and prayed with them all. And there was much weeping on the part of all; they embraced Paul and kissed him, being sorrowful most of all because of the word he had spoken, that they would not see his face again. And they accompanied him to the ship."[a] Yes, even the wolves pretended to love Paul the shepherd at that moment and remained covert like Judas until their plot became public.

EVIL PEOPLE

The Bible has many warnings about evil people: "Wisdom will save you from evil people, from those whose words are twisted. These men turn from the right way to walk down dark paths. They take pleasure in doing wrong, and they enjoy the twisted ways of evil. Their actions are crooked, and their ways are wrong."[b] Hundreds of times the Bible speaks of evil people as "the wicked."

Evil people are dangerous and cause harm intentionally. Often they have suffered abuse or trauma that contributed to bitterness and opened them up to demonic influence. If they don't heal from the hurt, the evil done to them can reside in them and work through them. Evil people respond to their own hurt by hurting others. They are tormented, and so they torment others. They live by the demonic values of fear and punishment and can be threatening, controlling, demanding, and domineering. With evil people, it is a win-lose war, and they want to win and make everyone else lose. Evil people have little to no compassion for anyone but themselves and are often unconcerned about the pain and harm they inflict upon others. Wise people live by the Spirit, foolish people live by the flesh, and evil people live by the power of demonic forces.

Evil people have three kinds of relationships. When you encounter an evil person, you must choose which kind of relationship you will have.

---

a Acts 20:36–38
b Prov. 2:12–15, NLT

1. Two evil people form a dangerous relationship like wolves form a pack.

2. An evil person and a foolish person have an abusive relationship like a wolf with a sheep.

3. An evil person and a wise person have a distant relationship like a wolf with a shepherd.

Christians think of sin in terms of *what* we do in life—doing a bad thing or not doing a good thing—but sin also includes (and often starts with) *whom* we do life with. Satan has a long history of working through evil people to try and build relationships with God's people.

This pattern starts when Satan shows up uninvited in the garden asking our first parents to partake in a meal together, which is how friendships form. The devil did the same thing with the Lord Jesus, asking to break bread after forty days of fasting. Satan also brought Judas to the Last Supper, and Jesus knew when to release the evil Judas. "Satan entered into him. Jesus said to him, 'What you are going to do, do quickly.'"[a]

Sometimes we have to release an evil person and simply keep our distance from them, no longer having a relationship with them.[4] No one is beyond *God's* help, but some people are beyond *our* help. Until they turn to God seeking His help, and possibly meet with a licensed professional, there is not much we can do to assist them.

CHURCH HURT

When they get into a church, the types of evil people we have studied in this chapter can cause church hurt. As a pastor's daughter I (Grace) have unfortunately experienced and witnessed the harm done by evil people many times. I remember a situation during my elementary school years when a woman in my dad's church told a lie about him. There was zero truth to what she said, but she convinced a faction of people to leave, which also meant I lost my closest friend. As a child this was so confusing and hurtful. I didn't understand why we couldn't be friends all of a sudden and why her mom would lie about my dad. The woman had her own pain and didn't want to deal with it, so she hurt others in return.

a John 13:27

About twenty years later she came to my dad and apologized for what she had said and done. I'm glad she finally repented, but the damage was done and the fact that so many families were impacted was very sad. My dad chose to forgive at the time it originally happened, so when she finally apologized, he wasn't bitter.

This situation somewhat prepared me for being a pastor's wife, but as a naturally trusting person I still got caught off guard by evil people. I have sadly learned that wolves *want* to harm, which is very different from people who don't intend to cause harm but do. They create so much confusion for the sheep in the church because they know how to manipulate relationships and scatter the church. I have learned that anytime I sense someone coming to "steal, kill, and destroy," there is a demonic element involved.

This is why church hurt is so common. I have had numerous conversations with people who are afraid of or opposed to trying church again because they are confused or have been hurt by wolves. The church is supposed to be a safe place for hurting people to heal, but evil people hurt them more. Sadly some people let this be a reflection of who God is instead of seeing it as a spiritual battle for which we should run to Jesus for help. Satan wants us to be isolated, not hear the preached Word, and not be in God's presence with God's people.

When people in the church hurt us, we can ask God to heal those wounds and bring healthy, wise people into our lives. They can help us discern the counterfeits to Christ, which we will study next.

CHAPTER 20

WIN YOUR WAR AGAINST COUNTERFEITS TO CHRIST

*The coming of the lawless one is based on Satan's working,
with all kinds of false miracles, signs, and wonders.*

—2 Thessalonians 2:9, csb

I N THE EARLIEST days of our ministry, the city we lived in was reported as a place of common coven activity and witchcraft. We saw many young people coming to Christ from backgrounds of witchcraft, deep drug use, and the occult. They shared about horrifying night terrors they were having and supernatural experiences they could not explain.

Among the most vivid was a young new mother. She literally grew up in a witchcraft store where covens met and spells were cast. She had been a practicing black witch from a young age but had gotten saved. She told us that her husband had looked in on her rocking their baby, and he found the rocking chair reportedly floating a few feet off the ground while she and the baby slept in it.

These kinds of things were fairly common in our first two decades of ministry—numerous demonstrations of spiritual power that were counterfeits to Christ. We've not seen nearly as much supernatural activity in our second church plant, likely because of a much higher concentration of mature saints who are devoted to praying for protection over our church.

God creates. Satan counterfeits. That simple truth is significant. Anything valuable is counterfeited—from Air Jordan shoes to women's handbags to financial currency. Since the kingdom of God is invaluable, it is not surprising that the devil and his demons counterfeit the works of God. The goal, like that of all counterfeiting, is to fool people into settling for what is fake rather than finding what is genuine.

God creates angels; Satan's counterfeits are demons. God creates truth; Satan's counterfeit is lies. God creates the kingdom; Satan's counterfeit is the world. God makes people Spirit-filled; Satan's counterfeit is making people demon-possessed. God makes covenants; Satan's counterfeits are inner vows. God creates blessings; Satan's counterfeits are curses. God brings Jesus with a spiritual Father and earthly mother; Satan's counterfeit is the sons of God seeking to conceive with the daughters of men.[a] God brings revival; Satan's counterfeit is a riot against the revival. The examples are nearly endless.

DEMONS IN EXODUS

We see the principle of spiritual counterfeits in the Book of Exodus, where a battle between the real God and Satan is on full display. Egypt is the manifestation of the kingdom of darkness counterfeiting the kingdom of God; Pharaoh is the counterfeit Jesus, worshipped as the son of the gods. Pagan priests counterfeit the real priests of God and perform counterfeit miracles to copy the mighty works of God. Exodus records forty years of this battle between the godly and genuine and the corrupt and counterfeit during the most active supernatural period of history recorded in Scripture.

Spiritually the Egyptians were such a polytheistic people with so many competing gods and priests that any attempt to sort out all of their demonic false gods and theologies is virtually impossible. There was no concept of a supreme singular God. Each place and object had its deity, and every phenomenon of nature was thought to be infused with a spirit that could choose its physical form (e.g., an animal, a mix of animals like the Sphinx, or a combination of animals and people like Thoth and Horus).

Egypt had no division between sacred and secular, leading to the creation of beautiful art and breathtaking architecture intended to bring people closer to the gods. Ra, the sun god, was the most important and was recognized as the giver of life.

---

a Gen. 6:1–6

The gods were housed in temples with special priests designated to serve them. Every morning, each priest awakened his god with a morning hymn, opened the shrine, cleaned and dressed the cult image, and presented offerings/breakfast to it. At midday the priest performed similar services. Some religious groups today have something similar in the form of small shrines to their demon gods in their homes or businesses.

Conversely, God's people who were slaves in Egypt had one God who did not need service but instead served people. Their God did not eat human food but instead fed His people with manna from heaven. Their God also lived in a tabernacle aimed not at housing Himself for leisure but instead inviting His people for rest and forgiveness of sin. A real priest conducted the service to this God. This priest labored for the people before God. As Christians, this is our God, and the one true God!

THE BATTLE IN EGYPT

The plotline of Exodus is nothing less than a cosmic continuation of the battle in heaven. Satan had formed the most powerful nation on earth—the mighty Pharaoh, the Egyptian army, a cast of sorcerers, and a pantheon of demonic false gods—to oppose the revelation of God and destroy His children. On the other hand, God, jealous for His glory and faithful to His promises, intervenes with speech and deeds that shatter that world and bring His authority and rule with force. He exposes the weaknesses of earth's most powerful people and spirits as puny and pathetic in His wake.

Moses and Aaron represented God; Pharaoh and Egypt represented Satan. One scholar says:

> [Exodus] is the only record of a power encounter in all of Scripture where the servants of the no-gods are allowed to duplicate the power demonstrations of the servants of God for a period of time.... The story does raise very controversial questions about the power of Satan and his demons to perform creative miracles.... God allows evil supernaturalism to work with the existing powers of nature and to manipulate them towards their evil and deceptive purposes. Thus they can cause storms, illnesses, and all kinds of damage, as the Scriptures clearly reveal. In the end time, the Antichrist will evidently possess greater miraculous powers than ever witnessed

before on the part of evil supernaturalism. He will come "in accord with the activity of Satan, with all power and signs and false wonders, and with all the deception of wickedness" (2 Thess. 2:9–10).[1]

The Ten Commandments in Exodus begin, "You shall have no other gods before me.... You shall not bow down to them or serve them, for I the LORD your God am a jealous God."[a] The gods are powerful but created and finite spiritual beings who have revolted against the Lord and have become corrupt, trying to establish their own power base in religions and nations. In a word, they are demons. Many theologians believe that the ten plagues God sent upon the nation were public defeats of specific demon gods worshipped by the Egyptians.[2]

God is abundantly clear that the conflict in the Book of Exodus is between the real God and the false demon gods. God says, "I will pass through the land of Egypt that night, and I will strike all the firstborn in the land of Egypt, both man and beast; and on all the gods of Egypt I will execute judgments: I am the LORD."[b] The word for *gods* is a general one that "can refer to foreign gods or idols (Gen. 31:17–35; Exod. 20:3), angels (Ps. 8:5), and spirits (1 Sam. 28:13)."[3] In the contents of Exodus the gods are demonic "deities other than the true God, which are falsely worshipped."[4]

Religion, politics, and morality formed a unified world system in Egyptian culture. The real God saw Egypt as a demonic system intended to replace the real God and His kingdom and bring harm to His people. Moses' father-in-law, Jethro, said after God's victory over the demon gods, "Now I know that the LORD is greater than all gods."[c] Moses added, "On their gods...the LORD executed judgments."[d]

The stage for the showdown between God and the demon gods was set when Pharaoh asked, "Who is the LORD, that I should obey his voice and let Israel go? I do not know the LORD, and moreover, I will not let Israel go."[e] The demons had made Egypt "free," the most powerful nation on earth, an empire of vast wealth, and the strongest military force on earth. By comparison it seemed that the God of the Hebrews was a nobody; His

a Exod. 20:3–4
b Exod. 12:12
c Exod. 18:10–12
d Num. 33:4
e Exod. 5:2

people were poor slaves, and He had no nation or army. Therefore, it made no sense for a "great" god like Pharaoh to obey a "lesser" God like Yahweh. God, however, made it clear that He is the only real God!

DEMONS LOVE RELIGION AND SPIRITUALITY

Powerful demonic spirits lead multitudes to follow them to hell forever through false religion and spirituality. In our modern, pluralistic culture it seems unkind to say that someone's religious beliefs or spiritual behaviors are wrong and dangerous. The general mood of most people tends to be "whatever works for you" without any consideration of what works for God. Because the God of the Bible loves people and knows that their eternity is at stake, He has a great deal to say about the demonic deception at work through counterfeits of Christ, as "Satan disguises himself as an angel of light."[a]

Throughout history religious sacrifices have been performed to counterfeit the Lord Jesus' one sacrifice for the sins of all. Sometimes these demonic sacrifices are things such as money, food, or other gifts left at shrines in homes to bring a blessing, or in a field to invite a great harvest, or near a worker's tools to invite a blessing on the business. In the Western world these include good luck charms and superstition, which is practiced by everyone from athletes to agnostics. We also know people saved from cults who have sacrificed animals at times. The Bible speaks about sacrifices not decreed by God or devoted to God in the most woeful of warnings: "So they shall no more sacrifice their sacrifices to goat demons, after whom they whore. This shall be a statute forever for them throughout their generations."[b]

From the Old Testament to the present day, some false religions practice illicit sex and child sacrifice as part of their rituals, according to people who reported being present for these acts before they were saved out of the occult. "They sacrificed their sons and their daughters to the demons; they poured out innocent blood, the blood of their sons and daughters, whom they sacrificed to the idols."[c]

The ancient demon god Ashtoreth (also called Ishtar) was the female deity of fertility and was closely linked with sensuality and sexuality. The

a 2 Cor. 11:14
b Lev. 17:7
c Ps. 106:37–38

ancient demon god Baal was her counterpart male deity. In ancient pagan temples they would worship this god and goddess with sexual perversion of every sort and kind, including religious prostitutes.

King Solomon brought this perversion into the nation of Israel.[a] This included worshipping the god Molech, to whom Solomon built a temple on a high place, which was an abomination, and "the worship of this god was particularly odious, as it required human sacrifice."[5]

Today we continue to commit abomination as we worship the same demons of sex. From porn sites to strip clubs, from sex trafficking and sexual assault to "friends with benefits," the same old demons have new names like love and freedom. Our modern culture also imitates the ancient practice of child sacrifice, which consisted of burning in the Old Testament but is now done chemically under the guise of medical waste.[b] We kill our kids in the name of *choice* and *abortion*—new names for old demons.

Demons also perform counterfeit miracles, as shown throughout Exodus. They are very willing to heal someone's body in this life in exchange for the destruction of his or her body and soul in the afterlife. Luke, a medical doctor, records that a powerful spiritual leader named Simon became famous by doing great feats and sought to buy the Holy Spirit so that he could also have the power of God.[c] Luke adds, "As we were going to the place of prayer, we were met by a slave girl who had a spirit of divination and brought her owners much gain by fortune-telling."[d] This poor girl was a physical slave of her master and a spiritual slave to her demon. The master made great riches through the demon who spoke through her, predicting some future event that the demon would then bring to pass by its power.

In various religions and spiritual groups demons fulfill dreams, heal sickness, lift torment, and answer prayers. Sometimes people are so desperate that they do not much care who or where their answer comes from. This leaves people vulnerable to making deals with the devil, largely unaware. Unfortunately these are all counterfeits from the kingdom of darkness to invite the demonic into your life and "false signs and wonders...wicked deception."[e] The Bible warns us of a tremendous demonic deception at the

a 1 Kings 11:33; 18:19
b Ps. 96:5; 106:37–38; Jer. 7:31; 19:5; 32:35; Mic. 6:7
c Acts 8:9–23
d Acts 16:16
e 2 Thess. 2:9–10

end of history as Satan and demons make their final push to defeat God and His angels on the earth to avenge the war they lost in heaven. "The beast was captured, and with it the false prophet who in its presence had done the signs by which he deceived those who had received the mark of the beast and those who worshiped its image."[a]

Anytime something spiritual happens, even if it seems good (like a healing, miracle, angel, or answer to prayer), we cannot overlook the possibility of demonic deception. "Beloved, do not believe every spirit, but test the spirits to see whether they are from God....By this you know the Spirit of God: every spirit that confesses that Jesus Christ has come in the flesh is from God, and every spirit that does not confess Jesus is not from God. This is the spirit of the antichrist....He who is in you is greater than he who is in the world."[b] To deal with the demonic requires discernment.

WHAT ARE THESE GODS DOING TODAY?

The false gods of our day are doing the same thing they always have, from promoting false religions to supporting evil political leaders, encouraging sinful social trends, and empowering godless forms of entertainment. Every culture worships counterfeit demon gods. Demon worship includes general spirituality, cults, and religions.

General spirituality is a broad category for an entire array of less-formalized spirituality. Examples include Wicca, New Age or New Spirituality, radical environmentalism that considers the world and animals as sacred, some deeply spiritual forms of martial arts, secret societies such as the Masons, Native American Shamanism, belief in everything from auras to mediums to horoscopes, and fascination with everything from crystals to angels. The entire town of Sedona, Arizona, near us has people come for pilgrimage from around the world to be in the presence of red rocks and experience what they report as the powerful energy of the topography and the vortexes.

Cults are demonic structures that claim to have come from within Christianity and be the new and true expression of Christian faith.

---

a Rev. 19:20
b 1 John 4:1–4

- Christian Science says Jesus is a wise man who teaches us to overcome sickness and death.

- Jehovah's Witnesses say Jesus is the first created being and an archangel.

- Unitarians say Jesus is merely a great man and a moral teacher of love.

- Mormons say Jesus is a man who became a god and sets an example for other men to do the same.

World religions make no claim to be Christian but are more formalized and governmentally recognized demonic power structures that make up part of the world system. Anyone who has traveled to nations where another religion dominates public and private life is quickly aware that something very spiritual is happening in every realm of society and culture. For example, a well-known demon spirit worshipped in ancient Egypt was named Isis and may be the force at work behind the terrorist group operating under that banner in the same region of the world to this day. The Bible is clear that demons work in politics and through nations because they do not see a distinction between sacred and secular or church and state.[a] No institution at work on the earth is spiritually neutral, and everything is part of a bigger story.

Muslims worship a god named Allah. Allah was a demon worshipped as a tribal deity in the ancient world.[6] *Islam* means to submit or surrender to the will of Allah, which is a summary definition of the religion. All that Muslims should do out of duty is called *sharia*. Counterfeiting the Christian Bible, they believe the Quran alone is without error and perfect. They also believe their prophet Muhammad is greater than Moses and Jesus Christ, whom they say is not God or the Son of God but rather a lesser prophet.

One thing that Mormons and Muslims hold in common is that they believe their founder received divine revelation for their religion through an angel. Muslims believe the angel Gabriel revealed the Quran. Mormons believe an angel named Moroni visited Joseph Smith and gave him the knowledge for the Book of Mormon. To this day Mormon temples have golden Moroni statues on top of their buildings as they are literally under demonic authority. One of the largest religions and one of the largest cults

---

a 1 Kings 22:1–40, 21–22; 1 Chron. 21:1; Deut. 32:8–9; Dan. 10:13–14, 20–21; John 14:30

both have demons masquerading as angels at their foundation, which is "a different gospel.... But even if we or an angel from heaven should preach to you a gospel contrary to the one we preached to you, let him be accursed."[a]

SYNCRETISM

Because people are arrogant and think we are more evolved, enlightened, and empowered than "primitive" people who came before us, we are prone to new spiritualities and beliefs. Demons don't mind creating new versions of old counterfeits, which God rebukes, saying, "They sacrificed to demons that were no gods, to gods they had never known, to new gods that had come recently, whom your fathers had never dreaded."[b] Sometimes the latest fads in spiritual and religious trends, from best-selling books to spiritual self-help seminars, are satanic.

Sadly it is quite common for believers to try to have a proverbial foot in both worlds. They like to try and keep parts of their Christian faith and marry it with non-Christian practice. "When you come into the land that the LORD your God is giving you, you shall not learn to follow the abominable practices of those nations....Anyone who practices divination or tells fortunes or interprets omens, or a sorcerer or a charmer or a medium or a necromancer or one who inquires of the dead, for whoever does these things is an abomination to the LORD."[c]

Academics call blending beliefs *syncretism*. God calls it adultery. The Bible says God is like a groom, and His people are like a bride. Therefore, to passionately pursue another god while in covenant with the real God is spiritual adultery.[d]

Syncretism is what happens when you combine true and false spirituality. Like gravity, everything in the world seeks to pull God's people into compromise and confusion. This will only become more intense as history moves toward the second coming of Jesus.[e] In an age of public shaming of Christians in the media and social media, the power of public approval is increasingly intense, especially in areas such as tolerance, gender, and

---

a Gal. 1:6–8
b Deut. 32:17
c Deut. 18:9–12
d Lev. 19:26, 31; 20:6
e 2 Thess. 2:9–10

sexuality. The pull of syncretism's demonic deception is well underway, especially among younger Christians.

When missionaries spread the gospel of Jesus Christ, they have two primary tasks: One, they *contextualize* the gospel to the local culture so that the people understand it in their language.[a] Two, they *contend* against false beliefs in the local culture so that one true gospel is preached rather than a corrupt version.[b] Syncretism happens when we contextualize but do not contend. Racism and cultural imperialism happen when we contend but do not contextualize. In every culture Christians have three reactions:

1. **Receive.** Because people are made in God's image, some aspects of the culture they create can be received by Christianity. For example, some cultures place a high value on family, which can be received by biblical Christianity as a shared value.

2. **Reject.** We must reject some things because they are against God. Examples include drunkenness, stealing, and all sex outside of heterosexual marriage—even if a culture widely approves of these things.

3. **Redeem.** We can use some things for God or Satan, and therefore Christians can redeem them for God's purposes. One example is Christmas, which was a pagan holiday that the early Christians chose to celebrate as the birth of Jesus because we don't know when He was born and we already had the day off.

Syncretism is what happens when we receive or seek to redeem things that we must reject. As one example in the Bible, the children of religious leaders were promoting syncretism when "Jeroboam and his sons cast them out from serving as priests of the LORD, and he appointed his own priests for the high places and for the goat idols and for the calves that he had made."[c]

Catholicism is notorious for syncretism, as it blended some Christian

a 1 Cor. 9:20–23
b Jude 3
c 2 Chron. 11:14–15

icons, images, and concepts with local pagan beliefs wherever it spread. Some younger Western Christians do this in the name of love, tolerance, and reconciliation. The Bible clearly says we are not to love sin, tolerate sin, or reconcile light and darkness. There are things, especially spiritually and sexually, that we must reject and not receive or seek to redeem.

RACISM AND CULTURAL IMPERIALISM

Admittedly, Christian missionaries have, at times, forced upon a culture some things that are not needed for a genuine expression of Christian faith. Sometimes missionaries bring not only the message of Christ but also the baggage of their culture. Denominational loyalties, narrow worship styles, modes of dress, and other cultural preferences are not necessary to walk with Jesus faithfully, and we should not impose them on every culture.

However, sometimes parts of a culture are darkness to be rejected. We tend not to see these areas where cultural preferences, entertainment, politics, social structures, and the like are darkness until we visit another culture. Christians who go on mission trips commonly see demonic work in the culture they are visiting because they have fresh eyes. They then return to their own culture more aware of demonic worldly structures in their own nation.

No culture on the earth is a full revelation of the kingdom of God. Every culture has worldly elements that go against God and harm people. However, some believe a person's culture is so sacred that to try to change it is a form of racism and cultural imperialism. This is an academic way of keeping people in demonic bondage.

Having spent our entire ministry career in areas with many Native Americans, we can provide an example that might help. There is a great divergence of beliefs among Native Americans, but as a general rule native spirituality teaches there is a Creator. In some traditions he is called the Great Spirit or the Father.

Under the Great Spirit is Mother Earth. This thinking is now carried forth by radical environmentalism based upon pantheism and panentheism, with bumper stickers that have a picture of earth and the words "Respect your Mother" or "Love your Mother."

Underneath the Great Spirit and Mother Earth is a human mediator—the medicine man, shaman, or witch doctor. He understands the secret: the earth and all that it contains are sacred and divine. What we see in the physical world is actually concealing a greater reality of the spirit world behind it. This is typified in the totem pole, where each animal is representative of a powerful spirit being, ordered from least powerful at the bottom of the totem to most powerful at the top.

It is said that the shaman can see through physical objects to their spiritual connectedness. He sees what spirit lies behind the mountains, wind, water, beasts of the field, birds of the air, and fish of the sea. The medicine man's job is to explain the spirit world and to appease the spirits or demons. Appeasing the demon spirits includes inviting them for a meeting by beating on drums, performing sacred dances, and entering altered spiritual states of consciousness through the pipe, sweet grass, tobacco, or sage.

To deal with sin, they suffer in the sweat lodge, deprived of nourishment. Their bodies are taxed, and they endure physical pain and suffering. Some say that the sweat lodge is the womb of Mother Earth, so they are going back into the womb to be rebirthed or born again.

Some tribal traditions include dances such as the Sun Dance, where a person is tied to a pole and pierced through the chest in a demonic counterfeit of Jesus' crucifixion. This dance was outlawed but is making a return without some of the piercing. We saw the dance performed at our state university's dedication of a new building for Native American studies.

In the Pueblo tradition there was something called a *kiva*. It was typically an underground meeting place where people would gather for sacred spiritual meetings to see demons and experience spiritual power. Like the sweat lodge, it represented the womb of Mother Earth. At the base of the kiva was a covered hole, and people would dance on it loudly and violently, seeking to awaken dead spirits. Then the covering would be removed, inviting the awakened spirits to roam among the living.

Tragically, when many Europeans arrived in America, they cheated and stole from native peoples, thereby turning people away from the Jesus they often claimed to worship. Today many college campuses sharply critique Christianity and emphasize the damage done to native peoples and cultures in the name of Christ. Some of these concerns have merit, but native people who are trapped in demonic spirituality still need to experience the forgiveness and freedom that Jesus Christ alone brings.

Many Americans and others in the West today think and act like native spiritualities and are simply pagans. In a study by the Pew Forum on Religion and Public Life reported in places like *USA Today*, the findings for all Americans were as follows:

- 92 percent believe in a god

- 70 percent believe that many religions lead to eternal life and you don't need Jesus

- 67 percent say they have had a spiritual experience seeing a spirit being

- 55 percent believe they have a guardian angel

- 52 percent believe in prophetic dreams where the spirit realm gives revelation[7]

Shockingly, many claiming to be Christians believe exactly what the ancient and native pagan peoples do:

- 20 percent believe there is spiritual energy in mountains, streams, and animals

- 16 percent believe in "the evil eye"—the ability to look at someone and cast a harmful spell on them

- 28 percent of Catholics believe in reincarnation[8]

Why does all of this matter? Perhaps a story will make the point best. There is a beautiful lake in the mountains where we enjoy spending summer vacations as a family. Some of our fondest memories are of renting a boat and pulling the kids around on inner tubes. One thing, however, continually threatens the lake. Several years ago someone brought a boat that had a strange algae from another body of water on the hull and dropped it in the lake without cleaning it first. That algae has since taken over the entire lake, choking out the fish life and costing huge sums of money to battle for the life of the lake. A foreign contaminant that started very small continues to grow and bring death with it.

The gospel of Jesus Christ is pristine, pure, and clean. The gospel of Jesus Christ was created by God. Satan counterfeits this gospel with unclean, impure, deadly false gospels that seek to do to the gospel what the algae is doing to the lake. This explains why Satan is always trying to contaminate what God created clean with his corrupting counterfeit. Thankfully, the kingdom of God will one day come and put an end to all counterfeits. That is the final subject, which we will study in the next chapter.

CHAPTER 21

ON EARTH AS IT IS IN HEAVEN

Your kingdom come, your will be done, on earth as it is in heaven.
—MATTHEW 6:10

THE BIBLE CLOSES with the final war of Jesus, which brings an end to all spiritual wars. This is the reason we decided to end this book by explaining Revelation.

Revelation is likely the most captivating and controversial book in the Bible. Some Christians see it as historical, recording what happened in the days of the early church. Some Christians see it as prophetic, foretelling events happening on the earth today. Some Christians see it as futuristic, revealing what the future holds. Without wading into all the complexities, they are all correct. To some degree Revelation is about all of that and much more.

Throughout this book we have explored two realms—the physical realm on earth, which we see by sight, and the spiritual realm in the kingdom, which we see by faith. These two realms are connected and continually working together for both good and evil. God sees both realms, and on occasion He shows us the past, present, and future of both domains through His eyes. This is the point and purpose of prophetic books such as Daniel and Ezekiel in the Old Testament and Revelation in the New Testament—to give God's perspective.

The Book of Revelation is primarily about one thing—the kingdom of God, with everyone and everything under the rule of God as King. The writing shifts between earthly scenes and heavenly scenes, between the seen and unseen realms, showing us what is simultaneously happening on earth and in the kingdom. This is crucial because although there are two realms, there is only one reality ruled by one God.

Some scenes are of the natural realm, showing what is happening on the earth in nations and churches as demonic and angelic forces collide in everything from conflicts within churches to wars between nations.[a] Some scenes are of the supernatural realm, showing worship and what is happening in the presence of God.[b] Revelation shifts between the two realms to reveal one reality.

Over everything in the book—churches, nations, angels, demons, and saints (living and departed)—is the throne. God's throne is revealed as the spiritual center of creation and history, the place where all wars started when Satan sought to unseat God and set himself on the throne.

Throughout the Bible a throne is mentioned roughly two hundred times, some two-thirds of which are in the Old Testament, with around one-third in the New Testament. The majority of mentions refer to God's throne, while others refer to thrones of human rulers and Satan. Of the roughly sixty-one appearances of God's throne in the New Testament, forty-five of them are in Revelation. In this great book of Jesus' war to end all wars, God's throne appears in seventeen of the twenty-two chapters, as all of human history is a war over who sits on that throne. Surrounding the throne is God's divine council, comprised of His two families—human beings and spirit beings—working together as one divine family.

In that day when people squatted, reclined, and sat on the floor, thrones were reserved for kings who ruled over kingdoms, priests who mediated between people and God, judges who rendered decisions regarding sin, and warriors who sat to rest after conquering an enemy and liberating a people. In Revelation, Jesus sits upon the throne at the right hand of the Father as our king, priest, judge, and warrior whose sovereign rule extends over all of His creation. Seeing Jesus upon His throne reveals His authority, power, majesty, and splendor.

His throne room is the center of history and creation, revealing the rightful place He is also to take as the center of our lives. As God is revealed from His throne room throughout Revelation, all of creation,

---

a Rev. 2–3; 6; 10; 12–13; 16–19
b Rev. 1; 4–5; 7; 11; 14–15; 19; 21–22

including angels, animals, and people, responds to Him in ways that bring Him glory, which is worship. As Jesus is revealed in resurrected glory, He is the source of inspiration for the songwriting and creative processes that surround Him. All artists (including visual and musical artists) should make note of the great songs and images in Revelation. God in glory is the greatest source for creative inspiration.

The book opens with John telling us, "I was in the Spirit on the Lord's day."[a] It was a Sunday, the day of Jesus' resurrection. John was an old man, the last living of the twelve disciples. He was the highest human spiritual authority alive on earth, exiled to a rocky and remote island called Patmos and no longer able to be in the pulpit as a pastor. We have visited Patmos as a family, and it is a desolate and barren place. Yet this is where Jesus came down in glory from heaven to visit His old friend John and give him a message to the churches about the kingdom.

ONE CHURCH IN TWO REALMS

The new covenant church of Jesus Christ began with the pouring out of the Spirit of God on the day of Pentecost. What happened that day "came from heaven" as the unseen realm flooded and invaded the world and included "a sound like a mighty rushing wind" (Spirit of God) as "tongues as of fire appeared to them and rested on each one of them. And they were all filled with the Holy Spirit."[b]

God intended that His two families—human and divine—live and work together as one united family. Sin caused humanity to rebel against God and side with Satan and demons, separating us from God, angels, and other divine beings. Everything changed with Jesus defeating the demonic realm on the cross and reclaiming us as His people. At Pentecost the two realms and families came together once again, as the divine council was present at Pentecost.

> The wind and fire in Acts 2 signified to readers informed by divine council scenes that the gathered followers of Jesus were being commissioned by divine encounter. They were being chosen to preach

---

a Rev. 1:10
b Acts 2:1–4

the good news of Jesus' work. The fire connects them to the throne room. The tongues are emblematic of their speaking ministry.[1]

The church in one realm is created by the kingdom in the other realm. It serves as the outpost for the kingdom, exists to witness to the kingdom, and is the beginning of the unveiling of God's kingdom across all creation. Starting at Pentecost, God intended that both His families would work together through the church until they were forever together as one united forever family.

THE SEVEN CHURCHES IN REVELATION

Revelation 2–3 identifies seven kinds of churches on earth. On a few occasions our family has visited these archaeological sites in and around modern-day Turkey with professors who helped us better understand their fascinating history.

1. Ephesus

The fundamentalist church is typified by Ephesus.[a] Jesus walked among this church spiritually, and the people were encouraged for serving faithfully, enduring hardship, having sound doctrine, and rejecting false teaching. Conversely, Jesus told them if they did not repent of their unloving and nonrelational Christianity, He would shut down their church.

2. Smyrna

The persecuted church is typified by Smyrna.[b] This city was the center for emperor worship. Those Christians who refused to do so were marginalized or even martyred. Jesus had no rebuke for this church and told them that though they were financially poor, they were spiritually rich and would be rewarded generously in the kingdom.

3. Pergamum

The heretical church is typified by Pergamum.[c] Jesus encouraged them that they had not completely abandoned their faith despite suffering both physically and spiritually. In their city Satan sought to establish the

a Rev. 2:1–7
b Rev. 2:8–11
c Rev. 2:12–17

headquarters of his demonic counterfeit kingdom and the place "where Satan's throne is" (Rev. 2:13). However, they were rebuked for allowing false-teaching wolves into their church who encouraged sexual sin and syncretism (living culture up instead of kingdom down).

4. Thyatira

The liberal church is typified by Thyatira.[a] This church was encouraged for its social justice work of helping those in need, being kind and relational, and having a growing ministry. On the other hand, it was rebuked for also tolerating sin (especially sexual sin) and demonic false teaching from a false prophet and false prophetess, which brought suffering upon the church.

5. Sardis

The dead church is typified by Sardis.[b] Jesus had nothing good to say about this church, as it was godless, dead, and no longer experiencing the life of the Spirit. Jesus said the people looked alive on the outside but were spiritually dead, and they must repent quickly or experience the death of their church and be sentenced to hell for eternity.

6. Philadelphia

The faithful church is typified by Philadelphia,[c] a wealthy city known for its wine and its chief deity Dionysius, the demon god of wine and debauchery. Despite enormous cultural and spiritual pressure, the church did not give in to the demonic seduction to sin. Jesus only had good things to say to this church, as the people had endured hardship and been publicly slandered yet remained godly and patient.

7. Laodicea

The lukewarm church is typified by Laodicea.[d] This was an arrogant and affluent city built on a high place. They literally and figuratively looked down on everyone else. Jesus had nothing good to say about this church, which was little more than a comfortable place for rich people to gather.

---

a Rev. 2:18–29
b Rev. 3:1–6
c Rev. 3:7–13
d Rev. 3:14–22

Jesus said their doors were basically locked and that even He had not been welcomed into their godless country club.

Which kind of church do you attend? Which kind of Christian are you?

Yesterday and today there is one church with members in the seen and unseen realms. Today we are spiritually seated with Jesus in the kingdom along with departed members of God's family.[a] Jesus is still walking in our midst among our local churches, seeing and knowing all that happens.[b] Today when the church on earth gathers for worship in the presence of God, the two realms come together as our worship and prayers join with those of the angels and departed saints who are constantly having church in the presence of God. In worship two realms unite into one reality in the presence of God.

WORSHIP

Revelation 4 shifts from the earth into the unseen realm. John is taken through a door into heaven, where he sees Jesus seated upon a throne in the divine council meeting with God's two families together as one. John strains with the limits of human language to express all that he experienced. This is why he uses words such as *like* repeatedly throughout his report.

Surrounding Jesus, seated on smaller thrones in the divine council, are twenty-four elders (leaders of God's people) who are likely the twelve disciples and the heads of the twelve tribes of Israel.[c] Similar to the reports of Moses, Ezekiel, and Isaiah, the throne explodes with lights superseding any worship concert, a shimmering sea of glass, and four angels flying day and night and singing about God.[d]

All authority comes from and all glory goes to God, who is seated on the throne. All of creation gathers around the throne to worship God. When we worship God on the earth, we are participating in the unseen realm. Our prayers and songs enter into God's throne room as the one church in two realms worships the one God together.

Western Christians have seen Revelation as a book about future things

---

a Eph. 2:6
b Rev. 1:12–13, 20
c Rev. 4:4, cf. Matt. 19:28
d Exod. 19:16; Ezek. 1; Isa. 6

(eschatology). They focus on the earthly scenes. Eastern Christians have seen Revelation as a book about worship (doxology). They focus on the heavenly scenes. Both are true. Today God is being worshipped in heaven and on earth. One day heaven will come to earth, and God will be worshipped on earth as He is in heaven. This is why one of the major themes of Revelation is "Worship God"; the book opens with John worshipping Jesus in the spirit and closes with a command to worship God until Jesus returns.[a]

Revelation contains some of the most beautiful and poetic imagery in all of Scripture, thereby demonstrating the lavish nature of worship. It also includes the composition of at least ten new songs featuring musical instruments, singing, shouting, clapping, kneeling, falling facedown, prayer, and the wedding feast between Jesus and His bride, the church. All of this worship is majestically directed to our exalted Lord, who is ruling and reigning over all of His creation, blessing His people and crushing their enemies from the throne.

THE HOLY SPIRIT

God loves and cares for local churches. It is important to understand that they are part of something much greater and grander—the kingdom of God. One day our local churches will be no more, but the kingdom of God will endure forever. In Revelation local churches are under the King and kingdom and commanded not to live "pew up," giving people want they want, but rather "throne down," doing what God wants. Local churches are commanded to "hear what the Spirit says to the churches."[b] Therefore, the first job of church leadership is to listen to the Holy Spirit and find God's will for that church.

The Holy Spirit is active throughout Revelation. John is "in the Spirit," sees God's Spirit raise the dead as the Spirit did Jesus, is "carried away in the Spirit," and knows that the heart of God and the church should be to invite people to Jesus as Lord, hearing "the Spirit and the Bride say, 'Come.'"[c] Regarding the Holy Spirit ministering between heaven and earth,

---

a Rev. 1:10; 1:17; 19:10; 22:9
b Rev. 2:7, 11, 17, 29; 3:6, 13, 22
c Rev. 1:10; 4:2; 14:13; 17:3; 21:10; 22:17

connecting the unseen and seen realms, He is referred to by seven, which is the number of perfection.[2]

ANGELS AND DEMONS

Revelation reveals that in addition to godly and ungodly people at work in the seen natural realm, so too godly and ungodly spirits are at work in the unseen supernatural realm. Each of the seven churches[a] is said to have an angel. Like we said earlier, the stars spoken of throughout the book are likely also angels, because that is common ancient language for the spirit realm. Stars are between the realms of heaven and earth connecting the two as angels do. The same is true today, as we do not fully understand how local churches have angelic support, but Revelation is clear that they do. Angels are sent from the throne room to the earth on a variety of ministry missions, including evangelism: "I saw another angel flying directly overhead, with an eternal gospel to proclaim to those who dwell on earth, to every nation and tribe and language and people."[b] [3]

Revelation reveals groups of angels working together on the earth for the glory of God and good of the church.

- Four angels are said to control activities on earth.[c]

- Seven angels stand before God and call forth judgment of sinful rebellion on the earth.[d]

- Seven angels oversee the seven last plagues and are sent from God's throne room to the earth to pour out the wrath of God in the great tribulation.[e]

- Lastly an angel will be sent from God's throne room to the earth with the keys to the abyss, which will be opened to bind Satan for a thousand years.[f]

---

a Rev. 1–3
b Rev. 14:6
c Rev. 7:1
d Rev. 8:2
e Rev. 15:1–7
f Rev. 20:2–3

God sends His unseen family to help His seen family, which means there is much more going on in the world, our churches, and our lives than we can imagine.

In addition to angels, demons also appear frequently. One theologian says, "There are more than one hundred references to demons in the Bible, most of them occurring in the New Testament. All the writers of the synoptic gospels report several cases of demon possession to demonstrate the power of Christ over demons. We may briefly state that all the writers (though not every book) of the New Testament, except the author of Hebrews, mention demons or evil angels."[4]

The revelation of demonic work on the earth in nations and churches appears all throughout the last book of the Bible. People are judged for counterfeit religion and spirituality, which is "worshiping demons."[a] Behind the supernatural events on the earth are unclean demonic spirits who deceive people by performing signs.[b] Some places filled with darkness are part of the spiritual Babylon, which is "a dwelling place for demons."[c]

In addition to a great deal of Old Testament imagery, the same demonic spirit of Jezebel present and at work through human leaders continues the plot of adultery and attack in the local church of Thyatira. Jesus says, "You tolerate that woman Jezebel, who calls herself a prophetess and is teaching and seducing my servants to practice sexual immorality and to eat food sacrificed to idols."[d] In this instance the unseen and seen realms are revealed to be working together, as a demon is leading a local church astray through a powerful woman.

Sexual immorality of any kind that is sanctioned in the church, starting with leadership, is a demonic spirit from Satan to destroy the work of God. In every age we find demonic, powerful, and even brilliant false teachers who want to replace repentance of sexual sin with the tolerance of sexual sin, claiming to be wise, enlightened, evolved, loving, and speaking for God. But they are academic antichrists. Demons are quite happy to make sure that their books sell, their messages are broadcast, and their platforms are built. Tolerance is the counterfeit of repentance.

When our kids were little, we often drove by a small church with a large

a Rev. 9:20
b 2 Thess. 2:9; Rev. 13:11–15; 16:13–14
c Rev. 18:2
d Rev. 2:19–24

rainbow banner hanging out front that said, "God is still speaking." One of our youngest children asked from the back seat, "What does that sign mean?" We answered, "That church does not believe the Bible. They believe that in the past God said that marriage and sex were only for one man and one woman, but that God has changed His mind and today says that marriage is not just for a man and woman and that sex is not just for marriage." The child then asked a great question: "Why do they still call it a church, then, since it's not a church anymore?" Exactly.

THE KINGDOM COMES TO EARTH AS THE REALMS REUNITE

As the story line of history in Revelation unfolds, in the middle of the book we find the announcement that the two realms of the seen and unseen will be brought together once and forever with the coming of King Jesus and His kingdom.[a] The full unveiling of the kingdom begins with an angel trumpeting to herald God overtaking all of creation. In response both realms stop to sing new songs of worship as Christians and angels stand side by side to rejoin the realms that sin separated.

Jesus Christ leads the coming of the kingdom and combining of the realms. Surrounding Jesus as He readies for war are musicians, songwriters, and singing, because worship is an act of war.[b] The war that Jesus won in heaven and won on the cross has one final battle before all wars—physical and spiritual—are no more.

Jesus then returns to earth on a white cloud of victory and purity, appearing like the Son of Man.[c] The second swing of Jesus' sickle is for the judgment of all the unrepentant sinners upon the earth, who are then thrown into a large winepress, where God stomps upon His enemies and their blood flows for two hundred miles as high as the bit in a horse's mouth. This is the war to end all wars!

In Revelation 15 the wrath of God is poured out upon the earth like it was in the days of Exodus. In Revelation 19 two scenes contrast the joys of heaven and judgments of earth. While worship takes place in heaven, war is carried out on the earth. Jesus rides a white horse from realm to realm as a triumphant kingly warrior, wearing a robe dipped in blood with a sword

a Rev. 11:15–19
b Rev. 14:1–5
c cf. Dan. 7:13; Rev. 1:7, 13

and "KING OF KINGS AND LORD OF LORDS" written on His thigh like a tattoo.

Throughout Revelation, scenes continually transition between heaven and earth. In the end God reconciles the two realms and reunites the two families forever. This will be our home forever as we live in beauty, unity, love, joy, and prosperity. In the middle of a great city will be a restored and more glorious Garden of Eden, a title which meant "garden of delight."[a] The place of God's divine council meetings with His human and angelic families will forever be open, and we can be in God's presence at any time. There the Father and Son will be sitting on their thrones, and we will see Jesus face to face as we eat from the tree of life to live with God forever. What God started in Eden, God will finish in eternity.

If you belong to Jesus Christ, what God has planned for you is not only more glorious than you think; it is more glorious than you *can* think. "What no eye has seen, nor ear heard, nor the heart of man imagined, what God has prepared for those who love him."[b] Not only did Jesus win your war, but He also has a future planned for you to become like Him, a person who is part of both realms for all eternity.

> In the beginning, God made humans to image him, to be like him, to dwell with him. He made us like his heavenly imagers and came to earth to unite his families, elevating humanity to share in divine life in a new world....Scripture is clear that immortality as a divinized human is the destiny of the believer, and that our present lives in Christ are a process of becoming what we are.[5]

After Jesus wins the war to end all wars, Satan's family (divine and human) will be sentenced to their eternal prison of hell. The two realms will be reunited, and God's two families reconciled forever. You will not be an angel or God, but you will be over the angels and more like God than you are today.

Forever you will be like Jesus Christ. "Beloved, we are God's children now, and what we will be has not yet appeared; but we know that when

a Rev. 22:1–6
b 1 Cor. 2:9

he appears we shall be like him, because we shall see him as he is. And everyone who thus hopes in him purifies himself as he is pure."[a] Today is the time between the times, when "our citizenship is in heaven, and from it we await a Savior, the Lord Jesus Christ, who will transform our lowly body to be like his glorious body."[b]

Admittedly this is a mystery, as the Bible is revealing a future state for you that is yet unrealized. The key to winning your wars until all wars have ceased is to look forward to the future God has planned for you and "only let us hold true to what we have attained."[c]

Today you are "a little lower than the heavenly beings" in God's order of authority.[d] However, when God is finished with glorifying you on the other side of the second coming, you will be in authority and "judge angels."[e] Your status will change eternally and include "authority over the nations" as you rule under God.[f] It is hard for the mind to receive the fact that just as Jesus won His war and then sat upon His throne, He says that you too can win your war and sit with Him. "The one who conquers, I will grant him to sit with me on my throne, as I also conquered and sat down with my Father on his throne."[g] In the kingdom you will be like Jesus and sit on a throne with Jesus ruling over angels and nations! This is what you are fighting for.

Until we see Jesus standing on the earth, we are to stand for Jesus on the earth. In the eminent passage on spiritual warfare in Ephesians 6 we are told no less than four times to "stand." As the kingdom of God marches forward, we are not to surrender in sin but to stand and worship God every moment of every day by living in light of the unseen realm amidst the seen realm. The word for *stand* is a military term for holding the line, not backing down or backing up. This is how you will win your war until Jesus shows up to win all wars.

Where do you need to stand? What is your war? Believe that "the God of peace will soon crush Satan under your feet."[h] Until then, stand your

---

a 1 John 3:2–3
b Phil. 3:20–21
c Phil. 3:16
d Ps. 8:5
e 1 Cor. 6:3
f Rev. 2:26
g Rev. 3:21
h Rom. 16:20

ground and win your war by worshipping your King and inviting His kingdom to reign down in your life as you fight in the realm you don't see for freedom in the one you do!

APPENDIX

SPIRITUAL INVENTORY

Satan might not outwit us. For we are not unaware of his schemes.

—2 CORINTHIANS 2:11, NIV

I F YOU WANT to consider the possible presence of demonic work in your own life, we offer the following as a self-guided Bible study. To help provide greater clarity and understanding, we encourage you to spend some time alone with the Lord, pray, look up the following Scriptures, and journal about the things that apply to your life.

Please read Galatians 5:19–21 and list each thing that has been a besetting or habitual sin for you.

Please read Colossians 3:5–8 and list each thing that has been a besetting or habitual sin for you.

Please read Mark 7:21–23 and list each thing that has been a besetting or habitual sin for you.

Please consider the following list and write each thing that has been besetting or habitual for you: sexual sin or deviancy (anything outside of heterosexual marriage); bad habits or addictions (drugs, alcohol, pornography); rage; blasphemy (swearing or vulgar language); violence; depression; suicidal thoughts; self-harm; eating disorders; mental illness; other dark behaviors or mental states that come to mind.

Please consider the following list of sins that may have been committed against you and list each thing that has been a besetting or habitual sin for you: rape, incest, molestation, other forms of abuse (i.e., physical, sexual, mental, emotional), as well as anything else dark or shameful that comes to mind.

Please briefly explain any involvement you may have had with the occult, witchcraft, or anything spiritual other than orthodox biblical Christianity.

Please briefly list any activity of your ancestors involved in the occult, witchcraft, other religions, drug use, alcohol abuse, sexual deviancy, rape, incest, mental illness, or anything else.

Please briefly describe your sleeping patterns, including any inability to sleep and ongoing nightmares or disturbances.

Please briefly list any paranormal/supernatural experiences you have had.

Please briefly list any voices you hear and what they generally speak to you.

Please briefly list the main two or three things that you would like resolved immediately.

Please read 1 John 4 slowly, praying each part that strikes you and honestly speaking with God about the things His Holy Spirit brings to mind. You can also journal about these things in the space provided. If you have trouble concentrating while doing this, please pray that the Holy Spirit would clear your mind and allow you to learn to read His Word and pray, and then continue.

NOTES

CHAPTER 1: WIN YOUR WORLDVIEW WAR

1. Mark Driscoll, Deepak Chopra, Annie Lobert, and Carlton Pearson, "Nightline Face Off: Does Satan Exist?," debate moderated by Dan Harris, *ABC Nightline*, ABC, March 26, 2009.
2. Heiko A. Oberman, *Luther: Man Between God and the Devil*, trans. Eileen Walliser-Schwarzbart (New Haven: Yale University Press, 1989), 104.
3. Mark Rogers, "'Deliver Us From the Evil One': Martin Luther on Prayer," *Themelios* 34, no. 3 (2009): 340.
4. Mark H. Creech, "The Night the Demon Visited," *Christian Post*, May 14, 2013, https://www.christianpost.com/news/the-night-the-demon-visited.html.
5. William Barclay, ed., *The Gospel of Matthew*, vol. 1, The Daily Study Bible Series (Louisville, KY: Westminster John Knox Press, 1975), 65; Scott A. Hendrix, "Legends About Luther," *Christian History* (*Christianity Today*), no. 34 (1992), https://www.christianitytoday.com/history/issues/issue-34/legends-about-luther.html; Helmut Thielicke, "The Great Temptation," *Christianity Today* 29, no. 10 (1985), 28, https://www.christianitytoday.com/ct/1985/july-12/great-temptation.html.
6. William Barclay, ed., *The Gospel of Matthew*, vol. 2, The Daily Study Bible Series (Philadelphia: The Westminster John Knox Press, 1976), 105.
7. William Barclay, ed., *The Gospel of Mark*, The Daily Study Bible Series (Philadelphia: The Westminster John Knox Press, 1976), 161.
8. William Barclay, ed., *The Gospel of John*, vol. 1, The Daily Study Bible Series (Philadelphia: The Westminster John Knox Press, 1975), 208.

CHAPTER 2: GOD WON HIS WAR

1. R. K. Harrison, *Evangelical Dictionary of Biblical Theology*, Baker Reference Library, ed. Walter A. Elwell (Grand Rapids, MI: Baker Book House, 1996), 21.

2. Leland Ryken, James C. Wilhoit, and Tremper Longman III, eds., *Dictionary of Biblical Imagery* (Downers Grove, IL: InterVarsity Press, 2000), s.v. "Angels," 23.

3. Michael S. Heiser, *The Unseen Realm: Recovering the Supernatural Worldview of the Bible* (Bellingham, WA: Lexham Press, 2015), 24. "At Ugarit the divine council had three levels: the highest authority (El, who did most of his ruling through a coruling vizier, Baal), the 'sons of El, and messenger gods (*mal'akim*). . . . All of this will sound familiar to someone who has read the Old Testament closely. The Hebrew Bible uses these same descriptions for the abode and throne room of Yahweh. And where Yahweh is, he is surrounded by his heavenly assembly, ready to conduct business (cf. Isa. 6; 1 Kings 22:13–28). The Old Testament has a three-tiered council structure like that at Ugarit. Yahweh is at the top. His family-household ('sons of God') are next in hierarchy. The lowest level is reserved for *elohim* messengers—*mal'akim* (the word translated 'angels')." Heiser, *The Unseen Realm*, 46.

4. "Since *elohim* is so often translated *God*, we look at the Hebrew word the same way we look at capitalized G-o-d. When we see the word *God*, we instinctively think of a divine being with a unique set of attributes—omnipresence, omnipotence, sovereignty, and so on. But this is not how a biblical writer thought about the term. Biblical authors did not assign a specific set of attributes to the word *elohim*. That is evident when we observe how they used the word. The biblical writers refer to a half-dozen different entities with the word *elohim*. By any religious accounting, the attributes of those entities are *not* equal.
   • Yahweh, the God of Israel (thousands of times—e.g., Gen 2:4–5; Deut 4:35)
   • The members of Yahweh's council (Psa 82:1, 6)
   • Gods and goddesses of other nations (Judg 11:24; 1 Kgs 11:33)
   • Demons (Hebrew: *shedim*—Deut 32:17)
   • The deceased Samuel (1 Sam 28:13)

- Angels or the Angel of Yahweh (Gen 35:7)." Heiser, *The Unseen Realm*, 30.

5. Heiser, *The Unseen Realm*, 323.

6. A. Colin Day, *Collins Thesaurus of the Bible* (Bellingham, WA: Logos Bible Software, 2009).

7. "Angels in the OT are often ranged in military and astral ranks known collectively as the heavenly host (Deut 4:19; 1 Kgs 22:19), or they are referred to individually as mighty ones. On occasion they intervened in Israel's wars (Judg 5:20; 2 Kgs 6:17). They were led by a captain or prince, who appears as chief angel (Josh 5:14)....In Daniel the national guardian angels are called...princes (Dan 8:25). The prince of Persia opposes Michael, who is 'one of the chief princes' (Dan 10:13). Michael is also Israel's guardian angel." Willem VanGemeren, ed., *New International Dictionary of Old Testament Theology and Exegesis* (Grand Rapids, MI: Zondervan Publishing House, 1997), 941.

CHAPTER 3: ADAM AND EVE LOST OUR WAR

1. Yeonmi Park, *In Order to Live: A North Korean Girl's Journey to Freedom* (New York: Penguin Books, 2015), 48–49.

2. Park, *In Order to Live*, 48.

3. Park, *In Order to Live*, 48.

4. Meadowdale High School, email message to parents, October 8, 2018.

5. Meadowdale High School, email message to parents.

6. Heiser, *The Unseen Realm*, 44.

7. In Genesis 3:16 the language for the husband and wife having conflict is the same as the conflict Cain had with sin in Genesis 4:7.

8. Heiser, *The Unseen Realm*, 121–22.

CHAPTER 4: JESUS WON YOUR WAR

1. C. H. Spurgeon, "Christ Triumphant," *The New Park Street Pulpit Sermons*, vol. 5 (London: Passmore & Alabaster, 1859), 387–89.

CHAPTER 5: WIN YOUR WARS

1. Clinton E. Arnold, *Powers of Darkness: Principalities and Powers in Paul's Letters* (Downers Grove, IL: InterVarsity, 1992), 67.

Chapter 6: Win Your War Against Demonic Influence

1. Oxford Living Dictionaries, s.v. "possess," accessed June 5, 2019, https://en.oxforddictionaries.com/definition/possess.

2. Kenneth O. Gangel, *Holman New Testament Commentary: Acts* (Nashville: Broadman & Holman, 1998), 82.

3. Heiser, *The Unseen Realm*, 277.

4. A. J. Maclean, "Abrenuntio," in *Encyclopædia of Religion and Ethics*, vol. 1, eds. James Hastings, John A. Selbie, and Louis H. Gray (New York: Charles Scribner's Sons, 1910), 38.

5. Maclean, *Encyclopædia of Religion and Ethics*, 39.

6. Madeline Farber, "What Causes Nightmares? Here's Why You May Be Prone to Scary Dreams," Fox News, October 13, 2018, https://www.foxnews.com/health/what-is-cause-of-nightmares-why-some-have-them.

7. Farber, "What Causes Nightmares?"

Chapter 7: Win Your War Against Idolatry

1. Brian S. Rosner, "The Concept of Idolatry," *Themelios* 24, no. 3 (1999): 28–29.

2. David Powlison, "Idols of the Heart and 'Vanity Fair,'" *The Journal of Biblical Counseling* 13, vol. 2 (Winter 1995): 35.

3. William M. Struthers, *Wired for Intimacy: How Pornography Hijacks the Male Brain* (Downers Grove, IL: InterVarsity Press, 2009), 79.

4. Struthers, *Wired for Intimacy*, 97.

Chapter 8: Win Your War Against Pride

1. Walter A. Elwell and Philip Wesley Comfort, *Tyndale Bible Dictionary* (Wheaton, IL: Tyndale House Publishers, 2001), 1072.

2. God speaks of a being called Leviathan five times, saying, "He sees everything that is high; he is king over all the sons of pride" (Job 41:34; 3:8; Ps. 74:14; 104:26; Isa. 27:1). One manual on deliverance and spiritual warfare says, "Leviathan was a spirit represented by the crocodile or a large sea serpent. In Isaiah chapter 27 he is called the 'piercing serpent,' the 'crooked serpent,' the 'dragon' that lies in the midst of the sea (v. 1, KJV). In Job 41:34 he is called 'king over all the children of pride.'" John Eckhardt, *Deliverance and Spiritual Warfare Manual* (Lake Mary, FL: Charisma House, 2014), 144.

3. Heino O. Kadai, "Luther's Theology of the Cross," *Concordia Theological Quarterly* 63, no. 3 (1999): 169–204; Gerhard O. Forde, *On Being a Theologian of the Cross: Reflections on Luther's Heidelberg Disputation, 1518* (Grand Rapids, MI: Eerdmans, 1997); Robert Kolb, "Luther on the Theology of the Cross," *Lutheran Quarterly* 16, no. 4 (2002): 443–66; Alister E. McGrath, *Luther's Theology of the Cross: Martin Luther's Theological Breakthrough* (Oxford, UK: Blackwell, 1985).

4. Gerald Lewis Bray, *Ancient Christian Commentary on Scripture, New Testament 7, 1–2 Corinthians* (Downers Grove, IL: InterVarsity Press, 1999), 132.

CHAPTER 9: WIN YOUR WAR AGAINST YOUR IDENTITY

1. Herod's homeland was Idumea, which is an area of Old Testament Edom.

CHAPTER 11: WIN YOUR WAR AGAINST DEFILEMENT

1. "In the OT the phrase 'the Angel of the Lord' occurs some sixty times. This angel is a special servant of Yahweh who helps accomplish God's will among his people. Thus he appeared to Moses at the burning bush (Ex 3:2), opposed Balaam (Num 22:22–35) and encouraged Gideon (Judg 6:11–16). He is said to have caused death among Israel's enemies (2 Kings 19:35) and in Israel itself (1 Chron 21:14–15), though he usually comes to the aid of God's people (Ex 14:19; Judg 2:1; 1 Kings 19:7; Ps 34:7). Often this angel cannot be distinguished from Yahweh himself (e.g., Gen 16:11, cf. Gen 16:13; Judg 6:12, cf. Judg 6:14)." M. J. Davidson, "Angels," *Dictionary of Jesus and the Gospels*, eds. Joel B. Green, Scot McKnight, and I. Howard Marshall (Downers Grove, IL: InterVarsity Press, 1992), 9.

2. Craig S. Keener, *Miracles: The Credibility of the New Testament Accounts* (Grand Rapids, MI: Baker, 2011).

3. Eckhardt, *Deliverance and Spiritual Warfare Manual*, 57.

CHAPTER 13: WIN YOUR WAR AGAINST UNFORGIVENESS

1. "Hatfields and McCoys," *Encyclopaedia Britannica*, accessed June 5, 2019, https://www.britannica.com/topic/Hatfields-and-McCoys.

2. "Hatfields and McCoys," *Encyclopaedia Britannica*.

CHAPTER 14: WIN YOUR WAR AGAINST LIES

1. Ryken, Wilhoit, and Longman, *Dictionary of Biblical Imagery*, s.v. "Jesus as Humorist," 410.

CHAPTER 16: WIN YOUR WAR AGAINST A FATHER WOUND

1. Jens Pulver with Erich Krauss, *Little Evil: One Ultimate Fighter's Rise to the Top*, electronic ed. (Toronto, Ontario, Canada: ECW Press, 2003).
2. Liam Resnekov, "Jens Pulver on Anxiety, Abuse, and the Fighting Spirit," Fightland Blog, May 22, 2014, http://fightland.vice.com/blog/jens-pulver-on-anxiety-abuse-and-the-fighting-spirit.
3. "Michael Servetus," *Encyclopaedia Britannica*, accessed June 5, 2019, https://www.britannica.com/biography/Michael-Servetus.
4. Henry Worsley, *The Life of Martin Luther: In Two Volumes*, vol. 1 (London: Bell and Daldy, 1856), 391; Andrew J. Lindsey, *The Life, Teaching, and Legacy of Martin Luther* (Bloomington, IN: Westbow, 2013), 72.
5. Michael Reeves, "Suffering Taught Him to Look to Christ: Charles Spurgeon (1834–1892)," Desiring God, October 19, 2018, https://www.desiringgod.org/articles/suffering-taught-him-to-look-to-christ.
6. John Piper and Justin Taylor, eds., *A God Entranced Vision of All Things* (Wheaton, IL: Crossway, 2004).
7. David Van Biema, "The New Calvinism," *Time,* March 12, 2009, http://content.time.com/time/specials/packages/article/0,28804,1884779_1884782_1884760,00.html.
8. Francis A. Schaeffer, *The Complete Works of Francis A. Schaeffer: A Christian Worldview*, vol. 3 (Westchester, IL: Crossway Books, 1982), 97.
9. Robert H. Stein, "Fatherhood of God," *Evangelical Dictionary of Biblical Theology*, 247.

CHAPTER 17: WIN YOUR WAR AGAINST FEAR

1. Elwell and Comfort, *Tyndale Bible Dictionary*, 479.
2. Mark Water, *Bible Promises Made Easy* (Alresford, Hampshire: John Hunt Publishers Ltd, 2001), 33.
3. Eckhardt, *Deliverance and Spiritual Warfare Manual*, 223.

CHAPTER 18: WIN YOUR WAR AGAINST DIVISION

1. *Rocky IV*, written and directed by Sylvester Stallone, MGM/UA Entertainment Company, 1985.
2. Jeffrey A. Kroessler, *The Greater New York Sports Chronology* (New York: Columbia University Press, 2010), 116.
3. Eckhardt, *Deliverance and Spiritual Warfare Manual*, 227–28.
4. Eckhardt, *Deliverance and Spiritual Warfare Manual*, 208.
5. Eckhardt, *Deliverance and Spiritual Warfare Manual*, 65.

CHAPTER 19: WIN YOUR WAR AGAINST WOLVES

1. "French Sheep Farmer Fighting Wolves," *Outlook*, BBC News, accessed June 5, 2019, https://www.bbc.co.uk/sounds/play/p01w7jzx.
2. Craig S. Keener, *The IVP Bible Background Commentary: New Testament* (Downers Grove, IL: InterVarsity Press, 2014), 529.
3. Jess L. Christensen, "How Can Jesus and Lucifer Be Spirit Brothers When Their Characters and Purposes Are So Utterly Opposed?," The Church of Jesus Christ of Latter-Day Saints, accessed June 5, 2019, https://www.churchofjesuschrist.org/study/ensign/1986/06/i-have-a-question/how-can-jesus-and-lucifer-be-spirit-brothers-when-their-characters-and-purposes-are-so-utterly-opposed?lang=eng.
4. Ephesians 5:7 says of evil people, "Do not become partners with them." Titus 3:10 says, "Have nothing more to do with him." Proverbs 1:15 says, "Do not walk…with them." Proverbs 22:24 says, "Make no friendship." Second John 10 says, "Do not receive him into your house or give him any greeting." Second Timothy 3:5 says, "Avoid such people."

CHAPTER 20: WIN YOUR WAR AGAINST COUNTERFEITS TO CHRIST

1. Edward F. Murphy, *The Handbook for Spiritual Warfare* (Nashville: Thomas Nelson, 1996), 236.
2. "The plague of blood, the first plague, was directed against the god Khnum, creator of water and life; or against Hapi, the god of the Nile; or even against Osiris, whose bloodstream was the Nile. The second plague, the plague of the frogs, was directed against Heket, goddess of childbirth, represented as a frog. The fifth plague, against the cattle, might have had in mind Hathor, the mother and sky goddess, who took the form of a cow; or against Apis, symbol of fertility, who took the

form of a bull. The seventh and eighth plagues (hail and locusts) were opposed to Seth, who manifested himself in wind and storms, or against Isis, goddess of life, or even against Min, who was worshiped as a god of fertility. Min is an especially good candidate for these two plagues, for he was widely revered in a 'coming-out-of-Min' celebration at the beginning of harvest. Darkness, the ninth plague, on the other hand, was directed against such deities as those associated with the sun— Amon-Re, Aten, Atum, or Horus. Finally the death of the firstborn could well be associated with Osiris, the judge of the dead and patron deity of the Pharaoh.... Mordechai Gilula, 'The Smiting of the Firstborn: An Egyptian Myth?' *Tel Aviv* 4 (1977): 94–95 notes three or four cases where the 'slaying of the firstborn' (Egyptian *smsw*, 'firstborn') occurs in pre-Mosaic texts about the death of the firstborn of the gods. They occur in the Pyramid Texts and Coffin Texts." Walter C. Kaiser Jr., *A History of Israel: From the Bronze Age Through the Jewish Wars* (Nashville: Broadman & Holman, 1998), 99.

3. "Divine Beings," in *The Lexham Theological Wordbook*, eds. Douglas Mangum et al., Lexham Bible Reference Series (Bellingham, WA: Lexham Press, 2014).

4. James A. Swanson, *Dictionary of Biblical Languages With Semantic Domains: Hebrew (Old Testament)* (Oak Harbor, WA: Logos Research Systems, Inc., 1997).

5. Harvey E. Finley, "Gods and Goddesses, Pagan," in *Evangelical Dictionary of Biblical Theology*, 303.

6. Tom Wallace, "Islam: Religion of the Devil," Fortress of Faith, July 19, 2017, https://fortressoffaith.com/islam-religion-of-the-devil/.

7. For more information, see Cathy Lynn Grossman, "Mixing Their Religion," *USA Today*, December 10, 2009, http://www.usatoday.com/NEWS/usaedition/2009-12-10-1Amixingbeliefs10_CV_U.htm; and Pew Research Center, "Many Americans Mix Multiple Faiths," Pew Forum on Religion and Public Life, December 9, 2009, http://pewresearch.org/pubs/1434/multiple-religious-practices-reincarnation-astrology-psychic.

8. "Many Americans Mix Multiple Faiths," Pew Research Center.

CHAPTER 21: ON EARTH AS IT IS IN HEAVEN

1. Heiser, *The Unseen Realm*, 297.

   "The first two points of the description that deserve attention are the 'violent rushing wind' and the 'divided tongues like fire.' Both are images in the Old Testament associated with God's presence—the disciples are being commissioned by God in his council like the prophets of old.

   "The whirlwind is familiar from divine encounters of Elijah (2 Kgs 2:1, 11) and Job (Job 38:1; 40:6). Ezekiel's divine commissioning likewise has the enthroned Yahweh coming with great wind (Ezek 1:4). The whirlwind motif is often accompanied by storm imagery, which can also include fire (Isa 30:30). Having 'wind' as an element in describing God's presence makes sense given that the Hebrew word translated 'wind' can also be rendered 'spirit/Spirit' (*ruach*).

   "Ezekiel's commissioning is particularly instructive since not only does Yahweh come to him with a wind, but with the wind there is 'fire flashing' (Ezek. 1:4). Burning fire is a familiar element of divine-council throne-room scenes (e.g., Isa 6:4, 6; Dan 7:9). It is especially prominent in the appearances at Sinai (Exod 3:2; 19:18; 20:18; Isa 4:5). Fire in the Old Testament was an identifier of the presence of God, a visible manifestation of Yahweh's glory and essence. It was also a way of describing divine beings in God's service (Judg 13:20; Psa 104:4)." Heiser, *The Unseen Realm*, 297.

2. "One unique aspect of the portrayal of the Holy Spirit in the book of Revelation is the reference to the 'seven spirits of God.'... It is therefore probable that the number seven is representative of perfection, and the NIV marginal note 'sevenfold Spirit' at Revelation 1:4; 3:1; 4:5; and 5:6 is an acceptable interpretation." Roy B. Zuck, *A Biblical Theology of the New Testament*, electronic ed. (Chicago: Moody Press, 1994), 202.

3. "Certain angels are designated by the activity they are assigned. There is the 'angel, the one who has power over fire' (Revelation 14:18). Another is called 'the angel of the waters' (Revelation 16:5). An unusual one is designated as 'the angel of the abyss' (Revelation 9:11). He is also specifically named as Abaddon in the Hebrew, and as Apollyon in the Greek. Both names signify the activity of destruction.... Finally, there is one described in Revelation 20:1 as 'an angel coming down from heaven, having the key of the abyss and a great chain in his hand.' This one will

bind Satan for the millennial reign of Christ (Revelation 20:2–3)." C. Fred Dickason, *Angels: Elect & Evil* (Chicago: Moody Press, 1995), 76.

4. C. Fred Dickason, *Angels*, 163.

5. Heiser, *The Unseen Realm*, 319–20.

ABOUT THE AUTHOR

WITH PASTOR MARK and Grace Driscoll, it's all about Jesus! Mark and Grace have been married and doing ministry together for over twenty-five years. They planted The Trinity Church with their five kids in Scottsdale, Arizona.

Mark has been named by *Preaching* magazine one of the twenty-five most influential pastors of the past twenty-five years. He has a bachelor's degree in speech communication from the Edward R. Murrow College of Communication at Washington State University as well as a master's degree in exegetical theology from Western Seminary in Portland, Oregon. For free sermons, answers to questions, Bible teaching, and more, visit MarkDriscoll .org or download the Mark Driscoll Ministries app. Pastor Mark's leadership resources and publishing projects can be found at theresurgence.com.

Together, Mark and Grace have authored *Real Marriage*. Pastor Mark has authored other books, including *Spirit-Filled Jesus, Who Do You Think You Are?, Vintage Jesus,* and *Doctrine*.

We are so happy you read our book.

We hope this book equipped you with tools to protect the four fronts of spiritual battle: your relationship with God, your identity, your family and friends, and your church.

As Our Way of Saying Thank You...

We are offering you a couple of gifts:

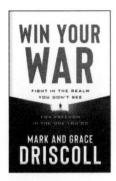

E-book:
Win Your War

5 Weekly Downloads: The Forgiveness Challenge

To get these **FREE GIFTS**, please go to:
www.driscollbooks.com/gifts

Thanks again and God bless you,

Mark and Grace Driscoll